JA

PORT ALBERNI

{ MORE THAN JUST A MILL TOWN }

HERITAGE

VICTORIA · VANCOUVER · CALGARY

{ To my husband, Raymond }

Copyright © 2014 Jan Peterson

All rights reserved. No part of this publication may be reproduced, stored in a retrieval system or transmitted in any form or by any means—electronic, mechanical, audio recording or otherwise—without the written permission of the publisher or a licence from Access Copyright, Toronto, Canada.

Heritage House Publishing Company Ltd.
heritagehouse.ca

LIBRARY AND ARCHIVES CANADA CATALOGUING IN PUBLICATION

Peterson, Jan, 1937–, author
Port Alberni : more than just a mill town / Jan Peterson.

Issued in print and electronic formats.
ISBN 978-1-927527-68-9 (pbk.).—ISBN 978-1-927527-69-6 (html).
—ISBN 978-1-927527-70-2 (pdf)

1. Port Alberni (B.C.)—History. I. Title.

FC3849.P56P485 2014   971.1'2   C2013-908560-2   C2013-908561-0

Edited by Renate Preuss
Proofread by Lara Kordic
Cover and book design by Jacqui Thomas
Cover photo by Martin Pedersen/Pedersen Arts Photography

The interior of this book was produced on 100% post-consumer recycled paper, processed chlorine free and printed with vegetable-based inks.

Heritage House acknowledges the financial support for its publishing program from the Government of Canada through the Canada Book Fund (CBF), Canada Council for the Arts, and the Province of British Columbia through the British Columbia Arts Council and the Book Publishing Tax Credit.

18 17 16 15 14   1 2 3 4 5

Printed in Canada

CONTENTS

INTRODUCTION 7

chapter one   **A NEW BEGINNING** 11

chapter two   **A MACMILLAN BLOEDEL TOWN** 16

chapter three   **GETTING TO KNOW THE CITY** 28

chapter four   **UNIONS AND FIRST NATIONS** 62

chapter five   **COMMUNITY RECREATION AND PRESERVING HERITAGE** 84

chapter six   **THE ARTS COMMUNITY** 100

chapter seven   **SUGAR IN THE FRIDGE; MICE ON THE TABLE** 128

chapter eight   **THE RECESSION HITS** 140

chapter nine   **FIGHTING BACK** 159

chapter ten   **FORESTRY IN THE HOT SEAT** 173

chapter eleven   **THE FLOODPLAIN DILEMMA** 190

chapter twelve	**A YEAR OF CELEBRATION**	198
chapter thirteen	**INTERVIEWS OF NOTE**	208
chapter fourteen	**PEOPLE OF THE ALBERNI VALLEY**	217
chapter fifteen	**A CHANGING FOREST INDUSTRY**	240
	EPILOGUE	253
	ACKNOWLEDGEMENTS	257
	ENDNOTES	258
	BIBLIOGRAPHY	262

MacMillan & Bloedel Ltd. company map showing the island divisions, ca. 1951.

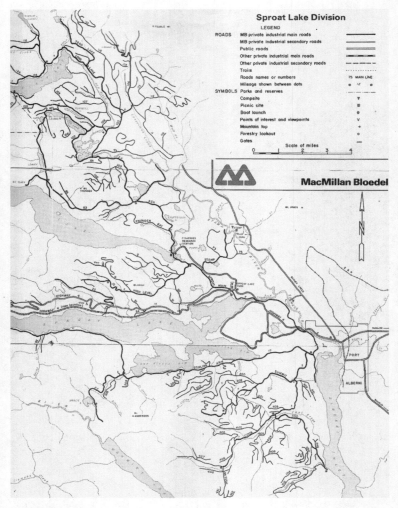

MacMillan Bloedel map of Sproat Lake division logging roads.

INTRODUCTION

The 1970s were perhaps the best of times in British Columbia. In a province where the past century had been marked by its share of boom and busts, the economy was considered good. The era of W.A.C. Bennett had come to an end in September 1972, when the New Democratic Party (NDP) under Dave Barrett swept into power. In Port Alberni Bob Skelly was elected under the NDP banner, his first foray into politics. Nothing seemed impossible.

It was with this air of optimism that our family decided to move to Port Alberni in 1972. At the time, forestry was an important economic factor in the lives of many families like ours in British Columbia. And Port Alberni, a city based on the forest industry, was thriving. Over the next three decades we would witness first-hand the boom-and-bust cycle so typical in resource-based communities.

In the NDP's first year in power, hundreds of bills were brought before the legislature. Many social services were reorganized. The sale of agricultural land was frozen, provincial employees were given full collective bargaining rights, rent controls were introduced, and a new labour code was drafted. All these changes left everyone breathless, but soon the NDP policies started backfiring. Barrett mistook the mood in the province and, with two years left in his mandate, called a snap election.

Without an heir apparent to W.A.C. Bennett, his son Bill was elected to his father's South Okanagan seat in 1973. Bill was a neophyte politically and his inexperience showed, but he had seasoned politicians behind him, and with his father at his side, he and the Social Credit Party managed to win the election. Barrett was personally defeated in his Coquitlam seat. In reflection, many believed the NDP's biggest mistake was attempting to do everything at once. But Barrett also had not taken into account, or had forgotten, the tenacity of the well-organized Socreds.

Bill Bennett was quite unlike his father. With his five o'clock shadow showing nightly on television, his seemingly dour, austere demeanour left many cool. And, very unlike his father, he did not seem to have a clear idea or plan for the future of the province. One plan that seemed like a good idea at the time went sour for everyone. The new premier established the British Columbia Resources Investment Corporation (BCRIC), a holding company that would invest in the province. Blustery talk-show host Jack Webster coined the nickname BRIC, and the name stuck. Five free shares were offered to any Canadian citizen resident in BC for one year. Over 85 percent took up the offer. Fathers and grandfathers bought shares for their children, thinking they were investing in their future. David Helliwell was placed in charge. The first two ventures he announced were the purchase of 20 percent of MacMillan Bloedel and an option for 22 percent of Kaiser Resources Ltd., a coal producing company. This purchase would have drained BRIC's cash reserves. Helliwell had no board experience in the resource industries, and the company soon headed for trouble. Later it was learned that Edgar Kaiser Jr., as CEO of Kaiser Resources, would have made millions on his own shares from the sale. Helliwell was fired and the BCRIC shares fell. Before long, they were just worthless pieces of paper.

For years, BC's economy rested with its natural resources—and with resource-based companies like MacMillan Bloedel. Mining, agriculture, and fishing were strong but considered secondary to forestry. It was the forestry sector that was the driving engine that lifted the economy and brought riches to the province. And Port Alberni reaped the benefits.

Surrounded by forests and mountains, Port Alberni is located in one of the most beautiful valleys in central Vancouver Island, with a gateway to the sea and a recreation wonderland of trees, lakes, and rivers. The town was first settled in 1860 when the Stamp Sawmill was established on the waterfront. The first big trees were felled by axe and crosscut saw to make ship masts. Some of the trees were so large it took several days to topple one. Wherever possible they were dropped into the water, since floating them was the only method of transportation. The sawmill lasted only four years and closed because it had, unbelievably, run out of available foreshore trees. Today, forests still cover the mountains and line the Alberni Inlet, the forty-kilometre deep-sea waterway to the Pacific Ocean that provides an important link to world markets.

Port Alberni had a population of around thirty thousand when we moved there; this included the smaller outlying communities of Beaver Creek, Beaufort, Cherry Creek, and Sproat Lake. The city was part of the larger Alberni–Clayoquot Regional District that included Tofino, Ucluelet, and Bamfield. Over the next decades, there were a number of developments and events that slowed the city's growth and demoralized forest workers, beginning with the recession in the early 1980s, then the Clayoquot Sound anti-logging protests, the sale of MacMillan Bloedel Ltd., and the changing of forest practices. As a contributor to the *Alberni Valley Times* newspaper from

1975 and then a reporter from 1981 to 1987, as well as an active member in various organizations, I witnessed and observed how these changes affected individuals and the community. I felt like I had a front seat to the developing history of the town.

This book is about living in a one-industry town in British Columbia. It is also about how world markets have an impact on everyday life and how decisions made elsewhere affect a community. It is about some of the city's trials and triumphs—and about the people of Port Alberni who strived to make life better.

{ *chapter one* }

A NEW BEGINNING

When our family moved to Port Alberni in 1972, some friends questioned why we would want to live there. "It's just a mill town," they scorned. The term seemed so negative, and conjured up images of the forest industry in the worst possible way. It was obvious the town had a reputation, but we also heard about the wonderful recreational facilities available. The city had the highest wage earners in the province. Driving through any residential area of town you could see evidence of this prosperity with campers, boats, and cars parked in the driveways of mill and forestry workers. This was MacMillan Bloedel's valley; if you didn't work for MB, the town's major employer, you worked for one of its related industries.

My husband, Ray, a professional engineer, had worked for MB's Vancouver Plywood Division, then MB Manufacturing Services, when he was offered a position as plant engineer in charge of maintenance at Alberni Plywood Division. The decision was easy. We had three small children and were willing to make the career move. Putting all negativity aside we remained positive.

We had visited Port Alberni briefly in 1964, the summer following the tsunami caused by an earthquake in Alaska. The tidal wave on Good Friday that year played havoc with the mills in low-lying and residential areas, tossing logs, lumber, houses, and cars all over the place. Fortunately there was not one single fatality. As we passed through town on the way to visit friends at nearby Sproat Lake we expected to see evidence of the destruction that had enveloped the community only a few months before, but the cleanup had been remarkable.

On that same visit, our friend drove us partly over the old switchback road to the west coast, where the view was simply spectacular. The Alberni–Tofino road that opened in 1959 had no similarities to the highway that exists today; it climbed 518 metres (1,700 feet) up a mountain. The lower route that eventually replaced it opened on October 12, 1972, when Bob Skelly's wife, Alexandra, cut the ribbon.

Ray began work at the Alberni Plywood plant in the fall of 1972. A month or so before moving, we checked out the housing available in town and discovered this was not going to be an easy task. It was quite common in those days for MB to move staff and workers around their divisions, and the company had recently moved an entire division from the Queen Charlotte Islands to Port Alberni. Those families had taken up many of the homes.

Real estate agent Ramon Kwok gave an introductory tour of the city, then asked which part we wanted to live in—South Port, Central Port, or North Port? Ramon explained there were once two cities, Alberni and Port Alberni, until they amalgamated in 1967. As we quickly learned, South Port refers to the former Port Alberni, which dates back to the first 1860 settlement, while North Port is the old town of Alberni. Ramon also pointed out that the community centre had a wonderful swimming pool, and that the police and hospital facilities were all located in the central part of town. Having already heard reports that Maquinna Elementary School was one of the best primary schools in School District 70 and that it was located in South Port on the edge of Maquinna Forest, this was the area we chose. After a day of viewing housing, we settled for a large comfortable home, built five years earlier, just a block away from the school. Our children could walk to school, and if all reports were true they were guaranteed a good education.

In the excitement of finding a home I had paid little attention to the weather, which on that particular November day was foggy. As we drove down into Port Alberni, fog totally immersed the city, blanketing everything for miles. Only the peaks of the mountaintops in the distance were visible from the summit above the fogbank. Driving into the fog felt like driving into a tunnel of grey darkness.

Before long, I learned that this approach to Port Alberni, travelling the mountainous Highway 4 over Mt. Arrowsmith from Parksville on the east coast of Vancouver Island, is called going "over the hump." Another localism is going "down the canal" for sailing down the Alberni Inlet to Bamfield or Ucluelet on the west coast. The inlet was once called the Alberni Canal. The name was changed in 1931 to reassure commercial ship captains they would not be charged a fee for sailing the waterway, as was done with man-made canals in some countries. The term "canal" is still in use by old-timers today.

The beauty of the town remained hidden until we moved into our new home on Boxing Day 1972. That day the sun shone and the picturesque scene of forest and mountains was revealed. From the living room window, we could see the sparkling waters of Alberni Inlet to the west, and to the north the Beaufort Mountain Range covered in snow. From the dining room window looking east was the stunning snow-capped peak of Mt. Arrowsmith. The mountain views were breathtaking, though eventually obscured as the trees in Maquinna Forest grew each year.

Most people anticipate moving day with trepidation, but we soon discovered a move with MB would be like no other.

The company took care of everything. Movers packed all our belongings, from linens to china to the children's toys. We just packed our suitcases and left. We stayed overnight in the Tyee Motel on Redford Street until our furniture arrived the next day at our new house. The moving company, Toms Bros. of Port Alberni, unpacked and placed furniture while I took care of the children. When Ray came home for dinner that night, all the beds were made, the dishes were unpacked and placed in the kitchen cupboards, and dinner was cooked. If there had been curtains, I am sure they would have been hung. The company also paid for drapes and provided an allowance for carpeting. It was an incredible move. You had the feeling that MB really cared about you and your family.

Our house was typical of those built in the 1960s. The builder, Danny Lee, worked at the Alberni Plywood Division plant, so there was lots of plywood used throughout construction plus a beautiful wall of cedar. The two-storey house had six bedrooms and three bathrooms, totalling three thousand square feet. Having come from a split-level three-bedroom house in Ladner, we felt this was enormous. The bedrooms were so large that on the day we viewed the house one of the rooms had three single beds lined up against one wall, each with ample space between. All the bathrooms had coloured fixtures, which was common in the sixties. Within a month, the drapes were hung and we had settled in.

The first few months in Port Alberni were spent getting the children settled in school, meeting our new neighbours, and finding our way around the community. We also found a doctor and a dentist. The partnership of Dr. Alan Philip Miller and Dr. Norman Jones served our medical needs. Their office was in the Credit Union Building at Fourth Avenue and Angus Street; both doctors were nearing retirement age, but in the remaining years they served our family well. Dr. Rollie Nystrom became our dentist; his young practice was above a store on Third Avenue. Our two oldest children enrolled at Maquinna

Elementary School, then under school principal Fred Bradley; our youngest joined Hilton School Kindergarten in the school annex on Tenth Avenue. The children were happy at school and settled in well, making new friends. An added bonus for me was that the two older ones could walk to their school unescorted, something almost unheard of today. Ray was also happy to come home every day for lunch, which he couldn't do when working in Vancouver. The only rush hour in Port Alberni was when the shifts changed at the MB mills.

Over the next decades, we would find there were many more benefits to living in this small vibrant community.

chapter two

A MACMILLAN BLOEDEL TOWN

A BRIEF HISTORY

The forests surrounding Port Alberni have been the mainstay of the city's economy from the start. In 1860 Captain Edward Stamp, an English shipmaster and entrepreneur, opened the first sawmill in the area. The mill was later sold to James Anderson and became known as the Anderson Sawmill. A small community of about two hundred people lived in the vicinity of the mill and made their living from forestry. In 1864, the mill closed because it had run out of available logs. The technology did not exist to log higher up the mountains, so only those trees close to the water were felled and dropped into the inlet. Workers left to find employment elsewhere.

The opening of the Canadian Pacific Railway (1886) across Canada created opportunities for immigrants, and those with farming skills began pre-empting land in the Alberni Valley. The Anderson Company, which still owned 1,000 hectares (2,500 acres) of land, began developing a townsite with the hope of selling land and recouping some of their investment.

The settlement was named Alberni, after the young Spanish lieutenant colonel Don Pedro de Alberni from the Nootka expedition to the west coast—though there is no evidence he ever sailed down to the head of the Alberni Inlet. Captain George Albert Huff built a wharf at the site of today's Victoria Quay that enabled supplies and mail to be shipped up-island from Victoria.

The next venture was a paper mill, the first of its kind in British Columbia, constructed by the BC Paper Manufacturing Co. Ltd. in 1891. It was built on the banks of the Somass River, where the present-day Paper Mill Dam Park is located. The first steamer to call at Huff's Wharf was the *Barbara Boscowitz* carrying supplies and equipment for the paper mill. Paper was then made from rags, but when the supply of rags ran out after four years the mill was abandoned. By 1896 another settlement developed south of Alberni. Entrepreneur Arthur E. Waterhouse arrived at the instigation of the Canadian Pacific Navigation Company to build a wharf; this he located at the foot of today's Argyle Street. He then opened a warehouse and a store that catered mostly to miners working in nearby China Creek. The rivalry between the two towns developed at this time due to competition in trade between the wharves. This new settlement was first named New Alberni, then changed to Port Alberni on March 1, 1910. The arrival of the Esquimalt & Nanaimo (E & N) Railway in 1911 benefited both communities by providing a further link to communities on the eastern side of Vancouver Island. Port Alberni incorporated in 1912, and the neighbouring settlement of Alberni incorporated in 1913.

Those early pioneers recognized the forests could be made to produce an economic product, and many small mills came and went. In 1904 the Barclay Sound Cedar Company was established on the site of the present Alberni Pacific Division. In 1915 Howard Dent leased the mill and changed its name to Alberni Pacific Lumber Company. He sold it in 1925 to an English lumber company, Denny, Mott and Dickson, which ran it until H.R. MacMillan Export Company bought it in 1936.

The two towns grew alongside the forest industry and other resource-based industries like mining, agriculture, and fishing, providing necessary jobs and an idyllic lifestyle only interrupted by the ebb and flow of the various industries.

THE MACMILLAN BLOEDEL ERA

There were other logging and sawmill operators over the years, but it wasn't until 1951—when Bloedel, Stewart & Welch and H.R. MacMillan merged their holdings to become one of the world's largest forest companies, MacMillan Bloedel Ltd.—that Port Alberni benefited from some stability and continuity in the forest industry. The corporate merger with Powell River Company in 1959 further secured a future for forest workers in both towns. By 1972 mills stretched along the Port Alberni waterfront, from the mouth of the Somass River at the north end of town to Polly Point in the south. They included Alberni Plywood Division (Alply), Alberni Pacific Division, Somass Division, and Alberni Pulp and Paper Division (Alpulp).

Public access to the Alberni Inlet was limited to the old wooden dock at the foot of Argyle Street, where the venerated *Lady Rose* anchored to pick up passengers and freight bound for points along the inlet out to the west coast of Barkley Sound. In 1973, Clutesi Haven Marina gave further access to the waterfront where the Somass River meets the Alberni Inlet. The marina offered boat ramps and docking facilities for leisure craft. It was here that fishermen brought their catch of giant salmon to be cleaned and weighed.

The waterfront in 1972 was a busy place; tugs, barges, and giant freighters were familiar sights in the harbour as they loaded forest products for delivery to all parts of the world. Floating log booms were common along the inlet, as were giant logging trucks on the highway and railway cars carrying freight on the E & N Railway to Parksville, then south to Nanaimo or Victoria. Residents were used to the constant sound—the hum of industry—their lives so intertwined with the forest industry.

Forests were vital to the city's economic stability. Trees surrounded the town; they grew up the hillside of Mt. Arrowsmith, which at 1,819 metres (5,968 feet) towered like a sentinel over the city; they grew along the mountains on both sides of the Alberni Inlet, and north to the Beaufort Mountain Range. There appeared to be a limitless supply of timber, and in earlier days few paid attention to planning or conservation. But in the 1970s there were those in the forest industry who began to fear for the future unless major reforestation took place. MB had already embarked on an intensive forestry program to ensure its future wood supply, but by the 1970s and 1980s logging was taking place higher up the mountains and in more difficult terrain, and stands of virgin old-growth were fast disappearing.

With a network of logging roads winding through hundreds of miles, the forests also provided residents with an accessible outdoor wilderness playground. Armed with MB logging road maps for each logging division, they would take to the woods on weekends in search of that idyllic spot for hiking, picnicking, or launching a boat or canoe in the rivers and lakes surrounding the town.

H.R. COMES TO TOWN

Harvey Reginald MacMillan, or H.R. as he was fondly known, was present at many of the milestones in Port Alberni's history. He and wife Edna's main residence was on Balfour Street in the Shaughnessy area of Vancouver, but he was a regular visitor to Port Alberni from his summer waterfront home, Greyshakes, in Qualicum Beach. In 1943 he added Arrowsmith Farm, in Qualicum, to his real estate holdings. For getaways at sea, he also owned the *Marijean*, a former US Navy minesweeper he picked up in Seattle at the end of the war and converted into a luxury yacht. He named the boat after his two daughters, Marion and Jean.

In 1947, H.R. bought another farm adjoining Arrowsmith Farm. This was a twelve hundred–hectare (three thousand–acre) model farm built at great expense by General Alexander D. McRae, a former senator. It had large barns for its purebred cattle, sheep, and pigs, and elaborate ponds for ducks and geese. The farm was a highly mechanized operation, utilizing the latest scientific methods, but still it lost money. H.R. was determined to make it profitable. Besides, it also gave him something to do with his leisure time when he visited Qualicum on weekends. Ken Drushka wrote in his biography of H.R.:

> *His early morning ritual now included a tramp through the fields with the farm manager, and an examination of livestock, during which he picked out turkeys and beef to stock the larders on the* Marijean, *his house in Vancouver and the kitchens of his daughters and friends.*[1]

On weekends at Qualicum, kilometres of forested logging roads beckoned H.R., not unlike his Port Alberni employees. Accompanied by forestry manager Ian Mahood, he would drive his Bentley over the unpaved rugged roads. As they inspected the young forests he passed on ideas on how to manage them for the future. Mahood told the story of how after one long weekend spent with H.R. at his home in Qualicum, he was rewarded with three quarts of fresh, warm milk from his dairy farm.

> *I took it home as a peace offering to my wife, but she was so angry that the weekends with the kids had been preempted by H.R., that the milk was never used and went sour! Happily, our marriage survived.*[2]

Occasionally there were trips into Port Alberni to buy groceries. Ken Hutcheson recalled seeing the forestry tycoon in the Super Valu store. His wife, Edna, filled her shopping basket with items they needed for their cottage in Qualicum, while H.R. trucked around his own basket, filling it with all the specialty foods he enjoyed, such as smoked oysters. The young man who carried the grocery bags out of the store to "that big gold jobby," the Bentley, received a five dollar tip.

Marie Jacobsen, who owned the Greenwood Hotel in the city, wrote in her diary about the time H.R. dropped in unannounced and was served a bowl of soup in the dining room. He looked around at the men sitting there and said, commiserating with them, "It is a dirty day in the bush today." The weather was bad and the men had had to leave the bush early. Marie remembered them sitting around grouching and complaining about having to work so hard to make money for H.R. MacMillan. He should come and cut his own logs, they said. Being unaware of who the stranger was sitting with them, they continued to bad-mouth H.R. with colourful language. H.R., agreeing with them, said, "I know that guy, he's a tough master. I don't think he's going to change his policies."

When H.R. finished his dinner, he returned to the kitchen and thanked Marie for the meal. "They are really having a good time in there," he said and laughed. Marie went into the dining room, and the men asked her, "Who was that bastard?" When she told them it was H.R. himself, the loggers thought they would all be fired the next day. "I doubt it," said Marie. "He came in for one purpose, to see what kind of meal and accommodation you were getting for $2.50 a day!"[3]

MB'S SOCIAL LIFE

The social life of Port Alberni was divided between the community and the MacMillan Bloedel divisions, with each plant having its own social club that organized dances, parties, and sporting events. Initially our introduction to the community was through the manager of MB's Alberni Plywood Division, Albert (Hoddy) Hodson, and his wife, Jean (née McPherson), whom he had met in high school. At various parties in their home, the Hodsons were perfect hosts, introducing us to staff members and people in the community. Hoddy always had a smile and a toothpick in his mouth.

The community identified with Hoddy as once being a member of the renowned "Termites," a Port Alberni championship high school basketball team. During the Second World War he joined the RCAF, reaching the rank of flight lieutenant. He received the Distinguished Flying Cross for his courage and bravery flying missions to disable enemy ships. After the war he and Jean married; they had four children: Brooke, Drew, Kent, and Tracy. Many of the war veterans from the old high school team revived the interest in basketball, and the Albernis became a hotbed of the sport when the Senior A Men's Alberni Athletics had everyone cheering for the home team in the old Alberni Athletic Hall. The games were broadcast over CJAV radio by Jim Robson, a young radio announcer who had been recently hired as a sports writer. Most of the athletes worked for MB. Today the town cheers for the Alberni Bulldogs, a BC Hockey League team that draws on that same community spirit.

Hoddy had a long career with the Alberni Plywood Division before becoming supervisor of the BC Forest Products veneer plant in Youbou. When he retired, there was no golden handshake, no gold watch, just a golden toothpick to mount on his wall.

Jean was as well known in the community as her husband, for her volunteer work with the West Coast General Hospital's Women's Auxiliary, an organization that provided many of the comforts for patients and specialized equipment necessary for diagnosis or treatment.

The Alberni Plywood mill was like a big family, and this started with the management team of Hoddy and Jim Olsen, the production superintendent. Ray Morris took care of personnel matters, and office manager Brian Hardy looked after the financial affairs of the plant. Don Gillis was in charge of the engineering department, and Ray (my husband) was plant engineer. The plant had three general foremen: Reg Morris, Ron Ritchie, and Rusty Allen.

At Christmas, staff members received a poinsettia plant delivered to their home courtesy of MB. Local florists must have loved this business; I know that I enjoyed the gift. Old-timers remember MB workers once lining up for free turkeys when the E & N Railway passenger train pulled into the Port Alberni railway station around Christmas time.

MB showed in many ways that it valued its workers. The MB Christmas parties were the biggest and the most memorable, and were usually held in Echo Community Centre. The event brought management and staff together socially, some coming from the head office in Vancouver. Occasionally there were gold wristwatches given for twenty-five years' service, or gifts presented to those retiring. The buffet table was placed down the centre of the Cedar Room, the largest room in the centre, with surrounding tables covered with white tablecloths and Christmas decorations. You could always tell the caterer by the traditional pile of dinner rolls at each end of the long table. Nettie's Catering did a wonderful job. After feasting, the buffet tables were cleared away and Silvereen was sprinkled on the floor making it ready for dancing. By this time, the band had set up on the stage.

Occasionally a popular local band named the Cavemen entertained; the musicians were music teachers and headed by Bill Cave. Alternately, DJs played the top hits of the day. During the 1970s the twist and jive were the rage. Elvis Presley brought everyone to the dance floor, and Neil Diamond had everyone singing along. Every taste was accommodated, from modern to old-fashioned waltzes, foxtrots, and polkas. Those fit enough sashayed under bars or poles to the Caribbean beat of the limbo. Women wore jumpsuits or mini skirts, while men were resplendent in their trendy knit shirts with polyester bell-bottom trousers.

The company liked to spread its business around, so other parties were held at the Greenwood Motor Hotel, in North Port. Carl Schretlen, who purchased the hotel from Marie Jacobsen in 1971, had been in the catering business in Vancouver's Gastown for twenty-four years.

The Alberni Plywood Division had many bowling teams, at one time eighteen. The team names were as colourful as the participants—Pin Sluggers, Duds, Gremlins, Donkeys, and Clippers, to name only a few. The only bowling alley, on Fourth Avenue, was well used by the whole community. There were also baseball teams and basketball teams, and always a healthy rivalry between the MB division teams.

MB also tried to look after its employees' inner well-being. The company endorsed the encounter movement of the seventies and urged managers and staff to participate in the program. The encounter group was an initiative to help individuals become more sensitive to their own and other people's attitudes and emotions, and more spontaneous in expressing their feelings. It was designed to promote leadership, authority, and the dynamics of change in an organization.

An encounter instructor with a retreat in Duncan gave sessions for MB staff at the Timberlodge Motel. Unfortunately some participants became more confused than liberated. Perhaps noticing the personality difference in staff after the sessions, wives were encouraged to take the course. Always interested in something new, I joined other wives at a Sunday session in the motel. Lessons were given on proper breathing. The image still remains with me of the wives lying flat on their backs on the floor being encouraged to breath using stomach muscle control, with the instructor checking each woman to make sure she was breathing properly. I am not sure the encounter worked for everyone!

EXPLORING MB'S FORESTS

MacMillan Bloedel's managed forest was open to the public to explore and enjoy, and everyone in region took advantage of the open roads, always mindful of active logging that might be going on in the area. Throughout the Alberni region there were hundreds of miles of logging roads, some in remote areas where logging in progress limited public access to non-operating hours. You ventured forth on a logging road at your own risk, always respecting posted signs that showed when roads were open.

Each forest area was marked with the date when the trees were planted, and MB guide maps were available for every division.

Franklin River Division, to the south of Port Alberni, had one of the oldest and biggest logging camps. It was named for Victoria auctioneer Selim Franklin, MLA, who promoted Dr. Robert Brown's Vancouver Island Exploring Expedition in 1864.[4] The first logs were taken from Franklin Creek in 1935 for the start-up of the Bloedel, Stewart & Welch's Somass sawmill. The camp gained a reputation for being the most dangerous place for accidents and deaths. Hard hats or "skull guards"—sometimes nicknamed "widow makers"—were introduced to the camp in June 1939 and saved many lives.

The camp became the largest railway logging "show" (operation) on Vancouver Island and had the distinction of being the first in North America to use power saws, and the first in the region to use logging trucks. The combined truck and logging show covered a total area of about 129 square kilometres (50 square miles) from the Beaufort Range to the Pacific Ocean and contained some of the finest timber found on the west coast.

The camp had a fair-sized village, with quarters for married men and their families and a one-room school for their children, and a boarding house for single men. When the school later closed, the children were bussed into Port Alberni. People who lived in camp said there was no life like it; they liked their independence and loved being in the forest, fishing in the rivers or boating in the inlet. Loggers were known to work hard and play hard.

Franklin River Division was easily accessed from Port Alberni. The road was partially paved to the community of Bamfield on the west coast. This was the only land route to the small picturesque village; the *Lady Rose* carried passengers and freight down the Alberni Inlet and made stops in Bamfield. The main road south wound past Coleman Creek, Franklin River, and Sarita River to Pachena and on through what would become Pacific Rim National Park Reserve on the coast. The scenery in this area is spectacular. In some places giant Douglas firs and cedars tower above the roadway; in others there are magnificent views of the Alberni Inlet.

Farther west and south of Nitinat Lake, some of the cedars are over a thousand years old. The Carmanah Giant (95.8 metres) is considered the world's tallest Sitka spruce and the tallest tree in Canada. In 1990 the province created a park to preserve the stand of trees. The lower part of the adjacent Walbran Valley was added in 1995 to form the Carmanah-Walbran Provincial Park.

If you were unlucky enough to land behind another vehicle travelling through this forest, it could be a pretty dusty and dangerous experience watching out for flying rocks. Passing a loaded logging truck on one of these roads was not for the faint of heart.

Sarita Division logging camp, an extension of the Franklin Division, gave access to the Sarita River. In 1948 a bug infestation played a role in the decision to start logging there while the dead timber was still in prime condition. The job of salvaging the 4,800 hectares (11,900 acres) of timber fell to Bloedel, Stewart & Welch, because it had the biggest stake in the infected area. The company also had the manpower and equipment to do the job.

Sproat Lake Division was close to Port Alberni on the west side and en route to the west coast. The lake was named for Gilbert Malcolm Sproat, who was sent to the area from London, England, in 1860 to oversee the Anderson Company operations in the Alberni Valley. Logging at Sproat Lake has been ongoing since the Sproat Lake Lumber Company, later Sproat Lake Sawmills, began operations in 1926. In the 1930s Bloedel, Stewart & Welch began logging in the area to feed the Great Central Lake Sawmill. Highway 4 cuts through the division, and then follows Kennedy River west toward Ucluelet and Tofino. The division included Sproat, Elsie, Dixon, Ash, and Great Central Lakes. Dixon Falls and the Ash River area are rugged, remote, and stunningly beautiful.

Kennedy Lake Division at Pacific Rim National Park Reserve included the forests from Ucluelet and Port Albion to Tofino, and east to Kennedy Lake and Clayoquot Arm, part of Tree Farm Licence 44, formerly TFL 21 and 22. This division became the setting for one of the most confrontational environmental protests ever seen in British Columbia history, one that directly affected Port Alberni.

Cameron Division encompassed Cameron Lake by Cathedral Grove, MacMillan Provincial Park, Mt. Arrowsmith, Mt. Cokely Park, and north to Horne Lake. The division logging roads followed Cameron River from its source at Labour Day Lake and the northeast slope of McLaughlin Ridge.

Northwest Bay Division was accessed from the Island Highway south of Parksville. Here the logging roads followed both branches of Englishman River. In the springtime Rhododendron Lake is alive with blossoms and quite beautiful. Mt. Moriarty looks over the area with Moriarty Creek flowing into Englishman River.

All these forests are critical to Port Alberni's prosperity. But the trees mean much more to the people of the Alberni Valley than just dollars; they are the cornerstone of outdoor recreation not only for residents in the area but also for those in central Vancouver Island. They are the foundation on which Port Alberni developed into a thriving community.

{ *chapter three* }

GETTING TO KNOW THE CITY

AMALGAMATED BUT NOT UNITED

In 1967 Alberni and Port Alberni were the first two cities in Canada to voluntarily amalgamate, becoming Port Alberni. This followed many years of discussion, but the divisions and rivalry between the twin cities remained. Alberni residents who were born and raised there found it difficult to now say they were from Port Alberni. For some they would forever be from Alberni. This fact was clearly illustrated at the funeral of one elderly woman. When the minister in charge of the proceedings unknowingly mentioned that the recently deceased had lived in Port Alberni all her life, a relative in the audience quickly jumped up to correct the minister: "She was from Alberni, not Port Alberni."

In theory the business community was united, but it remained divided with two business associations, the North Port and the South Port Business Associations. On the other hand, the Alberni Valley Chamber of Commerce spoke for everyone. And the two rival newspapers became one when Fred Duncan of the *Twin Cities Times* purchased Irving Wilson's *West Coast*

Advocate and named the new newspaper the *Alberni Valley Times*. The first edition came off the press on October 28, 1967, the day of amalgamation.

Perhaps the biggest uniting force for the twin cities was the Echo '67 Community Centre and the Centennial Pool constructed in the middle of town at the time of amalgamation. The centre included several social rooms, a lounge and kitchen, and offices of the Parks and Recreation Department. The Alberni Valley Museum was added to the complex in 1973; the two buildings were later joined by a branch of the Vancouver Island Regional Library.

Another common institution was the hospital. City fathers had not thought of amalgamation when they considered building a hospital, but good instincts and available land prompted them to build strategically in between the two towns. West Coast General Hospital (WCGH) was sited on Eighth Avenue to ease any friction between the two communities. Perhaps hoping to set differences aside, the *Alberni Advocate* reported in 1912 on the position of the hospital, "8,400 feet from the Alberni post office, 6,600 feet from the Port Alberni depot, and 10,000 feet from the Canadian Pacific Lumber Co. mill."[1]

Over the years the hospital went through additions and alterations, replacing the old facility with a new five-storey hospital in 1952 to maintain good health services for the communities in the area. The emergency department provided care for the entire west coast, from treating injuries suffered hiking the West Coast Trail to accidents at sea. MB also recognized the importance of fast available medical services for its workers in the woods or on the mill floor. Local doctors handled almost any emergency. Occasionally, a difficult case was transported to Victoria or Vancouver by ambulance, or in extreme cases by air ambulance. The community was well served by doctors working in various fields of medicine.

The hospital administrator, Malcolm Telford, worked with the WCGH board of trustees, whose representatives came from city council, the school board, the regional district, and the community at large. Laundry and meals were handled in-house. The bright and youthful candystripers assisted nursing staff. The Women's Auxiliary fundraised for necessary medical equipment and comfort care items, and also operated a lovely gift shop in the hospital lobby.

The big "H" on the roof of the hospital was a visible welcome sign when you drove into town. Residents have always considered the hospital a prized possession and have vigorously supported it financially. Getting good health care in a town geographically isolated with only one road access was important for everyone.

The central area on Sixth Avenue was also the chosen location of a new public safety building for the RCMP and a new city works yard built at amalgamation.

School District 70's administration office was in South Port, in the former Shop Easy food store building on Tenth Avenue, now the location of Quality Foods. Later a new administration office was built on the corner of Sixth and Roger Street. Bob Moss was then the school superintendent, with Harry Carroll maintenance superintendent.

Advanced education students had to travel to Nanaimo, Victoria, or Comox for further studies until 1976 when North Island College opened a satellite campus in the city in the former Smith Memorial School at the corner of Eighth and Maitland Street, a school once operated by the Roman Catholic Church. The original school had started with a number of old army huts joined together by a main corridor. When fire destroyed the centre portion in 1959, a new two-storey brick building was constructed the following year. Without financial aid from the Ministry of Education the school struggled financially, and in 1972 it became the first community-operated independent school in British Columbia. Four years later the school closed and the building became home to North Island College. Hardy Fink took over the gymnasium to house the gymnastic club, and Leanne and Gordon Jones operated a playschool in the library.

Joan Frohn-Nielsen became the first college director, a position she held until her retirement in 1991. Originally from Nelson, BC, she was educated at UBC in Vancouver, Queen's University in Kingston, Ontario, and the Sorbonne in Paris. She married in Denmark and had two sons, Thor and Per. In BC she taught in Squamish and the Kootenays before moving to Port Alberni in 1973 to teach at Mt. Klitsa School. She ran the Continuing Education Program before taking the North Island College position. Frohn-Nielsen loved to travel, her trips taking her to Africa, the Middle East, and Asia. She was a staunch supporter of the arts.

Understandably there were still two fire departments in the amalgamated Port Alberni—one in North Port and one in South Port. But the fire chief's office was in the newest station, built on Tenth Avenue in South Port at the time of amalgamation. Rusty Phillips was fire chief, with Ernie Rusel his assistant. On Argyle Street, just up the hill from the main post office, the old Port Alberni firehall remained with its distinctive drying tower looking down on the town. When we arrived in Port Alberni it was a forlorn-looking building, sitting derelict awaiting its fate. Many ideas floated about concerning what to do with the structure. In the end it was demolished.

There were also two post offices. North Port maintained a small red-bricked substation at the corner of Johnston Road and Gertrude Street. The residents of Alberni fought long and hard to maintain their small post office when there was danger of it being closed and all business being transacted in South Port. Alberni's feisty mayor Mabel Anderson, the first female mayor on Vancouver Island, is fondly remembered for her campaign in the early 1960s to keep the post office in her community.

The main Post Office and Unemployment Insurance Office on Argyle Street in South Port was a rather drab, institutional-type, grey-stone federal government building constructed in

1959 and located across the street from City Hall. It was a poor replacement for Port Alberni's beautiful old brick post office with its handsome clock tower that had once held pride of place on Third Avenue; after the 1946 earthquake in Comox damaged the building it had to be demolished, much to the dismay of many local residents.

The postmaster was Les Hammer, who would later be elected alderman in 1962, then served as Port Alberni's mayor from 1964 to 1967. He worked diligently with Fred Bishop in successfully negotiating amalgamation of the twin cities. Hammer had come to Port Alberni in 1946 to work for the provincial police force. Soon after, he applied for the postmaster's job and held that position for thirty-five years, retiring in 1981. He was active in the local branch of the Navy League of Canada, and in 1967 was awarded a life membership in that organization for his work with young people.

When I interviewed Hammer he told me about his other hobby, ham radio and communicating with other amateur radio operators. His hobby began when he took a wireless radio and communication course, graduating at the top of his class. This got him a job as a disc jockey in Vancouver, and then as a radio operator on the CP cruise ships, a lifestyle he enjoyed until the war interrupted his travels. He served in the air force, and remained an active member of the Alberni Legion, Branch 55, for forty-one years.

South Port had the largest shopping area, on Third Avenue, anchored on the east side by the Woodward's store, Fletcher's Furniture Store, and the Royal Bank of Canada, followed by a variety of small businesses and the Smoke Shop. On the west side was Saan, Fields, Nootka Gift Shop, and above it Miller's Paint; next door was the Pine Café, a Chinese restaurant, and then Woolworths. The Nootka Gift Shop was a destination spot for our family at Christmas time. It had one of the largest selections of Native arts and crafts on Vancouver Island, and also sold crystal, pottery, and beautiful books about the west coast.

Also located on Third Avenue was Port Alberni's only radio station. CJAV was jointly owned by Bill Gibson and Moe Inwards, who purchased it in 1972 from Ken Hutcheson. Hutcheson was a prominent member of the community who later became the economic development officer appointed by the city. Inwards, originally from Weyburn, Saskatchewan, started at CJAV in 1958 as a DJ, then moved into sales but remained an on-air personality. The BC Association of Broadcasters named him Broadcast Citizen of the Year in 1981 for his contribution to the community and the province. He sold his interest in the station in 1986 before moving into real estate.

Ike Patterson was another recognizable face associated with the station. With his hand-held tape recorder he did impromptu interviews and on-the-spot reporting. "Old Ike," as he was affectionately known, knew everyone in the community. There were few events he did not record in some form or another.

Most of the banks had their main outlets in South Port. Two of them, the Canadian Bank of Commerce and the Bank of Montreal, anchored the next corner on Third Avenue, at Angus Street. On the other corner was the old Beaufort Hotel built in 1913, once the largest hotel in both cities, with fifty rooms plus a dining room and lobby. The hotel also advertised having private baths, heating, lighting, and toilet facilities; it was quite advanced for the times.

Dissecting Third Avenue, which runs south to north, was Argyle Street flowing west from Eric J. Dunn Junior Secondary School down to the waterfront. At almost four lanes wide, it was one of the largest streets. Old-timers would tell of the wonderful times when they used to toboggan down the hill to the waterfront, probably before cars arrived on the scene!

At the bottom of the hill were the E & N Railway Station and the Carmoor Block, with the King Edward Hotel, dating from 1910, and the Somass Hotel nearby. Another destination shop was the Alberni Hardware on First Avenue operated by Charlie MacNaughton. In the early seventies, the old-style store still had sawdust on the floor, with boxes upon boxes of items you wouldn't find anywhere else. At first glance it looked a mess, but staff knew exactly where everything was and could easily find the item requested.

Port Alberni City Hall, located across from the main post office on Argyle Street, had opened in 1959. The honour of cutting the ribbon that day was given to Alice Crankenthorp, the first pioneer settler child born in Port Alberni. Architect Dexter Stockdill, of Wade, Stockdill and Armour, designed the building that also housed the Port Alberni Public Library. The *Columbus Tree* monument at City Hall is a section of a Douglas fir felled in the Nitinat Valley in 1957 and donated by MB for the opening. The giant timbers protecting the display once formed part of the Stamp/Anderson Sawmill in 1860.

In 1972 the Paramount movie theatre on Argyle Street was the only cinema showing current movies. The Capitol Theatre across the street sat empty awaiting its fate, having closed in the early fifties—as had the Roxy Theatre, in North Port, which was eventually demolished. The Capitol Theatre has now been refurbished as a live theatre, home to Portal Players, and a venue for small productions.

At the bottom of Third Avenue were a number of businesses, including Ken Barlow's Music Centre and Revelstoke Lumber Yard. The J & L Drive-In, still operating in 2013, is the oldest drive-in restaurant on Vancouver Island.

The Barclay Hotel, on Redford Street where Third Avenue becomes Gertrude Street, was gutted by fire in 1973. A small building was constructed on the site and became home for the first cable station in the mid-1970s. Walter Green operated it with program director Günther Smuda, whose programs were identifiable by the shaky camera work. Over the years I got to know both gentlemen and we had a good working relationship. If you were willing to do the work and put together a show promoting an event or exhibition, they would give you time on the air. Television on Vancouver Island was still in its infancy when we arrived in 1972. Cable TV only ran once or twice a week and without cable there were only two channels available: Channel 6 Victoria and Channel 12 Vancouver. Rabbit ears were still in use for some TVs, and test patterns were normal.

The *Alberni Valley Times* was located on Napier Street between Third and Fourth Avenues, around the corner from the Dairy Queen. The town's oldest newspaper can trace its beginnings back to 1907 when it was called the *Alberni Pioneer News*. There have been name and format changes over the years, with its current name adopted in the same year as amalgamation. But it always sought to reflect the voice of the community. The newsroom, administration, and print shop were conveniently located in one building in the lower floodplain part of town across from Dry Creek Park. The newspaper with its historic masthead of a snow-capped Mt. Arrowsmith became a daily in 1970 and was purchased three years later by Conrad Black's Sterling Newspapers. There were many dedicated publishers from 1970 to 1990, including Fred Duncan, Rollie Rose, Ron Nelson, and Nigel Hannaford. The newspaper recognized its place in the community and supported charitable community events, organizations, and sporting activities. There was always a healthy competition from the Vancouver and Victoria newspapers.

The MB Community Relations Office was in South Port, at the corner of Third Avenue and Kingsway Street. Bernard Kimble had been hired away from the *AV Times* to handle publicity for the company and improve public relations between local MB operations and Alberni Valley residents. Lillian Geigle, his secretary, remembers their office as a place where people felt free to express their complaints, to seek financial or material aid such as lumber or plywood for charitable organizations, to arrange tours of the mills and logging operations for special visitors and groups, and to forward news releases and literature. After Kimble and his wife, Peggy, retired to Schooner Cove in 1982, Jerry Peterson took over during a turbulent time, and the office was moved to the company headquarters on Sixth Avenue. Frank Hastings next filled the position as MB employee relations manager. He was well liked by everyone, and stayed in that position until retirement.

After amalgamation, North Port maintained its own small business district at Adelaide Centre on lower Johnston Road and along Gertrude Street. Anchoring the small shopping area next door to the bank and post office was St. Andrew's United Church and hall, built in 1939. Originally a Presbyterian Church that was built in 1892 and destroyed by fire in 1915, St. Andrew's was one of Alberni's finest buildings. The congregation used the church hall until a new church was built. It became St. Andrew's United Church in 1925 when four Protestant denominations merged to become the United Church of Canada.

The provincial government offices were on Elizabeth Street, where the government agent, Gil Mundell, had his office; it was one-stop shopping for birth, marriage, and death certificates plus driving licences. After amalgamation, the old Alberni City Hall at the foot of Johnston Road, on the banks of the beautiful Somass River, sat empty for some time. Later the building became the offices of the Alberni–Clayoquot Regional District.

Also on Johnston Road was the Arlington Hotel, built in 1893 by Matt Ward, which was once the social centre of old Alberni. Loggers, farmers, and fishermen have gathered at its Arli Pub for decades, sharing stories or news about the community. It was the second hotel built in Alberni, the first being the Alberni Hotel across from Kitsuksis Creek. The Royal Canadian Legion Branch 169 was built across the road. Port Alberni had its own Legion Branch 55 on Fourth Avenue. The two branches have since joined to become Branch 293.

A large store of note in North Port was Jowsey's Furniture and Appliances on Johnston Road. Customers came from across the island to shop for good furniture and appliances. Jack and Aili Jowsey started the store in 1947 as Jowsey's Home Variety and Electric, and the store remains in the family today.

WOODWARD'S:
RECOGNIZING THE POTENTIAL FOR PROSPERITY

Amalgamation did not change the shopping habits of residents in Alberni or Port Alberni. The dominant store for both communities was still Woodward's Department Store located in South Port on Third Avenue. No other community on Vancouver Island had a Woodward's, and Port Alberni was very proud to have it.

Decades earlier, a few of the Woodward's directors had favoured building in the larger, older cities of Victoria or Nanaimo, but they were out-voted. With considerable foresight, Woodward's realized that Port Alberni's potential for prosperity was greater than most places, and it would grow faster. Indeed, during the company's tenure in Port Alberni, the city would become British Columbia's third-largest-volume sea port; within 25 years 231 deep sea vessels would leave the city carrying 440,000 tons of lumber, 350,000 tons of paper, and 55,000 tons of plywood and shingles; the pulp mill would be equipped with a $23 million newsmachine producing 526 tons every twenty-four hours, thus becoming the world's fastest and one of the world's largest producers; and the lumber and paper mills would have a combined payroll of $42 million.[2] The company also judged the people of the Alberni Valley to be energetic, bold, and progressive.

But it was the friendship between Lieutenant-Governor W.C. "Billy" Woodward and H.R. MacMillan that brought the store to Port Alberni in 1948. Woodward had had requests from other communities to open stores. When asked about his decision to locate in Port Alberni, he pointed out the economics:

> *In 1941, the Dominion Bureau of Statistics quoted the Alberni district had a population of 6,584, and spent three million dollars, that is $462 per capita a year. Nanaimo on the other hand, had at that time a population of 6,635 and spent six million or $842 per capita per year.*[3]

This showed Woodward that a lot of money was being spent out of town because the community lacked facilities in Port Alberni. He speculated residents would prefer to shop at home. The company paid $15,000 for six lots on Third Avenue, three lots on Mar Street, and one lot on Fourth Avenue, all owned by Dr. Caleb T. Hilton. The good doctor took all the beautiful flowers from his garden and transplanted them into the garden of his new home on Bruce Street.

Woodward's was the first of the large chain stores to establish a branch in Port Alberni, followed by Eaton's, Woolworths, Simpson-Sears, and Zellers opening stores or order offices at intervals over the years. Fourteen Woodward's department managers were long-time employees. Jim Skinner, meat manager, and Bill Latimer, produce manager, moved to the city six months before the store opened. The first manager, Ken Whyte, was born and raised in Nanaimo and had already worked for Woodward's for sixteen years before moving to Port Alberni.

The *West Coast Advocate* called it "the most modern Department Store in Canada." When the doors opened on March 1, 1948, Mrs. C.N. Dane presented every customer with a rose.[4] The mayors and councillors from both cities attended. Woodward's Port Alberni served as a model for the Woodward's stores of the future.

Many of the small communities along the inlet and remote villages like Tofino, Port Albion, Long Beach, and Bamfield were served by a small cabin cruiser manned by Hazel Ritchie, a Woodward's personal shopper. The *Otter Point* skippered by Captain Richard Porritt loaded up with merchandise of all descriptions from the Port Alberni store. Woodward's looked on this as an innovative way to spread their service. Later when the road to the west coast was improved, the Port Alberni store became a drawing card for these residents and those from the east coast communities of Parksville and Qualicum. During the fishing season, crews from hundreds of fishing boats that docked annually in the harbour bought their food supplies at Woodward's.

When we arrived in 1972 Woodward's did have "something for everyone," as the old company slogan said. It carried a full line of merchandise: food, clothing, furniture, household supplies, electronics, garden supplies, and gas. You could purchase groceries, or fill up with gas and have your car engine checked at the gas depot. If you wanted a cup of coffee or a sandwich, the coffee shop in the store basement served your needs. The store also had an innovative service for grocery shoppers. After purchasing groceries you received a ticket identifying your food-cart; this allowed you to continue with your shopping elsewhere. When you were done, you drove up to a reception area by the grocery section, produced the ticket, and had your groceries delivered neatly into the trunk of your vehicle. No fuss, no bother, just another customer service. The store prided itself on service. Birthdays or Christmas gifts could be wrapped and conveniently mailed to other parts of Canada directly from the store. Woodward's was truly one-stop shopping.

Before each school year began in the fall, supplies were purchased on $1.49 day. The old familiar advertising jingle said it all: *$1.49 Day, Woodward's; $1.49 Day Tuesday*. On that particular day, the store was packed wall-to-wall with parents, all armed with the mandatory school supply list and vying for the same pens, pencils, and notebooks. Christmas time was also special, as the store had lovely window displays and was beautifully decorated.

The start of school always seemed to necessitate purchasing new shoes for the children. Woodward's had the distinction of having an x-ray machine in the shoe department. You placed your feet inside the machine then held down a button to see if your shoes fit properly. It was a great attraction for children who loved to look at their feet and wiggle their toes!

Manager Bill Patenaude was a tall man of good stature who walked with purpose through the store checking on the smooth running of each department. He and his wife, Helen, moved to Port Alberni in 1965 with their young daughter and two sons. In 1974 he was promoted to store manager, a position he held until his retirement in 1984.[5] Both Bill and Helen worked closely with the Lion's Club of Port Alberni.

A NEW SHOPPING EXPERIENCE

There was great excitement in the city when it was rumoured that Port Alberni might get a shopping centre with an indoor mall. Several had already been established in Nanaimo, and Royal Oak Holdings, a Vancouver-based company, had just opened a mall in Campbell River. Residents felt it was only a matter of time before Port Alberni would get one too. Just the thought of being able to shop indoors out of the rain during the winter months was enticing. As with all rumours, there was great speculation—in this case about where the mall would be located.

Until 1979 the main shopping area in town was on Third Avenue in South Port, anchored by the Woodward's store. But early in 1977, the Royal Oak company was approached by a group of residents about building an indoor mall in Port Alberni. They had the support of Port Alberni mayor Jim Robertson's council as well as the Alberni–Clayoquot Regional District and several retailers.

With approval in place, the company decided to locate the mall in a wooded area on the southeast corner of Johnston and Cherry Creek Roads in North Port, at the entrance to the city. It would be a perfect spot to catch the attention of visitors passing through town en route to the west coast. There was no opposition to the new mall but storeowners on Third Avenue could see the future retail market moving to North Port, just as the North Port merchants had felt back in 1948 when Woodward's arrived in town "like fifty small stores being planted in one place."[6] Still, Woodward's managed to hold its customers until 1993. Bill Patenaude believed it was the opening of the new Woodward's store in Nanaimo in 1981 that hurt his store, as a good percentage of his major appliance business went to Nanaimo. The Nanaimo Woodward's store anchored a new mall with about one hundred retail outlets, and created great competition for Port Alberni merchants.

The Alberni Mall opened with great fanfare on May 30, 1979, with forty-two stores and services.[7] These included a new Safeway, Kmart, Fields, Peoples Jewellers, Orange Julius, and Boots Drug Store. The opening drew a huge crowd excited to see the latest indoor shopping experience. The centre court became an ideal place for local performances, displays, sales, and other special events. On a cold wet wintry day, the mall became a destination either to shop or people watch.

Alice Chiko was hired as manager; under her direction the mall had a certain vibrancy that attracted customers. Chiko was a talented artist and a former schoolteacher who had served as alderman, worked with North Island College, and volunteered on many boards and organizations before starting up her own business, JAL Signs, a silkscreen shop, on Sixth Avenue. Her many contacts in town and throughout the region made her an ideal manager for the mall.

Many of the new stores ultimately fell victim to events happening elsewhere. Boots closed all its Canadian stores, and in Port Alberni was replaced by People's Drug Mart, only to be replaced by Pharmasave. When the anchor store, Safeway, closed in 1996, rather than let a competing food retailer into the space, it was leased to Liquidation World, and the mall lost a lot of its customers. Then the Hudson's Bay Company purchased Kmart with the intent of turning it into a Zellers and closing the rest of its stores. But when Kmart closed, the building was demolished to make way for a new Canadian Tire store. Hudson's Bay had already purchased the Woodward's store in 1993 and converted it to a Zellers.

The shopping experience has changed dramatically since then, with the construction across Johnston Road of the Pacific Rim Shopping Centre, which opened in 2005 with the big-box store Walmart and Extra Foods as its anchors. When the old

Alberni Mall reached its all-time low with only four stores left, it began to renovate and revitalize with new shopping opportunities for Port Alberni residents. Zellers in South Port is now closed; the building was purchased by Coulson Group of Companies.

COMMUNITY CONNECTORS

Anyone visiting Port Alberni is always amazed at the town's very wide streets, Argyle Street, Johnston Road, and Third Avenue are each as wide as a four-lane highway. Pioneer surveyor George Smith can be thanked for these splendid roads for it was he who, in the mid-1880s, surveyed the townsites and laid out the roads. City forefathers had grand ideas for the future of their town and planned accordingly.

However, the only connecting road between North Port and South Port remains Third Avenue/Gertrude Street, since the beautiful Roger Creek ravine separates the two communities. For many years there was talk of extending Tenth Avenue in South Port to join Ian Avenue in North Port by building a bridge across Roger Creek. When the Alberni Mall opened in North Port, an idea surfaced to construct a connector road along Twenty-first Avenue, but it too would have had to bridge the ravine and that was an added expense no one could justify. Those plans were put aside as the economic situation in the community declined.

The Horne Lake Road route was another connector road that was always a hot topic of conversation, especially during an election. Advocates wanted to build a road across the island to Horne Lake connecting to Qualicum; it would also shorten the route to Courtenay and Comox. The historic Horne Lake Trail to the lake can be hiked or travelled with a four-by-four vehicle, a distance of only a few miles. The argument was made that the only road in or out of the Alberni Valley to the east was Highway 4, and if that were blocked for whatever reason the town would be completely cut off. The general public would welcome a circular route.

The two Albernis were in fact cut off in 1948 when the famous landmark Angel Rock came crashing down, blocking the highway at Cameron Lake. Some theorized that the 1946 earthquake centred at Comox had weakened the rock. The Alberni Inlet offered an escape route by water, but few would venture out on the stormy waters of the Pacific Ocean in the middle of winter. There was a reason it was named the Graveyard of the Pacific.

In the 1880s the government had promised settler Charles Bishop a connector road inland from Cowichan to Courtenay. Fred Bishop, his grandson, initially led the campaign to build the link road and the family never gave up on it. Each year the Chambers of Commerce of Cowichan, Courtenay, and Port Alberni travelled in a cavalcade of cars and trucks to promote the road. The route required four-by-four vehicles, and only the hardy took on the task. Today, with the new growth in the communities of central Vancouver Island, the road still makes sense.

TOWN POLITICIANS

Both communities have strong ties to the past. Before becoming mayor of Port Alberni after amalgamation in 1967, serving until 1974, Fred Bishop had been the mayor of Alberni. His grandfather, Charles Frederic Bishop, had come to the Alberni Valley in 1886, having travelled across Canada on the first scheduled transcontinental passenger train from Montreal to Port Moody, then by boat to Vancouver. The Great Fire of Vancouver was still burning when the family arrived, and there was no place to stay, so they continued on to Victoria. The Bishops were attracted to the valley; they purchased 65 hectares (160 acres) and began farming.

The Bishops were a family dynasty, with three generations serving the Alberni community. In 1913 Charles Bishop became the first mayor of the new city of Alberni. His son Harold became an alderman in Alberni in 1919, and Harold's son Fred became mayor in 1962. Fred was a short, slightly balding man, smartly dressed, who exuded the air of a successful and respected businessman. He knew the town and its residents well. During the tsunami crisis in 1964, he as mayor of Alberni, and Les Hammer, the Port Alberni mayor, quickly called out police and rescue authorities. Their prompt action probably saved many lives. The community also loved him for promoting sports and bringing senior men's basketball to Alberni.

The years following amalgamation were no doubt trying for Mayor Bishop and his council, but they moved the town ahead and made the joining of the twin cities successful.

Despite a large labour-union force in town, it seemed to be conservative-minded mayors who got elected. Howard McLean followed Bishop as mayor in 1974. He was the grandson of Robert Bartlett McLean, the pioneer sawmill owner who built the R.B. McLean Lumber Company Sawmill.

McLean served as alderman from 1964 to 1973 and as mayor from 1974 to 1977. He was the local boy who stayed home and made good. His term as alderman was characterized by disaster but shored up by growth in the community. The disastrous tsunami alerted the city to an issue in the floodplain that was difficult to resolve. This, plus the amalgamation of the two cities in 1967, followed by the construction of major facilities such as Echo Centre and the police and court facilities, made it a difficult yet rewarding time in local politics.

McLean was a quiet man, very sincere and garnering respect; he was not easily influenced and not afraid of expressing his views. He was involved in service clubs such as the Rotary, K-40, and Kinsmen, and was a founding member of the Alberni District Association for the Mentally Retarded. He died in 1983 at age fifty-eight while vacationing on a cruise ship in the Panama.

His mother, Muriel, known as Amie to her friends, was one of the Alberni Valley's oldest residents, reaching the grand age of 107 before she died on January 5, 2008. Throughout her life she played the piano, and entertained at social events and at Fir Park Village retirement home. Amie worked diligently with the West Coast General Hospital's Women's Auxiliary.

Jim Robertson was elected mayor in 1978 after serving four years as alderman under Mayor McLean. Robertson was a successful real estate agent. He was a mild-natured man, quiet-spoken, short in stature, and always impeccably dressed.

In 1980, following one of the dirtiest election campaigns Port Alberni had ever experienced, Paul Reitsma knocked Jim Robertson out of the mayor's chair. Robertson had served only two years. Reitsma had begun his campaign for mayor the minute he was elected to his first term as alderman. The voter turnout was heavy in the November election, and turfed rival aldermen George McKnight and John Andrews out of office. Voters also rejected Bea Wilson as new faces filled the aldermanic seats—Len Nelson, Gillian Trumper, and Joe Stanhope, with Art Wynans topping the polls.

Reitsma was not a resident of Port Alberni but lived in Coombs with his wife and children. He was born in the Netherlands in 1948 and became a Canadian citizen in 1975. He divided his time between his businesses: Turner Brothers Travel in Port Alberni and R & R Travel Inc. in Parksville. He was a tall gangly man, with dark hair and a beard, who loved politics and supported the Social Credit Party. He was proud of his Dutch heritage, and spoke with a slight accent.

Reitsma liked to promote Port Alberni as a sports fishing destination that rivalled Campbell River for "Salmon Capital of the World." He even managed to garner a spot on the Jack Webster show on BCTV in 1982, where he presented the host with two twenty-pound spring salmon. One accidentally fell on Webster's desk, soiling all his papers. Somehow Reitsma managed to get Webster to hold up the two fish, which by this time were getting rather ripe, for the camera. Webster ultimately raffled off the salmon for $200, with the proceeds going to the Organization of Unemployed Workers group.

Reitsma would be elected mayor of Parksville in 1987, before jumping into provincial politics as the Parksville–Qualicum Liberal MLA. He will forever be remembered in BC politics for his letters to the editor of the Parksville newspaper, using the false name "Warren Betanko." He was ousted from the caucus after it was revealed he had been writing letters applauding himself and vilifying his political adversaries. This was the first time in provincial politics that a recall measure was used against a sitting minister. Parksville newspaper reporter Stan Gauthier led the "Recall Reitsma" campaign in 1998, collecting over seventeen thousand signatures. Reitsma resigned before the recall measure could be implemented, but the campaign was the only successful recall of a sitting parliamentarian in Canadian history to date.

Gillian Trumper won the 1983 mayoral election after a bitterly fought campaign against Reitsma. Before running for mayor, she had served two years as alderman and, before that, had given eight years of service on the board of trustees of School District 70, three years as chairman; she had also served four years on the board of North Island College. At the time she was first elected to the school board she had four children in the school system, and it seemed a natural thing to get involved. She was then critical of the Ministry of Education because schools were being asked to play a greater role in social concerns, which, she reasoned, put a strain on the system as teachers were finding less time for teaching.

In an interview prior to seeking election as alderman in 1981, she recalled the highlights of her eight years on School District 70. One was Port Alberni becoming part of the North Island College area. There were many in the community who did not agree with her and favoured joining Malaspina College in Nanaimo instead. It was a divisive issue within the school board and in the community. The deciding factor was that

Malaspina had stated that it would not provide courses and facilities in Port Alberni. North Island College has since built a beautiful new satellite facility in Port Alberni, providing valuable educational opportunities of students in the region.

Trumper was also proud of having championed a number of programs introduced during her tenure, including the Learning Assessment Centre, the French Immersion and the French Cadre programs, and the Family Life program. Offering French immersion and French as a second language presented some problems as well. The federal government grants for the introduction of French at the Grade 1 level sounded good, but it was up to the school district to finance the other grades as these students advanced. The French immersion program was so popular in Port Alberni that parents sometimes camped overnight just to get their child enrolled.

Reflecting on her years on the school board, Trumper recognized how difficult it was to get people to run for the position of trustee; perhaps she remembered her own busy life raising children and serving the community. Still, she encouraged others to seek election:

It is not such a tough job. The amount of time it takes is often a concern for people, but you must not look at it as a job. We have administration hired to do the job and we should allow them to do it.[8]

This experience on the school board made her well suited for the job as alderman, then later as mayor. There could not have been a more dedicated mayor; she was everywhere, at openings, dedications, services. Once she even brought cookies to a regional art exhibition being catered by Community Arts Council volunteers in the Cedar Room at Echo Centre. She well deserved the honour of being selected as Port Alberni Citizen of the Year in 1993.

Trumper's length of service and memberships is long. She had been a registered nurse before moving to the Alberni

Valley in 1969 with her husband, Dr. Mike Trumper, who also served the community through the Parks and Recreation Commission. During her term as mayor, and still serving as the local coroner, she would occasionally be called out from a council meeting to attend a sudden death. Trumper also served as president of the Union of BC Municipalities. In 2002 she was made a Freeman of the City of Port Alberni.

Trumper resigned her position as mayor when she was elected Liberal MLA for Alberni–Qualicum in May 2001. Her close friend June Kearney managed all her political campaigns. As MLA she held various portfolios such as Aboriginal Affairs, Parliamentary Reform, and Ethical Conduct, and also served on the committee reviewing the Freedom of Information and Protection of Privacy Act and was chair of the Women's Caucus Committee.

Ken McRae was the city's mayor from 2001 until losing the November 2011 election to John Maxwell Douglas. McRae brought new energy to the office of mayor. He led the community through some tough economic times as the forest industry declined. But he remained optimistic that the town would recover and, like others before him, he looked for ways to diversify the economy.

McRae had joined MB Alberni Plywood Division in 1957 and five years later went to work for Alberni Pulp and Paper. He took a two-year leave to work in the construction industry in New Zealand, and on return continued to work at Alpulp as a millwright until he retired in 1998. He served five years as president of the Port Alberni and District Labour Council, and has been a member of the Canadian Paperworkers Union for twenty-one years. In 2003 he was named Port Alberni Citizen of the Year.

In earlier times mayors and aldermen were elected yearly, usually in December, and taking their seat in January. This changed in 1989 when council was elected for a two-year term, then changed again in 1990, whereafter elections were held every three years.

Unlike the mayors and aldermen, city hall staff had more longevity. One example was long-time city manager Jim Sawyer, who had been city clerk in Alberni before amalgamation. He experienced first-hand the tsunami that swept through the city in 1964. He watched the river rise a foot a minute as he stood on the steps of Alberni City Hall. When it started lapping at the bottom step, he retreated across the street to join the rescuers manning a roadblock on the Kitsuksis Creek Bridge.

Before the two cities amalgamated, Sawyer worked with Port Alberni city clerk Dennis Thain, providing arguments for and against the union. They showed the benefits that would accrue to both cities and the differences in taxation, with Port Alberni having the highest percentage of industrial, commercial, and residential properties. After amalgamation, he became deputy city clerk, then eventually city manager, a position he held until retirement.

WACKY PROVINCIAL POLITICS

Provincially, British Columbia has a reputation for the wild and wacky rollercoaster ride of its politicians, but few could have predicted the outcome for Port Alberni's MLA Bob Skelly when he became leader of the New Democratic Party in 1984.

Skelly was only twenty-nine when he was first elected to the provincial legislature in 1972 as a member under NDP Premier Dave Barrett. He had been a schoolteacher before entering politics. He would serve the Port Alberni riding, provincially and federally, for over twenty years.

In 1984 he became the compromise choice in a leadership race to replace Dave Barrett. There was dissension in the ranks over Skelly's leadership, even talk of an NDP caucus revolt. Meanwhile Bill Bennett resigned as premier and Socred leader and was replaced by Bill Vander Zalm. Bennett would be remembered for building BC Place, Expo '86, and the Coquihalla Highway.

When Vander Zalm called an election for October 22, 1986, for Skelly "it was like jumping from the proverbial fire into the frying pan."[9] His campaign and news conferences were a disaster. Those who knew Skelly wondered where the confident, well-spoken, and thoughtful arguments and responses were. His nervousness in front of the cameras was captured on the nightly TV news reports. The NDP had trouble getting coverage over issues until near the end of the election campaign. The party failed to gain any seats, but they also didn't lose any.

Skelly's troubles took a back seat when Vander Zalm's bizarre policies and scandals forced him to resign over conflict-of-interest allegations regarding the sale of Fantasy Gardens. Rita Johnston took over as premier, albeit for just a short time.

Skelly resigned as NDP leader in May 1988—leaving Mike Harcourt, who had been sitting in the wings ready to take over as leader. Skelly may have had the legislative experience but Harcourt had the rapport with the press from his years as mayor of Vancouver. Harcourt defeated the Socreds in 1991, but faced difficult decisions regarding logging in Clayoquot Sound. He too resigned, over Dave Stupich's involvement with Nanaimo charity bingo operations.

The 1991 election brought Gordon Wilson into the fold as leader of the BC Liberal Party. He lobbied to be included in a CBC televised debate between Rita Johnston and Mike Harcourt. Wilson impressed many in the debate, resulting in the Liberals taking seventeen seats; Wilson was now leader of the opposition, and the Socred Party was gone.

Skelly ran federally in 1988 and was elected MP for the NDP in the Comox–Alberni riding. He served in that position until he was defeated in 1993. Interestingly, that was the same year his brother Ray was defeated after serving fourteen years as the NDP candidate in the Comox–Powell River riding. The

Skelly brothers served Vancouver Island well for many years. Bob Skelly retired to his home at Sproat Lake near Port Alberni.

Gerard Janssen succeeded Skelly in 1988 as the provincial NDP candidate for Comox–Alberni. Janssen was born in Holland and came to Canada with his parents in 1952. He lived at Whiskey Creek, a small rural community halfway between Parksville and Port Alberni, famous for its big ice cream cones. His wife, Flo, was a nurse at West Coast General Hospital. Janssen, a jeweller and watchmaker by profession, took over the jewellery business started by his parents in 1956. Janssen's Jewellers was located on lower Argyle Street. Before his election, Janssen was president of the Citizens First Committee and secretary of the Port Alberni Development Society; he also served two terms as president of the Alberni Valley Chamber of Commerce.

Janssen was appointed minister of small business, tourism, and culture on November 1, 2000. He also served as government whip and sat on the board of the Insurance Corporation of BC (ICBC). He held the seat until he was defeated by former mayor Gillian Trumper, then ran under the Liberal banner but a former Social Credit member.

FEDERAL REPRESENTATION

Port Alberni federal politicians have fared better than the provincial politicians, perhaps because they were far away in Ottawa out of the glare of publicity and public scrutiny. Comox–Alberni Liberal MP Hugh Anderson, agent for Thunderbird Insurance, was elected in 1974, replacing the popular NDP candidate Tom Barnett. Under the Pierre Elliott Trudeau government he held the position of parliamentary secretary to the minister of fisheries and the environment from 1977 to 1978, and then parliamentary secretary to the minister of Indian affairs and northern development until being defeated in the 1979 election.

Anderson was a large man, friendly, and easily accessible. With the 1970s, a time of great optimism in Port Alberni, thoughts turned toward building an airport. In 1976, Anderson managed to secure $250,000 in federal funding for an airport. But city council was split on the issue, three to three, with Mayor Howard McLean refusing to cast the deciding vote. This led to a referendum on the subject, where it was voted down. Needless to say, Anderson was very disappointed with the result. The final rub came when the Ministry of Transport said the money had to stay in the riding, but instead of going to Port Alberni it went toward paving Cassidy Airport in Nanaimo.

Unfortunately, the subject of an airport was frequently a hot political issue for local politicians. For years, planes had been landing and departing from a field on the Somass Delta, near the historic Somass Dairy Farm, and the subject of establishing an airport in the city had arisen several times. This invariably brought complaints about aircraft noise, traffic congestion, and anything else that could even remotely be blamed on an airport. It would take more than another decade before the Port Alberni Airport would be a reality.

Anderson also proposed a prison be located in Port Alberni, south of the city, at the site of the former Franklin River logging camp. He hoped the prison would boost the economy through government infrastructure projects. But public opposition shot down that proposal, too; forestry was booming at this time and there seemed no need to diversify the economy.

In the next election, Anderson was defeated in the new riding of Nanaimo–Alberni, but he continued to be active in the community serving as chairman of the Port Alberni Harbour Commission, now Port Authority. He re-entered politics when elected alderman in Port Alberni in December 1986, bringing his political experience to municipal government.

The NDP had a strong popular candidate to replace Anderson in Ted Miller, a teacher and guidance counsellor from Nanaimo. Miller held the riding from 1979 to 1984, when he was defeated by radio broadcaster and Progressive Conservative candidate Ted Schellenberg. Once again the riding was changed, this time to Nanaimo–Cowichan, resulting in a defeat for Schellenberg and a win for NDP Dave Stupich of Nanaimo. Schellenberg returned to his broadcasting career. Bob Skelly took the 1988 federal election for the NDP and held it until 1993.

COASTAL COMMUNITIES OF THE ALBERNI–CLAYOQUOT REGIONAL DISTRICT

Port Alberni is the centre of business and industry for a much larger geographic area on the west coast. Regional districts were created throughout the province to ensure that all residents had access to commonly needed services on a shared basis, regardless of where they lived. The Alberni–Clayoquot Regional District was established in May 1966. Geographically the region covered a huge rural area, including Clayoquot Sound and Barkley Sound, with diverse problems and concerns. The board represented the communities of Port Alberni, Beaver Creek, Cherry Creek, Beaufort, Sproat Lake, Tofino, Bamfield, Ucluelet, and Long Beach.

Meetings were held in the boardroom of the former Alberni City Hall at the foot of Johnston Road on the banks of the Somass River. Once or twice a year board members travelled to Tofino, Ucluelet, or Bamfield to hold meetings where local residents were encouraged to attend and voice their concerns. For regular monthly meetings west coast members made the long journey to Port Alberni. The Bamfield representative had to travel over a partly paved road or by the steamer *Lady Rose*.

The region also includes the Pacific Rim National Park Reserve, Canada's first marine park, which Princess Anne officially opened on May 4, 1971. The communities of Tofino, Ucluelet, and Bamfield are all within the park boundary. The park encompasses Long Beach, the Broken Group Islands, and more than a hundred small islands in Barkley Sound, plus the rugged and challenging West Coast Trail from Bamfield to Port Renfrew. Before the 1970s, six thousand hectares (fifteen thousand acres) of provincial Crown lands within the park were under tree farm licences (TFLs); those harvesting rights were bought back from the companies involved, or exchanged for other forested land.

Before the park designation, Long Beach was already a major draw, particularly for those with a different lifestyle. The "hippies" were concentrated on more remote sections of the beach. When Parks Canada administration took over, staff was given authority to evict the squatters; many of them remained in the area and became integrated into the Tofino population. Privately owned summer cottages that once dotted the shoreline of the beach were all expropriated. At this time the public had unrestricted access to Long Beach, meaning you could camp or drive your car on the beach. Some attempted to drive the length of the beach and became mired in the sand. Summer weekends were particularly busy; cars on the beach were sometimes three deep. The highway from Nanaimo to Long Beach was busy with cars, pickup trucks, and campers heading from the BC Ferries Departure Bay Terminal at Nanaimo to the west coast beaches—all, to the angst of Port Alberni businesses, driving right through town without a stop.

On the holiday weekend of May 24, 1973, an estimated ten thousand people were on the beach when two rival motorcycle gangs moved in and practically took over the beach. News reports of the incident stated there was a riot and that two vehicles had been burned. Police arrested eleven men. After that, it was inevitable restrictions would be made; Parks Canada closed the beach to traffic and no camping was permitted. Some locals were annoyed at the restrictions and felt this would discourage tourists, but it had the desired effect of driving the undesirable element off the beach and restoring order.

Sitting on a rocky prominence at Long Beach was the old wooden, weathered Wickaninnish Inn, which has since been transformed into the Pacific Rim Interpretative Centre. The old inn, which closed in November 1977, provided accommodation and storm-watching long before it was fashionable.

Tofino's Dr. Howard Richmond McDiarmid, who loved the west coast, can be given some credit for the establishment of the national park, for during his term as MLA for Alberni–Clayoquot he lobbied government for its creation. McDiarmid practised medicine at Tofino General Hospital for about fifteen years before going into politics. In 1966 and 1969 he ran successfully for the Social Credit government under Premier W.A.C. Bennett. McDiarmid moved away from the area for a few years, only to return in retirement to the family property at Long Beach, where he created today's new and popular Wickaninnish Inn.

Tofino, the western terminus of the Trans-Canada Highway, became a municipality in 1932. Once a small fishing village with a limited amount of logging in the area, today it is a prime tourist attraction with hotels filling travellers' needs. The resident population of approximately two thousand now almost triples in size during the summer, as tourists come to walk on the beach, storm watch, whale watch, or surf. The small airport caters to private and commercial flights.

A left turn at Highway 4 junction takes you to the Village of Ucluelet. The two villages, Tofino and Ucluelet, have a love/hate relationship that goes back many years. Now both compete for the tourism dollar. The *Canadian Princess*, docked in Ucluelet harbour in 1979, became a big draw for tourists. Owned by the Oak Bay Marine Group, the former *William J. Stewart* was built in 1932 and served forty-three years as a hydrographic survey ship. Here you could stay overnight on shore or on the ship, then board a smaller vessel to go out to the Broken Islands Group.

Before the Second World War, Ucluelet had a large community of Japanese fishermen who were part of the fishing bonanza in Barkley Sound. The fishing fleet was huge and provided a ready income for west coast residents. When the war intervened, the Japanese were removed to internment camps and their fishing boats confiscated and sold. A seaplane base was established during the war and a land base at Long Beach. The fishing fleet never regained its former glory, but on a smaller scale fishing still provides a good living for local fishermen.

Ucluelet is now a west coast tourist attraction like its neighbour Tofino, with hotels, beachfront cottages, and spectacular views of the Pacific. It is a naturalist's paradise.

Bamfield is a small, quaint west coast village with wooden sidewalks. Perched on the edge of the Graveyard of the Pacific, it is home to the Bamfield Life Saving Station, the Bamfield Marine Biological Station, and the Pacific Cable Station. What stories are etched into the village history—tales of wrecked ships, rescued passengers, and amazing heroism. The village marks the beginning of the West Coast Trail that winds along the rugged western edge of Vancouver Island south to Port Renfrew. Like Ucluelet, in the early days Bamfield shared in the rich fishing resource. The village is located on a protected inlet on the south shore of Barkley Sound, surrounded by Crown land, Native reserves, and the Pacific Rim National Park Reserve. It is divided into two sections, separated by the Bamfield Inlet; the west side has a boardwalk that connects homes and docks on the harbour side, while businesses occupy the east side. A water taxi connects the two.

NEIGHBOURING ATTRACTIONS

Surrounding Port Alberni are the rural communities of Cherry Creek, Beaver Creek, Beaufort, and Sproat Lake, each with its own distinct lifestyle. The first three were historic farming communities established when the first settlers arrived in the 1880s, whereas Sproat Lake had a brief history of sawmilling but always attracted the recreational visitor.

Klitsa Lodge at the south side of the lake once attracted the rich and famous from all over the world. During the thirties, it was operated by Mrs. Josephine E. Wark, a woman with indomitable spirit who was known to drive down to California each year advertising the lodge for fishing, hunting, and canoeing, long before anyone took notice of the potential tourism dollar. Writer and publisher Stuart Keate recalled that getting to the lodge was an adventure; since there was no road, visitors had to summon a boat from the lodge by ringing a bell or shooting a gun at Bishop's Landing.[10]

Today the lake's most famous occupants float in the waters at Weiner Bay; they are the famous Martin Mars water bombers, or "Gods of Rain" as they were affectionately nicknamed in Port Alberni. The flying boats splashed down on Sproat Lake in 1960, their purchase coinciding with the amalgamation of MacMillan & Bloedel and the Powell River Company in 1959. (The name was abbreviated to MacMillan Bloedel on May 10, 1966.) Just as the merger negotiations were underway, the bombers were on their way to the scrap yard in San Francisco to be smelted into aluminum ingots. The US Navy planes built by Howard Hughes had done their duty transporting troops and equipment during the Second World War.

Dan McIvor, a pilot with MB's Grumman Goose, happened to read a newspaper article about them and thought the planes could be the answer to the forest fire problem. He took his idea to the company and convinced them of its merit.[11] By August, six forest companies had staked $100,000 to purchase the four planes, the *Marianna Mars*, *Hawaii Mars*, *Philippine Mars*, and *Caroline Mars*. Statistically the bombers are legendary: 36 metres (120 feet) long, a 60-metre (200-foot) wingspan, a tail that stands 15 metres (48 feet) above ground, and wings that can withstand the weight of a D6 bulldozer.[12]

Tragically on June 23, 1961, the *Marianna Mars* plunged into a hillside near Parksville while dousing a forest fire on Mount Moriarty, killing all four of the crew. The next year, on October 12, the *Caroline Mars* was destroyed during Hurricane Freda.

The two remaining water bombers have provided safety in the woods for decades since. Each plane can carry 30 tons of water. They can scoop up this tonnage in just 22 seconds while skimming across the lake surface at 112.6 kilometres (69 miles) per hour. During a crisis the Mars could be in the air within 10 minutes and make a 23,000-litre (6,000-gallon) drop every 15 minutes. To be effective, water must be dropped from a height of just 46 to 76 metres (150 to 249 feet). The highly skilled pilots were experienced in all aspects of mountain and coastal flying.

Hugh Fraser, who piloted the *Hawaii Mars* and *Philippine Mars* from 1977 to 2010, said, "There's not an airplane in the world that can match what these can do under these conditions on Vancouver Island."[13]

It was a breathtaking sight to see these magnificent bombers flying overhead, or discharging a load over land or water. They are now owned by Coulson Forest Products and serve the industry both here and in the US.

After fifty years fighting forest fires, including the Kelowna fire in 2003, the *Philippine Mars* will have a new role to play as a tourist attraction at the National Naval Aviation Museum in Pensacola, Florida. The *Hawaii Mars* may look a little lonely sitting on Sproat Lake, but its presence is a reminder of the magnificent job the flying tankers did to keep the forests safe. Port Alberni is immensely proud of them.

Wayne Coulson, president of the company, understands how the people of Port Alberni feel about the Mars. He said,

> It's been a real honour and a privilege to own these aircraft, for everything that they stood for over the years between working for the military and on wildfires—they've done a wonderful job. In B.C. both Mars have made in excess of 8,000 drops with their 52 years of

history with the forest service. They are an icon in the province and they've certainly protected many lives and property over the years.[14]

Sadly the visitor's centre and tours of the Mars Bomber base shut down in 2013. However, all the memorabilia inside the base will not be lost to the community; it will remain in the Coulsons' possession, perhaps for a future exhibit.

FATEFUL VOYAGES

One of the most spectacular waterways on Vancouver Island is the Alberni Inlet that links Port Alberni to Barkley Sound and the Pacific Ocean beginning at the mouth of Somass River. This sheltered passage to the outside world can accommodate the largest freighters carrying lumber to markets around the globe; even the ill-fated *Ocean Ranger,* the largest oil-drilling rig in the world, made the journey up the inlet in 1978 to be serviced in Port Alberni. It was a sight to behold sitting in Stamp Harbour dwarfing the mountains on either side. From our home, we could see it in the evening lit up like a Christmas tree. The rig left Port Alberni for the Hibernia oil fields off Newfoundland, where it met its fate in 1982 when it capsized taking eighty-four lives down with it.

The year after our arrival the town still buzzed about the wreck of the *Vanlene* out on Austin Island in Barkley Sound. It had become a bit of a tourist attraction. The Panamanian-registered freighter went aground on the island on March 14, 1972, carrying a cargo of three hundred Dodge Colt automobiles from Japan. The freighter had lost its way when navigation instruments broke down, leaving the captain with only a compass to find his way in dense fog along the west coast. Fortunately there was no loss of life, and many of the cars were recovered. For months the wreck sat grounded and exposed to the elements, suffering the indignity of scavengers who carried away bits and pieces for souvenirs. What they didn't finish, the sea did. A year later the main body of the ship broke apart from the bow section, which remained embedded in the shoreline of Austin Island for some time.

For years people had heard or read about the historical west coast shipwrecks; now they could see first-hand what the turbulent sea and the rugged coastline could do to a ship in trouble. Capitalizing, or opportunistic, the skippers of the *Lady Rose* took curious Sunday excursionists from Port Alberni to the site of the wreck. Many joined the day cruise and took photos, and had stories to tell their grandchildren.

The *Lady Rose* was so much a part of life in Port Alberni, and I felt a personal connection to her as she was built on the famous Scottish Clydeside shipyards in 1937, the same year I was born only fifty kilometres southeast of Glasgow, at Strathaven. When the sturdy little vessel was built, she was named the *Lady Silvia*, and plans were to operate her on the Howe Sound run. Her name was changed shortly after her arrival in Vancouver to avoid duplication. Before her arrival in Port Alberni in 1960, she had a proud record of service from the war years carrying military personnel and equipment.

Her owners Dick McMinn and John Monrufet happily served the communities up and down the Alberni Inlet, gaining a reputation for running "the best little ship on Vancouver Island." Whenever visitors arrived, a trip "down the canal" was a must. They watched in awe as freight was expertly unloaded either to small craft or rickety docks, and kayakers were carefully deposited or picked up in the water. Salal Joe was an added attraction, tourists eagerly taking photographs of the famous west coast hermit as he pulled alongside the ship with his bundles of salal destined for the flower shops in Vancouver.

Perhaps the most unusual cargo was a number of goats imported to a lodge on Clarke Island. The owner had tired of cutting salal—which grows everywhere on the west coast—and decided the only solution was to have a few goats that would happily graze on the plant. Unfortunately they ate everything except the salal, and eventually swam to another island and were never seen again.

McMinn gained a reputation as the "wheelhouse poet," a hobby that kept him occupied between stops along the inlet. He and Monrufet retired in 1982 after a long and happy association. The *Lady Rose* is now retired too, but her memory lives on. Today, the *Francis Barkley* continues the tradition of carrying passengers and freight down the Alberni Inlet to Bamfield and Ucluelet, and all stops in between.

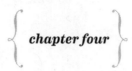

UNIONS AND FIRST NATIONS

Port Alberni is known as a strong union town; it also has a large population of Native people, with two bands living in the vicinity of the city. Both groups have a large number of people working in the forest industry and are an integral part of the community. Unions have fought a steady battle for improved working conditions and higher pay. In some instances they brought the forest industry to a standstill in an effort to achieve those goals.

Natives suffered the indignity of being taken from their homes, denied their language and culture, and placed in the Port Alberni Residential School. They were segregated and suppressed in the grand design of assimilation. The land claims issue has always been foremost in their fight with provincial government politicians, who were reluctant to change history, and with federal governments, who had them tied up in the tangled web of the Indian Act.

The struggles of the unions and the First Nations people, and their interaction with each other over the years, have made both groups stronger and the community richer.

LABOUR UNIONS

As the forest industry grew in Port Alberni so too did its unions. In 1986, the Port Alberni and District Labour Council had twenty-four affiliate unions under its umbrella, representing 5,700 workers in the forest industry. Over many years these unions fought a hard battle for improved benefits and working conditions. One of the largest unions was the International Woodworkers of America (IWA) Local 1-85.

When the IWA was formed in 1937 the average wage was about $1.10 an hour. By 1986, a worker in one of MB's divisions could expect to make anywhere from fourteen to seventeen dollars an hour, with added benefits. Tradespeople's wages were even higher. The first IWA strike took place in 1946; it idled 37,000 workers and brought in the forty-hour week. It wasn't until 1955 that the coast industry saw a two-year contract signed. The first major strike in the British Columbia pulp and paper industry was in 1958 when an eighty-three-day strike cost the industry $50 million and the International Brotherhood of Pulp, Sulphite and Paper Mill Workers and the United Papermakers and Paperworkers lost $6 million in wages.

Often the union strikes crippled Port Alberni, and sometimes the entire province. But union workers grudgingly gave credit to MB, the company that buttered their bread.

There were many socially conscious union leaders who left their mark on the community—Earl Foxcroft, Larry Baird, Dave Haggard, Henry Nedergard, Mark Mosher, Walter Behn, and George McKnight, to name only a few. Some were labelled communists or socialists because of their stand on certain issues. The Alberni District Labour Council usually offered up a slate of candidates for the position of alderman. Nedergard, Behn, and McKnight, whose political persuasions were left of centre, all served as aldermen at various times. Often their combined vote on an issue split city council, leaving the mayor to cast the deciding vote.

George McKnight was a dedicated servant of the community. He came from the Kamloops area where his family had a 526-hectare (1,300-acre) farm. His uncle Ed Hoffman, who was a millwright at Great Central Lake Sawmill, persuaded him to come to the Alberni Valley in 1941. McKnight worked in the Alberni Plywood Division from March 31, 1942, until his retirement in 1983. During those years, he was a labour leader, politician, and musician; he also served as chairman of the Alberni–Clayoquot Regional District and chairman of the board of West Coast General Hospital.

Showing an amazing determination to become an alderman, he ran for city council thirteen times before finally being elected. Thereafter he topped the polls in every election. This civic position suited him well, as he was on constant nightshift at Alberni Plywood so could give time to committee work during daylight hours. He served with four mayors over a period of fifteen years.

McKnight was a tall man with a commanding presence and a good speaking voice; he could easily sway an argument one way or another and was always an advocate of the working man. In retirement he became an author and historian. His love of music remained throughout his life. In his younger years with his band the Rhythm Riders, he played the accordion at dances throughout the Alberni Valley.

One of McKnight's earliest causes was the campaign to get the old army camp barracks converted to housing. One of those huts, when converted, became his home in the Glenwood area. His second wife, Edith, was always by his side giving support and encouragement whatever the cause, and he was proud of his four sons, George, Jim, Harry, and Bill.

McKnight once advocated for the province to adopt a six-hour day to help provide employment in the face of new technology and job reduction, and suggested salaries and wages should be increased by the same percentage that the hours are reduced, so that living standards can be maintained. Thousands of people who were on welfare and unemployment insurance would be working for wages, paying taxes, and keeping the economy going.¹ He conceded that Sweden had tried the six-hour day with 250 employees in Kiruna but had abandoned the idea after sixteen years, saying it didn't work and was too expensive. Today other countries and labour organizations still advocate for a shorter workday, so McKnight may have been ahead of his time.

Walter Behn, McKnight's friend and ally on city council, came to Canada from Germany in 1951 with his wife, Charlotte, and their three children. He worked for a time at Camp One and at the Alberni Pacific Division before transferring to Alberni Pulp and Paper Mill in 1957. Behn was first a member of the IWA, then later a member of the Canadian Paperworkers Union (CPU) Local 686, and was a founding member of the Alberni and District Labour Council (ADLC). He served as alderman and was on the board of West Coast General Hospital. He helped establish Fir Park Village and Echo Village, two senior-care facilities. Behn once said he had spent five years destroying the world—he had been a German paratrooper—and thirty years building it up.²

Behn told the story of how Canadian Labour Congress president Joe Morris had been a big stumbling block in the formation of the ADLC. Morris was of the opinion that a labour council for a city the size of Port Alberni would be ineffective and virtually impossible to finance. Behn said it took two years to convince the Labour Congress that it would work.²¹ Dan Connell became the first president, with Behn as first vice-president. Behn later became president.

In his career as a politician, Behn received many commendations. However, the one he was most proud of was a letter from NDP leader Dave Barrett, thanking him for his years of effort in helping workers.

Mark Mosher was first a union leader before joining the Communist Party. In the period after the Second World War when union organizers were perceived as being communist, many were blacklisted, a term reminiscent of the name of the Black Agency in Vancouver, which did the hiring for logging camps. Mosher was then working in logging camps doing various jobs until he was certified as a steam locomotive engineer. He became shop steward, and worked hard selling memberships in the IWA.[3]

In 1946 Mosher heard Tim Buck, leader of the Communist Party, speak to a crowd in the Capitol Theatre in Port Alberni. He was so impressed that he joined the party. At that time he was secretary of the IWA. After a turbulent episode in that union's history when the union was torn apart internally over a move to disaffiliate with the US-based IWA and create a Canadian union, Mosher was blacklisted and never worked in IWA camps again. This particular incident, and the ongoing struggle for better wages and working conditions, perhaps earned the Port Alberni local a reputation for being radical.

Dave Haggard was another well-known labour voice in Port Alberni who spoke for the IWA 1-85. Born in Kamloops and raised in Barriere, he came to Port Alberni in 1973 to work as a welder for MB. He became a full-time officer of the IWA and camp chairman of MB's Franklin River Division in 1985. Haggard served five years as president of the IWA 1-85 in Port Alberni, and in 1996 was elected president of the union. He also sat on the executive council of the Canadian Labour Congress and was an officer of the B.C. Federation of Labour.

There were many meetings in the IWA Hall where Haggard showed he was destined for a larger audience than the Port Alberni forest workers. Like other labour leaders in the province, his language could politely be described as "colourful," much like Jack Munro's, when he was trying to make a point. He entered politics by, oddly, running for the federal Liberal Party.

In 2007 he was appointed to the B.C. Treaty Commission, replacing Jack Weisgerber on the committee that was responsible for treaty talks. He told reporters that he had become much more diplomatic over the years after leading his union, the IWA, through eight years of its toughest times in the history of the forest industry in the province.

The IWA was the largest trade union in the province, and the one with the biggest clout politically. President Jack Munro, or "Big Jack" as he was fondly called, visited Port Alberni on several occasions. The outspoken, larger-than-life union leader could cause many to rethink their positions on any issue, and always gave the *Alberni Valley Times* gripping headlines. At union or public meetings held in the Alberni District Secondary School (ADSS) auditorium, or in the IWA Hall on Montrose Street, Big Jack would storm across the stage, cussing and swearing at the newspaper and its editor for its slant on a specific story, which always seemed to differ from his opinion. Munro's language was not always complimentary; he was loud, and proud of his working-class roots, and he could hold an audience with his oratory skill. Munro was a match for any of the MB executives. But he knew his own weaknesses. In his book *Union Jack* he said:

> *My language isn't all that good at the best of times, but when I get upset and angry it really goes all to hell. In one speech to the employers I guess I really got wound up. One of the guys on our negotiating committee said I used the f-word 32 times in one speech.*[4]

Munro was born in Alberta and dropped out of school in Grade 10. He joined the IWA while working in a sawmill in Nelson, at the start of a long career in the forest industry. Before long he was an official within the union. He ran unsuccessfully for the provincial New Democratic Party in 1966. Two years later he was an executive of the union, and by 1973 its president. He became known throughout Canada when in 1976 he became vice-president of the Canadian Labour Congress. He was and still is considered one of the last of the old-time labour leaders. And he cared a great deal about the province of BC.

DEALING WITH AIR POLLUTION

The Alberni District Labour Council was an umbrella group of representatives from various unions whose aim was to advance the economic and social welfare of workers in the community. One of the labour council's first resolutions was to protest fly ash, fallout, and air pollution in the city. Despite Port Alberni's wonderful scenic location and amenities, the town once had a bad case of air pollution from the pulp and paper mill. There were times when a wash was hung out to dry, only to be brought in later in the day completely black. One year when it snowed, the snow turned black. Windows were constantly washed. Residents accepted the accumulation of black grime on almost everything; it was a problem they dealt with daily. The pulp mill smell, some bragged, was "the smell of money."

The labour council reacted by researching air pollution, and within six months had enough information to present a brief to the provincial minister of the environment, Ralf Loffmark. The minister remarked that the council possessed more information than the provincial government. The brief was the first of its kind by any organization in British Columbia on the problem of air pollution. As a result, new rules were passed and MacMillan Bloedel was ordered to install pollution abatement equipment.

There are many stories about the arrival of the smell in the community. George McKnight told the story about an old Scottish pioneer who was driving past the pulp mill around the time the first batch of pulp was blown. The old-timer, who lived on Mary Street in North Port near the mill, was returning home from shopping with his wife and daughter just at the precise time to get the full benefit of the new aroma. He mistook the origin but said nothing until he stopped the car in front of their home. As they got out of the car, he said in his broad Scottish accent, "Aw r-r-right, which one of you was it?"

Another story tells of a housewife who also lived in North Port, downwind from the mill, and was never allowed to complain about the terrible smell, or the bad air, because her husband worked there. She was reminded that work at the mill was their bread and butter. North Port suffered the most from the air pollution, with South Port getting some—depending, of course, on which way the wind blew.

Air pollution was particularly hard on car and boat dealerships, where the exposed metal corroded and specks of red rust appeared on paintwork. Car dealerships had the most difficult time, having to wash the cars in their lot almost daily. MB helped its employees with the ash problem by installing wash sprays at each of the mills. A drive through one of these ingenious showers took away most of the fallout, and a good wash on a weekend took care of the remainder.

The black plume rising from the mill, the fly ash on the car in the morning, the smell—all of these concerned the residents. But many felt they had little power to change things. The pollution, it seemed, was part of the life and prosperity of Port Alberni. Some citizens believed there were health concerns and became quite vocal about it, but they were labelled environmental activists. MB was also concerned, not only from the public relations point of view but also for the health of its workers, and spent millions trying to improve the air emissions from the pulp mill smokestack.

During the 1970s, another form of pollution would engulf the town in the fall—smoke. On a beautiful day, the sky would turn red and hazy from slash fires burning in the forests. Smoke filled the air, making eyes water and breathing difficult for those with respiratory problems. This aspect of logging practices made researcher Paul George angry. He worked for the Nuu-chah-nulth Tribal Council, and was involved with the planning aspect of forestry. He complained, "It takes years before the nutrients return to the soil. It is crazy to slash burn. Along comes a heavy rain and everything is washed down the hillside."[5]

Often the slash burning continued for several days before the fires burned out and the air finally cleared. Eventually forest companies were required to stop or curtail slash burning.

Another homegrown pollution problem was the smoke from the chimneys of wood-burning fireplaces in homes throughout the valley. No one complained, until years later when the smoke was recognized as a health hazard; its resolution became a cause championed by Mayor Gillian Trumper. During the 1970s, though, when the price of heating oil escalated, everyone burned wood. In fact, happiness was a neatly stacked woodpile with enough firewood to last through the next winter.

Every spring the sound of wood being split was heard around town. As the weather improved, the slo-pitch league started, the snow came off the Beaufort Mountains to signal that gardens were ready for planting, the lawn mowers came out—and electric saws were dusted off and readied for action. On Third Avenue there was a steady stream of pickup trucks loaded down with blocks of wood. "There goes a nice load," one old logger nodded to another as a truck rumbled along. "I wonder where they're cutting?" Before long, everyone would know!

There was little doubt that felling trees, bucking them into usable lengths, then splitting and stacking, provided vigorous outdoor exercise that was healthy and satisfying. With the proper equipment and convenient access to the forest, anyone could harvest a cord of wood a day. It sounds quite idyllic, while in reality it was plenty of hard work, especially if the wood being cut was some distance from the road and had to be lugged to the roadside for pickup. Men teamed up and made a day of it, complete with a six-pack or a flask of coffee and sandwiches.

Transporting the wood to the carport or backyard was hard work, but the real artistic challenge came with stacking. Not every woodpile was the same. You could tell an old pile from a new one just by the colour of the wood. A drive through the residential areas showed some woodpiles neatly edging the driveway and others stacked up in carports. Some would be meticulously piled in the backyard providing a privacy screen for the family barbecue, or they were stacked against the fence or house. A beautiful woodpile was a work of art and a source of great pride and comfort for the winter months ahead.

Concern over environmental issues grew over the years as individuals and groups became more educated on safety conditions in the workplace as well as air and water pollution.

The frustration was shared equally with the company. MB's top environmental specialist Al Chmelauskas said, "Trying to meet anti-pollution standards was rather like shooting at moving targets."[6]

The environmental control programs for Alberni Valley mills were complicated by two problems: their location at the mouth of the Somass River, which is an important salmon spawning run; and the poor ventilation capacity of the valley, which affected dispersal of air emissions from Alberni Pulp & Paper Mill. The right to clean air and clean water was a clause in a contract negotiated by workers at the mill, and workers and management worked together to improve conditions. But the pollution problem did not go away easily.

Today it is unlikely that permission would be given to build a pulp mill in the same location. Before Bloedel, Stewart & Welch built it in 1946–47, the Department of Fisheries was requested to do an investigation into the effect on the Alberni Inlet. Dr. John Patrick Tully with the Pacific Biological Station in Nanaimo was assigned to do the research. Tully and Henry Vollmers fitted up a laboratory aboard Vollmers' trolling boat, where they lived and worked accumulating and analyzing data.

They made a model of the upper end of the inlet to confirm water movements complete with tides, river flow, and winds. With that, Tully could predict the dispersion pattern of pulp mill effluents and ensure measures were taken to reduce damage to the fisheries.[7]

Today there is no pulp being produced in Port Alberni. The mill is now known as Catalyst Paper Port Alberni, a name that reflects both the change in product and the change of ownership.

THE NUU-CHAH-NULTH PEOPLE

The 1970s was a time of great change for Natives in the province. The West Coast Allied Tribes incorporated in 1973, becoming the District Society of Indian Chiefs. Six years later, on April 2, 1979, this became the Nuu-chah-nulth Tribal Council with George Watts as chairman. Watts grew in status from his involvement in these processes and became an outspoken advocate for his people.

There are fourteen Native bands within the council, in a territory that stretches along 300 kilometres (186 miles) of the west coast of Vancouver Island, from Brooks Peninsula in the north to Point-no-Point in the south, and an inland area within the Port Alberni district. Two reserves are in the vicinity of Port Alberni. The Tseshaht, the larger of the two, occupies an area on the south bank of the Somass River by the Orange Bridge on the western outskirts of town, while the Hupacasath reserve is situated on the north bank of the river. The latter was the original occupant of Sproat Lake and the surrounding area. In earlier times, the Tseshaht lived in the Valley during the fall and early winter, spending the spring and summer at their reserve sites along the Alberni Inlet and in Barkley Sound.

When incorporated, the organization provided programs and services to approximately eight thousand members. In an effort to keep them informed, it began publishing the *Ha-Shilth-Sa*. With its first edition on January 24, 1974, it is Canada's oldest Native newspaper. Since then the paper has informed, celebrated and reported on people and issues that affect the region. Bob Soderlund was editor for twenty-five years, and during that time he documented the political growth and cultural changes within west coast communities.

A collection of photographs taken by Soderlund formed an exhibit in 2007 at the Alberni Valley Museum entitled *How We Are: How We Want to Be . . .* The curators of the exhibit were sisters Dawn Foxcroft and Kelly Poirier, both members of the Tseshaht. Covering most of the Nuu-chah-nulth territory, it showed food fishing, sporting events, political protests, daily family life, and dancers in ceremonial costumes. The exhibition was so successful it was shown in several communities before moving on the following year to the Canadian Museum of Civilization, now the Canadian Museum of History, in Gatineau, Quebec.

GROWING NATIVE LEADERSHIP

George Watts was a respected chief of the Tseshaht. He spent most of his life on the Port Alberni reserve except when he attended the University of British Columbia where he majored in engineering and education. He served as chairman of Nuu-chah-nulth Tribal Council until 1993, and also filled a dual role as band manager from 1970 to 1980.

Watts worked hard for the Tseshaht people, but his interest and recognition of aboriginal rights took him even farther—to Victoria and Ottawa to lobby federal and provincial politicians. He was known to be a hard-driving negotiator who could use colourful and sometimes inflammatory language. You always knew where he stood on an issue! Perhaps his biggest legacy was when he represented the Tseshaht as chief negotiator in the treaty process.

In 1984, the year the National Indian Brotherhood reconstituted itself into the Assembly of First Nations, Watts was interviewed March 5 on CBC radio about land claims. He said:

> *We take the position that we are sovereign nations, that our existence stems from the fact that we were the first peoples here, that we have the aboriginal title to the land.*

> But that sovereignty is one, which could coexist along with the rest of Canada. We're not talking about being sovereign nations as far as having post offices, armed forces and monetary systems of our own. What we're talking about is having Indian governments within the Confederation of Canada.

When a proposed treaty with the Nuu-chah-nulth Tribal Council collapsed, he resigned as chief. Twelve of the bands rejected it. When the ratification collapsed both provincially and federally, Watts helped resurrect the talks that took four more years of hard work to rebuild the scaled-down deal. He warned Premier Gordon Campbell, "We will do harm to this province if you do harm to us. If you want a fight, you are going to get it."[8]

Watts was front and centre in the battle to protect Native interests when the battle over Meares Island went to court. If the Nuu-chah-nulth Tribal Council won the court battle, he promised, his council would save Meares Island for tourists. It was a small part of the country but, he vowed, Native people were not going to be taken advantage of there.

> I'm not an outside agitator; I have been involved in tribal politics for half my life and Meares Island is about people living in this country and being able to live in this country.[9]

The ultimate ruling that MB could not log Meares until the Native land claims were resolved elated him: "I feel like David did when he beat Goliath."[10]

Watts served on a number of provincial committees and boards, including Forest Renewal BC, the Premier's Forest Sector Advisory Committee, and the Loan Board of the Nuu-chah-nulth Economic Development Corporation. He was a board member of BC Hydro from 1993 to 1997.[11]

Both the Tseshaht and Hupacasath were very much a part of life in Port Alberni. Their presence was felt throughout town, particularly in the fishing and logging industries and culturally in the arts and crafts industry. However, a division existed between status and non-status Indians—those who lived on and those who lived off the reserve.

One facility in town brought both together for meetings and cultural events. The Friendship Centre, once located on Second Avenue, was the centre of Native activity within the city. Mayor Les Hammer recognized the need for such a facility the year the tsunami struck the town in 1964. With the support of all fourteen bands plus the local Lions Club, and both the Alberni and Port Alberni city councils, the centre became a reality. The old Eric Graf Hall, formerly the Workers' Hall, was leased for a dollar a year. Eric Graf was a logger who had been blacklisted; the hall was named in his honour as a symbol of the long struggle for workers' rights.

The Indian Friendship Society operated the hall. Dr. Harry Webster was the first chairman of the board that included Jessie Hamilton, Dolly Watts, Alex McCarthy, Charlie Sam, Keitha Adams, Sherman Lauder, and Les Hammer. The centre provided counsellors on drug and alcohol abuse, and help for Native people moving into the city. There were also social events and drop-in programs.

A new, beautifully designed Friendship Centre opened on November 21, 1987, on lower Fourth Avenue. This facility continued to provide the same services as the old. The eight thousand–square-foot building included a gymnasium-type hall complete with kitchen, a youth room, two common rooms and a boardroom. It is one of twenty-five such facilities in BC, and is administered by a non-profit society duly elected by the membership. However, with a growing urban aboriginal population of over two thousand people, and 60 percent living off the reserve and in the city, there is a need to expand.

Natives excelled athletically at many sporting events, but in school there was a large dropout rate. Originally Native children were banned from public schools and forced to attend the Alberni Residential School, then operated by the United Church of Canada. This sad event in Canadian history has been well documented. In the seventies only the old gymnasium remained as a reminder of the residential school on the Tseshaht reserve, but for many Native people it will take some time for the scars to heal.

In an effort to stem the dropout rate, a Native Awareness Society was formed in 1976 recognizing a need for students to feel they were a part of the school population. Dolly Watts, who was a home-school coordinator and a Native Studies teacher, did a survey of Native education in the Alberni Valley. The results showed that 50 percent of Native students dropped out of the school system in Grade 8. Watts also found in her survey there was a desire to be recognized for achievements, and so the Dr. George Charles Clutesi Scholarship Fund was established to give financial assistance and encouragement to students. This fund was enhanced by a grant from the H.R. MacMillan Trust fund.

Sadly, despite the large number living on and off the reserve, few Natives were employed in local stores or businesses or in the mills. There were exceptions, such as Tseshaht chief Adam Shewish who worked in the Alberni Plywood Division for forty-four years as a sander operator; he had actually helped on the mill construction when he was only twelve.

The Shewish family followed the seasonal rounds of their traditional territories in the Broken Group Islands. Adam was born at Dutch Harbour in Barkley Sound on April 18, 1920. His parents, Jacob and Eva, taught him about living a life dedicated to serving and caring for his community. Eva died when he was twelve, and his aunt Mabel Taylor took over the role of teaching him traditional values to love people, to show generosity, and to share with his fellow man. She taught him patience and to take pride in whatever he achieved.

Mabel Taylor lived out her life on Polly Point, a reserve adjacent to the Alberni Plywood Division. She was a familiar face to those who worked in the mill, since she occasionally came in to use the telephone. Mabel was a noted basket weaver and an extraordinary woman. She had travelled thousands of miles translating legends for anthropologists and was an inspiration to many young Natives.[12]

Adam Shewish became chief of the Tseshaht following the death of his father in 1951. All his life he loved the Broken Group Islands; his biggest dream was that the Tseshaht would regain control of their birthplace. Every song that was sung, every prayer, and all his teachings were in the Tseshaht dialect. He said that people should care about each other and share what they had in good times and bad. He married Margaret Jackson of Neah Bay, and they had one child, Edward; Margaret already had four children from a previous marriage. Adam always took an interest in young people and believed you taught children not by telling them but by example, just as his father had taught him.[13] The elementary school on the reserve was named the Shewish House of Learning in his honour.

Adam was a pleasant man, always joking, and he loved telling stories. When I called him on the phone, as I did on several occasions, he always answered with "Boy you're looking good today!" followed by his familiar laugh. When I visited his home on the reserve, he welcomed me with a big smile and the offer of a cup of tea. As we sat down to talk, he pointed with pride to a plaque on the wall showing his ancestral family tree dating back hundreds of years.

Then his face saddened and voice softened as he talked about Margaret. He told me how he cared for her for five years after she had a stroke and was partially paralyzed. A year after her death in 1988 he held a memorial potlatch for her, his aunt Mabel Taylor, and his grandson, Norman Smith Jr. Over a thousand people attended.

Before I left, he proudly showed me his workshop where in retirement he carved beautiful paddles, some painted with traditional Native designs. We had visited for about two hours when I commented on how quickly the time had passed. He laughed, "I should have been at a meeting an hour ago." Time did not matter to this kind and gentle man.

Port Alberni's most famous citizen was Dr. George Clutesi, who was also a student at the Alberni Residential School. He put aside all the hurt and discrimination of that institution to become a leader among his people. He was raised on the Tseshaht reserve, although his mother was of the Hupacasath band. His parents, George and Kathleen, opened their son's eyes and heart to traditional values and a deeply felt religion. His interest in art was inherited from his mother, who died when he was a child.

Clutesi's marriage to Margaret Lauder on February 5, 1937, produced six children: George, Edward, Guy, Joy, Barbara, and Carol. He worked in a variety of jobs, including fishing and pile driving. A workplace accident changed his life forever when he broke his back. During a long stay in hospital, he began to paint. Many of these works of art formed the first exhibition of his work, in 1944, at the Royal British Columbia Museum in Victoria.

His nephew Randy Fred remembers his first encounter with his uncle in the Alberni Indian Residential School in the early 1960s.

> *By the time I attended, the school was massive with a half a dozen or so large outbuildings, but it was a much smaller building during his schooldays. Being a creative soul with a great sense of humour, Uncle George left the traditional Tseshaht mark on the school. Between the boys' side and the girls' side was an auditorium capable of holding more than 300 people. There was a foyer outside*

the auditorium door. This is where the rope was to pull the large bell to signal for mealtimes, church times, etc. On the foyer floor George created a beautiful motif using the floor tiles. It was an image of a whale with a thunderbird on its back. This motif within a circle is what our tribe, the Tseshaht, still to this day use as our logo. I believe it was Uncle George's way of marking the spot as traditional Tseshaht land.[14]

Clutesi met Emily Carr when she was a very old and sick woman. She encouraged him to keep painting and showed him her unsold paintings. She told him she couldn't get ten cents apiece for them. Carr willed her brushes and paints to him.

Clutesi has been named one of Canada's most prominent artists; he used words, paint, and dance to record the myths and legends of his people. His West Coast Dancers included in their repertoire the *Lightning Snake Dance*, the *Woodpecker Dance*, and the *Medicine Man Dance*, all performed at social events around the island. He acted in several movies, playing the leading role in *The Dreamspeaker*, a movie made for CBC television.

As an author, in 1967, he published *Son of Raven, Son of Deer*, and two years later *Potlatch*. Both books are now textbooks in schools. Clutesi's work as an author was not always well regarded by his people. Some felt he was selling out their culture. When *Son of Raven, Son of Deer* was first published, he was not regarded as a hero on the reserve. But slowly the Tseshaht people took pride in his accomplishments.

The University of Victoria gave him a honorary doctor of law degree in 1971, and in 1973 he was presented with the Order of Canada. That same year, Port Alberni honoured him by naming the new marina on the Somass River, just a short distance from where he was born, the Clutesi Haven Marina.

When I was renovating a building that became known as the Rollin Art Centre, on behalf of the Community Arts Council, Clutesi paid occasional visits just to see how work was progressing. Sometimes he stopped by Echo Centre Lounge where other works of art were displayed. He always showed an interest in the arts.

When he died in February 1988 at age eighty-three, hundreds gathered to say farewell to this soft-spoken and talented man who had not only introduced a generation to Native dance, music, film, and art but also influenced the next generations. I was privileged to attend, and to hear the music and stories told that day. He would have been pleased to be remembered in this way.

Randy Fred, Clutesi's nephew, was one of twenty-eight survivors of the residential school who sued the federal government and the United Church of Canada for their suffering as students in the school. Fred was taken from his family at age five, abused by an older student when he was six and by a dormitory supervisor when he was eight. He turned to alcohol at age twelve, but overcame his addiction as an adult. He has had retinitis pigmentosa all his life, and although he is now legally blind, he continues to be involved in publishing and consulting. He founded Canada's first aboriginal-owned publishing company, Theytus Books, in Nanaimo in 1980. In 2005, he received the Gray Campbell Distinguished Service Award for his outstanding contribution to the development of writing and publishing in BC.

MEMORABLE NATIVE WOMEN

There were many strong Native women in the community. Agnes Dick, or Aggie as she was fondly known, was another student from the Alberni Residential School. She graduated from Civil Defence as a home nurse in January 1959 in Port Alberni and then continued training in the Nanaimo Indian Hospital, becoming a certified nurse and social worker. She was a health and welfare coordinator for the Tseshaht band and a respected elder in the community.

There were times when she thought the job as health and welfare coordinator was a thankless job. She said she was called a lot of names, even by her own people, but she was thrilled when those who called her names came back to ask for help with their problems.

When she retired on March 31, 1976, after a long career of service to her people, she wrote a letter to the editor of the *Alberni Valley Times* about the work she had tried to do for neglected children and for juveniles who got into trouble, and about her work with government agencies.

She often expressed the difficulty of living between two worlds. She didn't expect her people to return to the "old ways" after having a taste of the way things were now. Aggie believed that their future was with their children and grandchildren. Even after her retirement, she continued to work on behalf of Native people, serving as president of the Native Indian Homemakers Association, and with various other organizations. There were few events in the community that did not have her involvement.

Aggie was a friend and a regular caller to the newspaper. Occasionally she just wanted to talk, or express concern about something, or tell me about a grandchild's achievement. She loved children and was surrounded by them when I interviewed her in her home on the reserve.

Aggie's concern for Native women was evident when Rose Charlie, who was then the founder and president of the Indian Homemakers Association of British Columbia, was invited to speak to the local women's group headed by Aggie in the Friendship Centre. Charlie told how difficult life was for Native women and children, and expressed her concern about drug and alcohol abuse within the population. She was married, with six children and nine grandchildren, and lived in Harrison Mills. Aggie's local of the Homemakers Association wanted better housing, water and sanitation systems, and education for their children. This was the first time I had seen a talking stick used at a meeting. The stick was passed around from member to member allowing only the person holding the stick to speak, giving everyone present a chance to have their voice heard in the discussions. The stick was very effective—except when someone didn't want to stop talking.

Rose Charlie received an honorary doctor of law degree from UBC in 1989 and in 2003 was awarded the Order of British Columbia. Her work helped restore First Nations status to over 16,000 women and 46,000 first-generation individuals of mixed ancestry.

Jessie Hamilton was an elder and the second female Hupacasath chief her grandmother was the first. Jessie was active in the community working for many years with West Coast General Hospital Women's Auxiliary. Her years spent at the Alberni Residential School, where she was not allowed to speak her language, made a lasting impression on her. Afraid her Native language would disappear forever, she began documenting the dialect for future generations. She said:

I was about seven or eight before I started to learn English. The language was spoken in our home when my mother was with us. She died in 1967. To me, it has always been important to know who I am, where I came from and what our people did before the European people came. It makes me sad to see so many of our old ways going.[15]

Hamilton produced a series of books preserving the language of her people and has been recognized by the federal government for her work.

Judith Sayers is another woman from the Hupacasath who has become a leader within the wider aboriginal community. Her mother a Hupacasath and her father Cree, she grew up with the Mormon faith. She left home in Port Alberni to attend

Brigham Young University, where she earned a law degree. She kept her connection with the Mormon Church until she was twenty-five.

Sayers was involved in international politics from 1983 to 1994. She married and had two children, Alayna and Cole. When she returned to Port Alberni in 1990 as a single mother she established an all-woman family law practice. In 1993 she received an honorary doctorate from Queen's University for her work in international and constitutional law. She began to focus on treaty issues and the conditions of her people.

In 1995 she was elected chief councillor of the Hupacasath; her enthusiasm and powerful personality challenged local attitudes in both Native and non-Native communities. Working together she brought change and built partnerships; she sat on a number of boards and committees in Port Alberni, and looked to improve living and working conditions for band members. She remained chief for fourteen years, being elected five more times, each one contested. Sayers continues to be a thorn in the side of government as she fights for the future of her people.

Now a professor at the University of Victoria, Sayers has the power, knowledge, and instincts to influence another generation of young people. She will continue to be a powerful voice for the future of aboriginal people in Canada.

{ *chapter five* }

COMMUNITY RECREATION AND PRESERVING HERITAGE

In Port Alberni both community recreation and heritage preservation came under the jurisdiction of the Parks and Recreation Commission, a municipally appointed board with its own budget and mandate. The city was blessed with excellent sporting facilities, giving residents many opportunities to participate through community programming, or through those offered by the MB mills. The Alberni Valley Museum also came under the Parks mandate; a member of the commission sat on the museum board, providing first-hand communication and relaying concerns about heritage activities.

RECREATION

In the 1970s there were many changes happening within Parks and Recreation. The arts community wanted to be part of that change, so it lobbied to have someone appointed to the commission to represent it. This was unheard of! Normally city council decided who sat on the commission, and they did not want someone with an axe to grind. After much lobbying by the Community Arts Council, however, city council, then under Mayor Howard McLean, reluctantly agreed to look at a list of candidates. My name was chosen from those submitted.

At my first commission meeting, chairman Bill Gibson's opening remarks made it clear that everyone at the table was there to represent the entire community, not just one small part of it. I knew he was referring to me and to the arts community. Gibson was co-owner of CJAV radio station. He retired as Parks chairman at the end of 1975 and was replaced by Helen Patenaude, with Dr. Mike Trumper as vice-chairman. Around the board table were two representative aldermen from city council, Bryan Latham and Jim Robertson, plus community appointees Rob Jones, Dave Nelson, Doug Brinham, June Kearney, and myself. The superintendent of parks and recreation at that time was Larry Beres, who like me was a newcomer to Port Alberni, having arrived about the same time. Beres was knowledgeable about recreation in the province, and one of the first things he did was design a Master Recreation Plan for the city.

The Parks and Recreation Commission meetings usually were a hotbed of discussion and open to the press, sports groups, and interested residents. There was opposition to any increase in fees for the rental of playing fields or facilities, and concerns were sometimes raised about the conditions of playing fields and the need for more programs for young people. The press gave good coverage and generated a lot of community debate. The department did get high marks with everyone for the excellent school program that provided swimming lessons for every child in school. Living close to rivers, lakes, and the ocean, it was considered essential that children know how to swim.

There was also an excellent school skating program delivered at the Ice Arena in Recreation Park. The building was shared, with the ice arena in one half and the AV Curling

Club in the other. When it came time to put a new roof on the building, there was heated debate about who should pay for it.

Within the department there were a number of young people with backgrounds in recreation programming. Doug Brimacombe started as a young man, later replacing Larry Beres as superintendent when he accepted another position in Victoria, and Gary King was community program coordinator. Ron Doetzel had big success with a weekly floor hockey program for teens and other recreational programs at Gyro Youth Centre in Recreation Park. Kenn Whiteman, the youth coordinator also working from Gyro, received wide acclaim for one of his most innovative and successful programs, the Port Alberni Clown College. The program was designed to give young people an opportunity to learn about makeup, mime, magic, and the art of clowning. With this knowledge they entertained at children's parties and community events and in parades, and most importantly developed good self-esteem. I had first-hand experience with this program through my children, who all participated at one time or another. Clown makeup and wigs were the norm in our house during their teen years. Our daughter entertained many as Clarence the Clown.

The commission maintained soccer and baseball playing fields, the ice arena, and Glenwood Centre, a large all-purpose hall that was also used as a roller-skating rink. Originally it was the RCEME Hall during the Second World War when the army base was stationed in town. In 1949 it became the Glenwood Sport Centre. There was also the outdoor swimming pool at Recreation Park, plus the indoor swimming pool at Echo '67 Community Centre and the centre facility itself. The Sunshine Club, a seniors group, used Echo Centre for most of its activities and contributed financially to upgrades in the building. Teresa Kingston became the senior coordinator when Anne Morrison left to take another position on the mainland. The department also coordinated the use of school playgrounds and gymnasiums and organized community sports programming.

The Parks and Recreation summer programs were some of the best in the province with a calendar full of exciting outdoor events, canoe excursions to Sproat Lake or Barkley Sound, hiking, and camping, plus arts and crafts programs for children in the city.

Echo Centre was the hub of all recreational activity. In the 1970s Kay Pickles was a familiar face at Echo Centre Lounge, where she dispensed information, gave advice on federal and provincial programs, and provided help for seniors. She had come from Yorkshire, England, to Port Alberni in 1950. After her husband died she began using her stenographic skills by writing a senior citizens' advice column for the *Alberni Valley Times*. She was also one of the founders of the Sunshine Club in 1967, and took an active interest in the Intermediate Care Home Society.

Regional recreation was a big headache for the city. While the city had all the recreational facilities and local taxpayers paid for their upkeep, residents in the outlying areas of Cherry Creek, Beaver Creek, and Sproat Lake used the facilities free without taxation. Twice residents in those areas defeated a regional recreation referendum to share in the costs—who wanted to pay more taxes?! Eventually the subject was resolved by charging users in the outlying area an extra fee to use the facilities.

One of the most difficult and major discussions during my term with the commission was the closing of the outdoor swimming pool in Recreation Park. The pool was a popular place in the summer, but it had deteriorated to such an extent that authorities considered it a health hazard. The city faced a difficult choice between building a new pool, rebuilding the old one, or just closing the old. It chose the latter, much to the dismay of children living in the city who had no transportation to Papermill Dam Park on the Somass River, or Sproat Lake Provincial Park in the summer.

COMMUNITY FAIRS

There were three community events held each fall that brought the community together—the Salmon Festival, the Fall Fair, and Logger's Sports Day. These events fell on consecutive weekends. The Salmon Derby on Labour Day weekend attracted hundreds to the Clutesi Haven Marina to participate either as fishermen or observers.

The town can thank the former owner of the Greenwood Hotel, Carl Schretlen, for being one of the founders of the Salmon Festival. He noticed during his first year in town that there was nothing happening on holiday weekends. What was needed, he thought, was an event that would keep residents in town and also bring people in, and so the Salmon Festival was initiated. He recalled the first committee received good support from the community. Later, in 1972, the group formed a non-profit society with the hotel as headquarters for the festival.

Since then the event has grown tremendously. The harbour is a sea of fishing boats of every size—almost anything that floats, in some cases. China Creek Marina and Campground to the south of the city is also packed with eager fishermen from other parts of Canada and the US who come to take part in the fishing derby.

At Clutesi Haven Marina the smell of barbecue salmon whets the appetite of anyone within range. Furniture businessman and former alderman Art Wynans was famous for guarding his secret, prized barbecue sauce, despite numerous requests for the recipe. There was entertainment over the three-day event, and thousands of dollars in prize money awarded for the biggest fish. Sometimes the top fish would be around forty or fifty pounds in weight. Today the fish seem smaller, but the Salmon Derby is as successful as ever.

The annual Fall Fair held at Glenwood Centre grounds followed the next weekend. Dating back to the early 1900s, it was similar to other events held throughout the province to promote agriculture. The Alberni Valley had lots to boast about in farming. Some farms dated from the 1880s and have gained provincial heritage status. The first Alberni Fall Fair was held in 1904, organized by the Industrial and Agricultural Association of the Alberni Valley. Three years later it had six hundred entries, which was double that of the previous year. The motto for that year was Watch Alberni Grow.

Two world wars interrupted the fair, and by September 1946 the Kinsmen Club of Port Alberni had taken over hosting the event. Since then it has grown in size and now has several permanent buildings located at Glenwood Centre grounds.

The Fall Fair gave city children a chance to pet a farm animal or view competition between farm animals, as well as enjoy the midway, merry-go-round, and concessions. Alberni Valley folks competed for prizes in home baking, flower and vegetable growing, plus arts and crafts. Businesses rented booths in the Centre to promote their enterprise or product. Front-and-centre at these events were Miss Port Alberni and her entourage.

The Miss Port Alberni Pageant was a big event that started in 1978 in the ADSS auditorium. The originator was Stella Teindl, who worked hard to bring the event to fruition. At its inception she did the speaker's circuit, talked up a storm, and convinced everyone of the merits of the pageant. Initially there was opposition and objections from feminists, but she stood behind the event. The first pageant was free and drew a large crowd. Each year thereafter the event grew in popularity until it just "packed them in." Teindl organized the first two pageants herself, then got some much-needed volunteer help from Cindy Zajes, and from Ron Baker-Smith of the Alberni Valley Chamber of Commerce.

Teindl felt the benefits to young women from the public experience were many. They gained self-confidence and poise, and increased their public speaking abilities. She said,

When these kids register, they are scared. They don't know if they want to go ahead with it or not. You can see it in their faces. But come the night of the pageant it is a different story. They have made new friends, a bond has been developed between them and they are full of self-confidence. They feel good about themselves and anything that can do that for a girl is not all bad."[1]

The Miss Port Alberni Pageant grew to be one of the highlights of the year in the community.

Logger's Sports Day was held on the last day of the Fall Fair, usually on a Sunday. This colourful event attracted thousands to the Glenwood Centre grounds where loggers strutted their stuff, from log rolling and cutting to axe throwing and speed climbing, showing what working in the woods was all about.

One family, the Boykos from Sproat Lake, dominated the logger's sports competition year after year. Alan Boyko was a logging sports legend who had worked at MB's Sproat Lake Division for twenty-six years. Each year he thrilled the crowd with his axe skills. He also travelled the logging sports circuit, eventually winning the world championship. Queen Elizabeth was entertained by his axe throwing on her 1971 royal visit to British Columbia. His son Mike was also a champion logroller, as were daughters Janice and Brenda.

Watching a man climb a tree at breakneck speed, then shimmy down in record time was thrilling. Some tried it, but few could compete with Les Stewart, a faller, also with the Sproat Lake Division, who could climb to the top of a hundred-foot pole and back down again in thirty-six seconds. He was consistently the winner at speed-climbing events, and won the Canadian championship three times. His son Wade was also a tree speed-climber.

PRESERVING VALLEY HISTORY

As Canada's centennial celebration approached in 1967, pioneers in the Alberni Valley had begun to look at the past hundred years and decided it was time to begin collecting and preserving what remained of valley history before it was forgotten.

With this in mind, some descendants of those pioneers met on March 31, 1965, in the old Alberni City Hall on Johnston Road, and formed the Alberni District Museum and Historical Society, electing Keitha Adams as its first president. Adams was the daughter of the Reverend Frank Edwin Pitts, once a principal at the Alberni Residential School. Also present was Lila McKenzie, wife of Ken McKenzie and granddaughter of the pioneer Kenneth and Alexandrina McKenzie family who arrived in the valley in 1883. The McKenzies cleared land on the east bank of the Stamp River and began farming. There have been over 150 descendents of the family—six generations, five of them born in the Alberni Valley and many still living here. Other co-founders of the society included Meg Trebett, Helen Ford, and Richard Hilton. Trebett was the former editor of the *Twin City Times* and granddaughter of pioneer Joseph G. Halpenny, who farmed in the Beaver Creek area in 1892. Helen Ford's father, Frederick Charles Manning, had purchased Sproat Lake Sawmill in 1930. Richard Hilton was the son of Dr. Caleb Thomas Hilton, the pioneer doctor who arrived in the community in 1908; he built a home and office at the corner of Third and Mar Street where Woodward's eventually located.

The society dedicated itself to working toward the establishment of a museum and archives. Adams said at the time: "If we are to chart a wise course in the future, it is necessary to understand our past . . . If we are to grow, we must know where our roots lie."[2] The group incorporated in 1967, the year of Canada's centennial celebrations and the year of amalgamation.

At first the old army camp firehall at the corner of Roger and Tenth Avenue was used to store some artifacts and as a workshop to sort, file, and record archival material. From these cramped quarters and a few filing cabinets the society began collecting community records. Larger artifacts were stored in the basement of the old Alberni post office. The volunteers who worked in this small space were dedicated and never lost sight of their goal.

This goal was realized somewhat in 1971 when the Alberni Valley Museum was officially opened and the artifacts as well as the photograph collection were transferred to the museum. John Sendy was the first museum curator, followed by John Mitchell. But the move still left the society preserving what it called its "paper treasures" in the old firehall. It was not until 1982 that a museum expansion allowed the Historical Society's archival collection and its volunteer workers to move into the museum. Over the years, a good working relationship developed between museum staff and the society volunteers. Museum staff are paid by the city, taking care of the artifacts and photographs, while the society members work as volunteers in the same building with a separate function caring for the archives, the written treasures. It is a system that has worked well.

The Alberni Valley Museum was built adjacent to Echo Centre on Wallace Street, providing easy access to the community. Various curators have served the museum well over the years, carrying on the commitment made by countless volunteers in establishing the facility. Long-time curator Jean McIntosh arrived in 1980 as a summer student to work under curator Nathalie Macfarlane, taking over from her when she left in 1986. Many others helped move the museum forward, including Charlene Garvey, Lillian Weedmark, and Shelley Harding, who remains as education director. McIntosh retired in 2013 and Dr. Jamie Morton has now filled the position.

The expansion in 1982 transformed the museum by implementing the unique concept of visible storage, with everything on display, touchable, and workable. At the opening, Helen Ford and Keitha Adams, two of the society's co-founders, officially cut the ribbon, assisted by MLA Bob Skelly and Mayor Paul Reitsma. Displays depict Port Alberni's long history with the forest industry, fishing, agriculture, and pioneer settlement. Panels from the exterior of the old Bishop store were displayed high above the balcony overlooking the industrial display area.

The museum expansion was a milestone event in recognizing and drawing awareness to Native artists in the region. Officially opening the museum's Temporary Exhibit Gallery, Dr. George Clutesi paid tribute to young artist Ron Hamilton, whose work was exhibited in the gallery. Joan Frohn-Nielsen, a member of the museum advisory committee and director of North Island College's Port Alberni campus, introduced Nitinat carver Art Thompson, who then unveiled the first in a series of panels he carved for the exterior of the museum.

Not all artifacts can be neatly packaged or displayed within a museum. The town had much larger items of historic significance and helping to collect and preserve these artifacts was the Western Vancouver Island Industrial Heritage Society. The group initially formed to restore the old 2-Spot, a rusting Shay logging locomotive that had tested time and rested in a dedicated green space at the foot of Redford Street, across from the pulp mill. H.R. MacMillan had presented the 2-Spot as a gift to the city in 1954, Mayor Loran Jordan accepting on behalf of the community. The locomotive was much loved by the community and reminded residents of their past, a time when railway logging was the norm. Unfortunately, by 1976 the years of exposure to the elements had taken a toll, and concerned old-timers called for its restoration.

Action was taken to move the locomotive to a new location on Tenth Avenue near Echo Centre. There it was still exposed to the weather, but the location was better for restoration and closer to the Alberni Valley Museum where John Mitchell took it under his wing. After plans were worked out and a committee formed, the government, industry, and businesses were approached for funding and volunteers began dismantling the old Shay. They stripped her down and found to their amazement that the boiler and firebox were still in pretty good shape; all they needed were more parts, so the search for parts was on! Old railway men like Bob Swanson came to the rescue to lead the restoration. Over many years Swanson had restored eight steam locomotives; his most well-known project was the restoration of the Royal Hudson steam locomotive that carries tourists from Vancouver to Squamish. His knowledge as a boiler inspector provided valuable assistance to the Port Alberni group.

Restoration took until 1984 when the locomotive was ready for a test run at the opening of the new Alberni Harbour Quay development on the waterfront. The venerated 2-Spot was placed on the E & N railway tracks at Roger Street, and after a few hiccups and some angst among the crew, the old engine inched slowly alongside the railway station. When the train whistle blew, there were a lot of happy faces of railway enthusiasts in the crowd who had given countless volunteer hours restoring the old engine.

With the 2-Spot project completed, the Industrial Heritage Society then turned its attention to the E & N railway station at lower Argyle Street. Built in 1911, the station saw the first passenger train arrive in Port Alberni in 1912, and the last passenger train pull out for Victoria in 1957. Since then the station had sat empty and neglected. After the city acquired the building, the Industrial Heritage Society set about restoring it to its original condition. The station became the society's base of operations not only for restoring the old station itself but also in the restoration of other pieces of railway rolling stock, a steam donkey at the McLean Mill, and various other pieces of industrial heritage. Today the station is fully restored and still used by the society to run excursion trains out to the McLean Mill National Historic Sawmill.

THE McLEAN MILL

The McLean Mill, as it is known locally, is situated about 12 kilometres (7 miles) from Port Alberni, on 12.8 hectares (31 hectares) in the Beaver Creek area. The old sawmill sits deep in the forest in the shadow of the Beaufort Mountain Range. Robert Bartlett McLean purchased timber rights to about 120 hectares (300 acres) from pioneer Bobby de Beaux, and built the steam-powered sawmill in 1925. McLean and his wife, Cora, were originally from New Brunswick and had operated a sawmill in Cloverdale in the Fraser Valley for ten years before a scarcity of timber forced them to look for another opportunity. At this time the forest industry in the Alberni Valley was growing, with three new sawmills built within a period of two years. The McLeans' three sons—Walter, Arnold, and Philip—also moved to the valley; they were all married but left their wives behind until houses were built for them at the mill site.[3] (Philip and Muriel's son Howard would become mayor of Port Alberni in 1974.)

A spur line was added to the sawmill from the E & N track between Bainbridge and Alberni, and water was diverted from Kitsuksis Creek to make a log pond. A small village took shape when log cabins were built to accommodate the McLean families, and a bunkhouse and cookhouse to house single men employed in logging or working in the mill. Management for the mill was divided between the sons: Arnold was mill manager, Walter looked after logging, while Philip managed a subsidiary in Cumberland. Their father stayed only a few years before returning to Cloverdale. Life was not easy for the young McLean families. Without electricity or running water, living in primitive two-room log cabins where the wind often whipped through the cracks was a pretty rugged existence—and there was the isolation of being away from family and friends.

A number of Japanese families with children moved to work at the mill, and in 1929 a one-room schoolhouse was built along with accommodation for the teacher. Those who lived there have happy memories of a rich social life of parties, concerts, and dances held in the small schoolhouse. The school closed in 1942 when the Japanese families were evacuated. The remaining children were driven to school in Alberni in the jitney, a small bus open on both sides.

When the mill ceased production in 1965, it sat derelict for a number of years before the McLean family donated it to the City of Port Alberni, including all the equipment. It was some time before restoration began, and in the interim scavengers and souvenir hunters took advantage of the mill's isolation. In 1988, the City of Port Alberni, through donations from the McLean family and MB, became the owner of the mill site. Restoration now proceeded under the direction of the Alberni Valley Museum. The community began to sit up and take notice of what a wonderful tourist opportunity the mill presented. Countless hours of work by volunteers brought the old mill back from obscurity.

Dave Lowe worked on the mill for twenty years, ten as a volunteer and ten as project manager. During that time, he met some of the former employees of the mill, such as Kermit Green who had been the head sawyer until it closed. Green and others provided valuable information about the operation of the mill. The museum acquired most of the company records and photos that proved invaluable. In the meantime, Jean McIntosh, Alberni Valley Museum director, made arrangements for university students to make drawings of the mill, while she negotiated with Parks Canada to join in the restoration. Lowe also made drawings of all the buildings on the site. Convincing Parks Canada to help restore the mill to operating condition was difficult; it did not believe it could not be done. Lowe told its officials that the word "can't" did not exist in his vocabulary. He recalled:

We invited them to the mill and cut board [lumber] by using air in the main steam engine. From that point on they worked closely with us. It was challenging but enjoyable.[4]

Lowe always welcomed visitors and could be relied upon to give a knowledgeable conducted tour of the site. During the restoration I visited the site several times. On my first visit I was astonished to see the old sawmill village sitting in isolation in this remote location with most of its buildings still intact. There was this feeling of stepping back to an earlier time in history when the giant trees in the nearby forest were being felled and the mill was producing lumber. One could almost imagine hearing the train whistle as it neared the site.

A few years later I was privileged to visit the mill with Muriel McLean and friend Dorrit MacLeod, both in their nineties. The women gave a running commentary about each of the houses, including who lived where, and provided a personal look at the history of the mill. To see Muriel rush excitedly toward the log pond, then scurry over to the sawmill and poke her nose into each building while Dorrit added her own perspective about each of the pioneers was an incredible experience not to be forgotten.

Parks Canada assumed responsibility and in 1989 the sawmill and village was designated a National Heritage Site. An agreement was reached in 1996 between the city and the federal government: Ottawa would contribute $2.6 million toward the restoration and preservation of the mill as a National Heritage Site for forty-two years. The museum was tasked with overseeing the preservation and safeguarding the equipment, artifacts, and records. The city owns the mill, the museum, and the railroad, and it contracts with the Western Vancouver Island Industrial Heritage Society to run the mill and the railroad.

The McLean Sawmill is the only remaining steam-operated sawmill in Canada. The mill now produces lumber for the specialty market, netting almost $600,000 a year. Wood from the mill has been shipped to the eastern US and other parts of BC and Canada.

The success of the mill as a tourist attraction shows the degree of commitment by all concerned. During the summer months, Alberni Pacific Railway Engine No. 7, which once served the logging industry, pulls five converted transfer cabooses full of passengers out to McLean Mill. There is a gift shop and a café, and the gently restored original buildings house exhibits of their history. Visitors can see the mill and the restored steam donkey in action.

PRESERVING MARITIME HISTORY

While the Industrial Heritage Society was busy restoring pieces of old railway rolling stock and collecting industrial artifacts, another group focused on the region's maritime history. Those interested in maritime history had been meeting regularly and had begun collecting information and artifacts. They turned attention to restoring the largest artifact: the old Bamfield Lifeboat, formerly based in the Canadian Coast Guard Station at Bamfield and retired from service in 1969. For two decades the gallant little vessel had answered distress calls on the dangerous waters off the west coast. When its restoration was complete the ship was put on display at Alberni Harbour Quay. At the same location, a beautiful mural was painted depicting the heroic steamer *Valencia* that was wrecked on January 20, 1906, on its way to Victoria carrying 164 passengers and crew. Only thirty-eight people survived. The mural served as a reminder of the tragedy and of the region's rich maritime history.

After many years, the group formed the Port Alberni Maritime Heritage Society in 1989 as a non-profit society with the purpose of working with the museum and the community to preserve and present the maritime heritage of the west coast.

Twelve years later the Port Alberni Maritime Discovery Centre was completed on the waterfront south of Alberni Harbour Quay. Ken Hutcheson was foremost in promoting and collecting maritime history over the years; the Hutcheson Gallery at the new centre is named in his honour. The Bamfield Lifeboat was moved to a new home alongside the lighthouse at the Discovery Centre.

Dr. Harry Webster helped form the Maritime Heritage Society and for many years passionately promoted the idea of building a replica of the Spanish sailing ship *Santiago*, which once sailed the west coast waters. His idea was to have the ship located on the Port Alberni waterfront as a tourist attraction, perhaps even have it sail the Alberni Inlet.

The original frigate *Santiago* was built and launched in San Blas, in October 1773, for the first Spanish expedition north to the west coast of Vancouver Island. The 225-ton vessel was well armed, and captained by Juan Perez, the senior naval officer at San Blas. A second voyage took place in 1775. But there is no indication of a ship of that nationality sailing to the head of the Alberni Inlet. Port Alberni's name is Spanish, but the city was named for Don Pedro de Alberni, a lieutenant colonel in charge of the small military force accompanying the 1790 expedition to Nootka by Francisco de Eliza.

Despite all of Dr. Webster's hard work in trying to get the project underway, it never came to fruition. On the other hand, he was successful in urging the city to buy the local waterfront property that eventually became the Alberni Harbour Quay development. Dr. Webster practised family medicine in Port Alberni for thirty-four years. He was a member of the Kinsmen Club and served two terms as alderman. Retiring from full-time practice, he and his wife Louise moved to Nanoose Bay, where he continued to enjoy his garden and his boat.

{ *chapter six* }

THE ARTS COMMUNITY

When I first moved to Port Alberni I was amazed at the vibrant arts community that existed in the town and the high level of volunteerism. There was something about living in a small community that encouraged you to get involved. On my arrival, as the movers carried my paintings into our new home, they suggested I might want to show my paintings at Echo Centre, or even give art lessons to the community, both of which I did within a few years. Several weeks later, my new next-door neighbour invited me to join the Alberni Valley Art Group. Before long I was totally immersed in the life of the arts community.

MUSIC, THEATRE, AND VISUAL ARTS

In the 1970s Port Alberni was blessed by having the largest performing arts theatre on Vancouver Island, with one thousand seats, at the Alberni District Secondary School (ADSS) auditorium. The Alberni Valley Musical Theatre performance held every year around Christmastime packed the theatre.

The cast included an eclectic group of teachers, lawyers, clerks, mill workers, housewives, and businessmen. They staged such musical theatre shows as *White Horse Inn, Brigadoon, Hello Dolly, My Fair Lady, South Pacific,* and *Fiddler on the Roof*, to name only a few of the wonderful performances.

The crowd cheered when George Marshall danced across the stage in many of the shows. Marshall, who worked at the Alberni Plywood Division, was a trained dancer and had performed several summers in the Butchart Gardens show in Victoria and at various venues in Vancouver. The audience was just as thrilled to hear Dr. Alan Markin, a professor at North Island College, sing "If I Were a Rich Man" from *Fiddler on the Roof*. Retired teacher and real estate agent John Andrews directed and sometimes acted in many of these productions. Pat Cummings and her daughter Alison Cowan, from the Pat Cummings School of Dance, offered their dance expertise, and teacher Sam McKimm directed the choir, while musician Phil Wallbank conducted the orchestra.

Other performances held at ADSS included concerts by the senior choir, which was aptly named Timbre! (with the exclamation mark). The mixed choir attracted large audiences in whatever venue it sang, whether theatres, churches, or community centres. Formed in 1972, it remains one of the top choirs in the province. In the early days Jim Nolan shared conducting expertise with Art Tinney, and later with Dave Morgan. In 1973 Nolan became sole director, and under his leadership the choir flourished. A year later the choir had grown so large a decision was made that everyone had to audition and be able to sight-read. Michael Oczko directed from 1981 to 1983, then music teacher Pat Miller took the baton from 1983 to 1996. Robert Comejo succeeded Miller for two years before Miller returned to the choir in 1998. She continues to lead the choir today. Under her direction the choir performed atced the first Canadian Choral Celebration at Carnegie Hall in New York. In January 2011, Miller was awarded the Amy Ferguson

Award by the British Columbia Choral Federation for fostering outstanding vocal practice in BC's choral community.

Pat Miller (née Auld) was born in Estevan, Saskatchewan, and came to Port Alberni at the age of fourteen. She then studied at the Musical Conservatory of Toronto and the Banff School of Fine Arts, and on her return to Port Alberni taught piano.[1] She continued her musical education as a choral conductor, starting a young choir that became the Port Alberni Community Choir. She often joined her husband, Barry, in producing musical concerts for the community.

In fact, the husband-and-wife musical team of Pat and Barry Miller is considered a community treasure. Both have participated, promoted, taught, and been part of the music scene in Port Alberni for decades. They were made Citizens of the Year in 1992. While Pat taught piano, Barry was the music teacher, first at Eric J. Dunn Junior Secondary School, then at ADSS. He organized the School District 70 Stage Band composed of music students from ADSS and three junior secondary schools—Eric J. Dunn, Mt. Klitsa, and A.W. Neill. The stage band concerts were sold-out performances. Barry also initiated a high school bell-ringing ensemble, making every Christmas concert special.

In Barry's spare time, if he had any, he played in a weekend band named the Cavemen, led by trumpeter Bill Cave who once taught with him at Eric J. Dunn Junior Secondary before moving to Kwalikum Secondary School in Qualicum Beach. The drummer was Rick Acres, and the other part of the quartet was Steve Jones, who was band director at Mt. Klitsa Secondary School and now teaches at Vancouver Island University in Nanaimo. The band played for MB Christmas parties and was much in demand at other venues around Vancouver Island. An offshoot of the Cavemen was the Arrowsmith Big Band, created by Bill Cave in 1975.

Barry and his brother, Terry, were sons of Dr. Alan Philip Miller and wife Evelyn, who had come to the community in 1934 to practise medicine. Evelyn was a member of the Alberni

Valley Art Group, and did beautiful floral watercolour paintings; she was also an active member with the WCGH Women's Auxiliary. Dr. Miller was in partnership with Dr. Norman Jones, who cared for our family well until they both retired.

Community theatre had many ups and downs, always with one strong person leading the way but unable to maintain a strong program. The lack of a small theatre venue was always troubling, and the Community Arts Council looked at various locations. There was hope of turning a movie theatre, such as the boarded-up Capitol building, into a performing art space. The council also examined the old hydro building, on Fourth Avenue, for a possible theatre, but the idea never took root, and the old industrial building with its beautiful rustic red bricks was eventually demolished. The bricks were used at the Qualicum Museum.

Mildred Milliken ran a theatre program for young drama students through a Parks & Recreation program, while teenager Cindy Zajes struggled to establish an independent amateur theatrical group called Backstage. Today Portal Players Dramatic Society performs in the renovated 230-seat Capitol Theatre on Argyle Street. Cindy Solda (née Zajes) is now a respected alderman for the City of Port Alberni, and continues to support live theatre.

The annual spring Craft Fair held in the mid-1970s in Recreation Park was a wonderful family event that gave artists and craftspeople an opportunity to sell their work and meet the public. The event attracted talented artisans from across Vancouver Island. Everyone was responsible for his or her own display. Families came for the day. Picnics were laid out on the grass with activities planned for children. The Alberni Valley supported a large number of visual artists as well as craftspeople ranging from potters, weavers, and batik and fabric artists to wood and bone carvers and a glass blower, plus Native artists such as Ramona Gus and Charlie Mickey.

At that time Recreation Park still had the outdoor pool and while parents attended the Craft Fair, their children enjoyed the pool adjacent to the ice arena and Gyro Youth Centre. After the pool closed, a splash pool was built for the younger children. There was also the usual playground equipment. Recreation Park was a wonderful venue for a family event. Everyone prayed for sunshine, but spring weather could be unpredictable, and eventually the Craft Fair was moved inside the ice arena after it had closed for the season. Being under cover may have been less stressful for the artists and craftspeople to display their work, but the fair lost its family ambience and outdoor picnic atmosphere.

There was something about Port Alberni that made you want to give back to the community. Perhaps it was the isolation of the town and a willingness to make life better, but newcomers soon found themselves immersed in clubs, societies, and organizations that made the town hum. When I joined the Alberni Valley Art Group in 1973, I met many local artists with the same interests.

This painters group had been in existence since 1944 when Merwyn McVicar, Ken Caufield, Rose Colpman, Betty Crozier, and Jack Flitton brought some like-minded individuals together to paint, exhibit, and bring in visiting artists and shows. Dr. George Clutesi was one of the club's earliest members. The group took great pride in participating in art exhibits displayed in Echo Centre Lounge. Once a week members painted together in a room at the centre, and occasionally sponsored visiting artist workshops. San Francisco artist Warren Brandon and David Anderson of Victoria both visited several times, sharing their talents and critiquing club members' work.

In 1974 Faye Marcellus was president, with Bubb Bottner as treasurer and myself as secretary. The Art Group membership list had a diverse group of artists, including Evelyn Miller, Gen Bellamy, Muriel Harding, Monika Coulombe, Isobel Monson, Muriel Harding, Rie Snikkers, Mary Earl, and Dorothy Symons. There were few men in the group, although founder Merwyn McVicar continued to offer support.

Each spring members participated in the Craft Fair. If members sold one painting they were happy—if they sold two or three, they were ecstatic. After the entry fee was paid, there was always enough profit to buy more paint or canvasses. The opportunity to discuss art with the general public or exchange views and ideas with other artists was very worthwhile.

Also well received by the community were visits from the Victoria Art Gallery and the Emily Carr College in Vancouver bringing travelling exhibitions into Port Alberni. Occasionally workshops were arranged to coincide with these exhibits.

The Art Group was affiliated with the Alberni Valley Community Arts Council (CAC), an umbrella organization for groups who belonged to various disciplines from theatre, dance, and music to the visual arts. It also included the Alberni District Historical Society and Mt. Klitsa Garden Club. Each member group paid a small fee to belong to the council.

The CAC formed in 1966 with Robert Aller as president. The following year the 1967 Centennial Fund was established in the province. This fund later became known as the BC Cultural Fund and was administered by the newly formed British Columbia Arts Board. The arts community had often felt that sports organizations got a bigger share of the financial pie, so hopes were high that for the first time something positive was being done to help promote the arts in the province.

The CACs in the province were each given a grant to award member groups or individuals for performance or exhibition, but there was never enough money to fund every application. And the board had no teeth; it could only do what government said within its very limited budget. The council could also act as an advocate for a group or add its support to a specific cause, celebration, or event.

When I joined the Alberni Valley CAC in 1974, Woodward's employee Paul Squires was president. He was enthusiastic about furthering the arts in the community. Meetings were held in

Echo Centre and concentrated on local concerns. There were approximately seventy-five other CACs scattered throughout the province, some of which shared their newsletters. The council decided to select items from these newsletters and incorporate them with regional events to create a relevant local newsletter. In this way members would learn about other councils while also publicizing local events.

And so the newsletter *Tawasi* was born, and I became its first editor. The title *Tawasi* was a Native name meaning "friend and helper." The name seemed appropriate!

In the first issue, published in October 1974, there was news from Nina Baird, the provincial cultural animateur, on a report she had produced named "Access to the Arts." It laid the foundation for an arts policy for the province, BC being one of the few provinces in Canada that did not have such a policy. *Tawasi* also announced that Dr. George Clutesi had been elected to the board of governors of the Canadian Conference of the Arts. The local drama group was casting for *The Ecstasy of Rita Joe* under the direction of Jack Ashbridge. Twenty members of the pottery group had just had a Japanese Raku firing at the home of Elspeth Watson. A creative writers' group was being organized, and there was a list of upcoming exhibitions at Echo Centre. There was also a poem by Pat Grace entitled "Day's End." Pat Grace was the *nom-de-plume* of Dick McMinn, a part-time poet and the owner and skipper of the *Lady Rose*, the sturdy little vessel that transported passengers and freight from Port Alberni to Bamfield and Ucluelet.

Assembling information for the monthly newsletter gave me an appreciation for writing and publishing and perhaps whetted my appetite for a future career. Unlike today with easy access to computers and printers, in the 1970s the hard copy had to be carefully typed on stencils, then run off on an A.B. Dick offset machine. The newsletter took hours to produce, then more hours to fold, staple and stamp, then mail to the membership and other CACs in the province. Initially my three children and Charlene Wetick, volunteer CAC secretary to president Paul Squires, helped with the assembly. Charlene was also a secretary at the pulp mill.

When Squires was transferred to the Woodward's Penticton store in 1976, John Parker briefly held the position of CAC president before I was elected president. There was talk of Woodward's building another store on Vancouver Island, possibly on the outskirts of Nanaimo, but that seemed a long way into the future. The fate of the CAC was now in my hands.

The newsletter led to opportunities to promote the arts, including a local cable television show entitled *Tawasi Review* with Günther Smuda behind the camera. This was followed by a local radio show on CJAV named *Tawasi Report*. Next came a weekly column *B.C. Arts Scene* for the *Alberni Valley Times*. Ruth Roberts, a reporter with the newspaper, was a big supporter of the arts and always gave her time to promote a cause.

During the 1970s, the arts in the province thrived. New CACs were being formed, and theatres, art centres, and galleries were being built, thanks to financial assistance from the provincial and federal government, and those infamous Local Improvement Project (LIP) grants courtesy of the federal Liberal government under Prime Minister Pierre Elliott Trudeau. The growth in the arts reflected a thriving provincial and federal economy.

FROM GARDEN TO GALLERY

In the late spring of 1976 when I was serving as a member of the Parks and Recreation Commission, a note came from city council requesting the commission look into the value of the gardens of the late Fred Rollin, a pioneer of the Alberni Valley who had recently died. In his will he had donated two garden lots to the city; these were adjacent to his residence, which had been willed to his nephew. The nephew didn't want the building and offered it to the city, which eventually purchased it for

$24,000. Now the city owned three lots: two in garden and one containing the residence. Rollin had bequeathed another lot on the south side of the building to Eighth Avenue Elementary School located next door.

Parks and Recreation had the grounds evaluated by its foreman, and a report came back to the commission stating the garden was of little value but the grounds had good topsoil and the department wanted first chance at it. Alderman Jim Robertson, a member of the commission who had been a friend of Fred Rollin, asked me to take a look at the site and see whether it would be of interest to the Alberni District Historical Society, one of the CAC-affiliated groups. He thought perhaps the building would make an interesting pioneer-type museum.

My first venture to the grounds of the Rollin property, at Eighth Avenue and Argyle Street, was quite memorable. The garden was alive with spring blossoms, tulips, daffodils, and azaleas, and the dogwood tree was in full bloom. The site was stunning! Sixteen fruit trees shared space with some holly, spruce, and two huge Port Oxford cedars, and the biggest monkey puzzle tree I had ever seen sat at the entrance. Unfortunately, Mr. Rollin in his declining years had been unable to maintain the property, and the garden was now overgrown with weeds and the residence neglected. But there was a peaceful atmosphere about the old place that appealed to me. I could see the love that had gone into the garden, and there was an air of seclusion, even though the site was only two blocks from downtown and on one of the city's main streets, Argyle Street. An artist friend Marianne McClain joined me in the garden and we discussed possibilities for the site. If the Historical Society wasn't interested, then perhaps it could become a centre for the arts.

The Historical Society wasn't interested in the building, but members like Dorrit McLeod had many exciting stories to tell about Fred and Ellen (née Ohlsen) Rollin. The family's history in Port Alberni went back a long way. Fred's father, James, had built the King Edward Hotel in 1910. Fred, who had worked at Alberni Pacific Lumber until retirement, was an outdoorsman, an amateur naturalist, and a keen gardener. There was a large set of horns mounted on one of the trees in the garden, evidence of an earlier hunting trip.

Mrs. Ellen Rollin was a member of a prominent Victoria family. She studied music in Germany and had once been a concert pianist. She gave music lessons to Port Alberni children, including Alan Wright who became a local wildlife artist. Her grand piano, which had been shipped around Cape Horn, took up most of the living room. Dorrit McLeod lived only a short distance from the Rollin residence and knew the family well. Her stories and the beauty of the gardens helped convince me of the need to save this site from the bulldozers.

The CAC gave overwhelming support to proceed with negotiations with the city to save the building for an art centre. In August 1976 a fundraising committee was formed in anticipation of securing the lease. My children formed their own fundraising committee and went door to door in the Maquinna School neighbourhood raising money for the centre. These few dollars were the first donations received for the project.

After many meetings with city council, and joint meetings with School District 70 and the Parks and Recreation Commission, public hearings were held to rezone from residential to recreational use. A five-year lease of one dollar per year was signed in January 1977.

A NEIGHBOURHOOD TRAGEDY

There was one tragedy that affected the entire community at this time and diverted my attention away from the Rollin Art Centre to my children, who attended Maquinna Elementary School.

On April 14, 1977, Carolyn Lee, a student at Maquinna Elementary School and a friend of my daughter, was abducted while walking the four blocks between her afternoon dance class at the Pat Cummings School of Dance and her family's restaurant. The family reported her missing that evening. The following day, her beaten and partially clad body was found by a local farmer on his property near Cox Lake, south of Port Alberni. The community felt shock and horror that such a thing had happened here. The police began an intensive investigation into the murder. The Chinese community, which the Lee family was part of and which had been so friendly, outgoing, and welcoming to everyone suddenly became wary.

All newcomers to the valley were questioned; the police obviously thought it was not a resident who had committed this terrible act. One young man from Quebec whom I had recently hired to work at the Rollin Art Centre renovations was questioned. He was cleared of any wrongdoing and work proceeded, but the tragedy unsettled everyone.

On the day of Carolyn's funeral, her cortège slowly passed her home and Maquinna Elementary School where she had so many friends and classmates; this was a tradition in the Chinese community. The Lee murder was one of the most sensational murder stories in the province at the time, and it remained unsolved for almost two decades.

A few years later when I was working as a reporter at the *Alberni Valley Times*, I got a call at my home one evening. A woman wanted to speak to me about the murder. A little shocked at the call and the subject, I wondered how to approach the caller and silently questioned whether I should believe what she had to say. The woman was calm while she explained how her husband had come home the evening of the murder and told her to clean the back seat of the car because it was all bloodied. He had told her something about having been hunting and killing a rabbit. She proceeded to clean up the mess, unaware that she was actually cleaning away evidence in a murder. It wasn't until some time later that she connected the dots and realized what she had done. During this conversation I had automatically taken notes, but we agreed to meet the next morning for a more in-depth interview at her home. I had a sleepless night thinking about our conversation and its implications.

At work the next morning I told my editor of the conversation and he was as surprised as I at the disclosure. He agreed I should follow through with the interview. About fifteen minutes before I was due to leave the newsroom I got a call from the local police asking me to drop the interview as it would conflict with their investigation. The man was a suspect, but they did not have enough to convict him as yet. I was shocked and conflicted but understood the consequences and agreed to forego the interview. The written notes of my conversation with the woman were filed away in the newsroom for use at some future date.

Some time later the case was assigned to a special division of the Royal Canadian Mounted Police, along with other unsolved murder cases. This was to be the first case cracked by this special division.

On March 13, 1997, twenty years after Carolyn's body was found, the police charged Gurmit Singh Dhillon, a foundry worker and a resident of Port Alberni, with first-degree murder. After a month-long trial the jury convicted him, and the judge sentenced him to life imprisonment with no chance of parole for twenty-five years in the abduction, rape, and murder. It was his former wife who had telephoned me; she later testified against him at the trial. He had been an early suspect but gave an alibi for the time of the murder. The police never gave up, and it was new advanced DNA testing that led to his conviction.

The murder of Carolyn Lee in 1977 affected everyone in the neighbourhood. Margaret Kelly, who lived in the Maquinna School area, felt deeply about the young girl's death, and when children were afraid to go back and forth to school, she decided to do something about it. In an interview she said:

> I had heard about a Block Mothers program in Marysville, near Everett, Washington, where we had

lived for a year, so I wrote to the school district for some information about it. Then the Canadian Safety Council Block Parents program came to my attention.[2]

Within two months Kelly had the program installed in the Maquinna School area, but it was about a year later before the Alberni Valley was fully covered with five hundred Block Parents. There was some opposition to the program, but the RCMP encouraged her and was very supportive.

With the success of organizing the program behind her, Kelly ran for school board and was elected for a two-year term. She resigned in September 1982 when her husband, David, accepted a position at Kitimat pulp mill.

ROLLIN ART CENTRE

While the lease for the Rollin Art Centre was being negotiated, I applied on behalf of the CAC for a federal LIP grant to upgrade the building. The grant was for six labourers and a part-time bookkeeper. Before the application could be submitted there had to be a guarantee that the CAC would get the lease of the building. When the city granted the lease, our application was accepted and we received $24,000 for a period of six months.

The lease was signed on January 17 and work began on the Rollin residence on February 1, 1977. Port Alberni architect Ian Niamath kindly redesigned the building and provided building plans that kept the charm of the old house while at the same time making it workable as a public art building.

Unfortunately LIP grants had their good and bad points, the bad sometimes outweighing the good. The six labourers were all young unemployed males under the age of twenty-one, with no experience in construction or anything else. The CAC member who was to oversee the project suddenly left the pulp mill and went to seek employment elsewhere.

Nonetheless, in the spring of 1977 work proceeded in upgrading the Rollin building. It needed to be completely rewired, the furnace removed and heating systems installed, and gyproc applied on all walls. As it was now to be a public building, doors had to be re-hung to swing outwards, public toilets and a new plumbing system plus sprinkler system had to be installed. Many people told me the CAC was crazy to attempt such a renovation—that the building should be condemned; we would be further ahead building a new one. However strong their arguments, they hadn't considered the determination of a vibrant arts community. There were only a few leaders, but everyone threw themselves behind the project and the fundraising effort. My stalwart volunteers included Roy Innes, Laura Evans, Margita Hartmann, Marianne McClain, Meg and Gordon Scoffield, and many others too numerous to mention. I kept track of all volunteer hours—essential statistics to have when applying for grants, as this showed good community support.

CAC treasurer Roy Innes and I supervised the renovations, instructed the students, and dealt with the building inspector, the fire marshal, Manpower and Immigration, etc. I was optimistic the project would be finished in the summer of 1977 so went ahead and applied for a Young Canada Works grant to hire students for summer employment at the Rollin Art Centre. Classes were organized in theatre, dance, and art for young and old during the summer months. To my absolute amazement, this application was also successful. A grant of $16,000 was received to hire nine students: three in theatre, one in dance, two in art, a gardener, a bookkeeper, and a project manager. However, before the students could begin work, an occupancy permit was necessary, and with the building still unfinished there was little hope of getting that. Fortunately the city had an understanding building inspector who was very generous in his recommendations to city council. The occupancy permit arrived a week before the grant started. There was much to be learned about renovating an old building.

A Canada Council Explorations grant of $7,600 paid for a token year's salary as administrator, but what it really paid for was office equipment, a desk, a filing cabinet, a chair, and a duplicating machine. I felt it important that there was a presence in the Art Centre during business hours. The CAC newsletter *Tawasi* was published from the centre; Laura Evans took over as editor for two years, freeing my time to focus on the centre. I now worked full-time, Monday to Friday.

The summer works students were marvelous. They were all dedicated and enthusiastic young people, and happy about being in at the beginning of the Rollin Art Centre. Cindy Zajes, a high school graduate, was a very capable project manager. Her interests lay in theatre, and at the time she was trying to establish Backstage, a young theatre group. Lois Watkin-Jones led the dance class. Karen Poirier led an art class for young students. By the end of summer we hoped that everyone in town knew or had heard about the Rollin Art Centre. The students had done a wonderful job of promotion. They went into the shopping areas, put on impromptu performances, and generally let everyone know that the town now had an art centre. This made my job as director that much easier.

When September 1977 came, our student teachers returned to school. I was alone in the centre without heat and working in an unfinished building. I had undertaken this project and wanted to make it work; I was determined not to be discouraged. Last year's willing volunteers now became very reluctant volunteers. They were tired, very tired, and made no bones about the fact they didn't think it was going to work. This was a very difficult period, and somehow I had to find a way to make it happen. We needed publicity!

I began writing a column in the *Alberni Valley Times* called the Rollin Art Centre Report. This kept the public informed about what the CAC was trying to do, and included news items about affiliated groups. I wrote that the centre needed heaters—these arrived and were installed by a generous benefactor. With the upstairs now heated, programming began for the season offering courses in theatre, dance, and silkscreening. Working with little or no budget, local artists were persuaded to offer instruction on a 60–40 split of registrations; the centre got the 40. This worked well—too well, so that now CAC groups wishing to use the centre couldn't because of the classes. We had to chart a new direction. The CAC had to decide where its priorities lay.

When a local church was disposing of some pews, a member quickly secured a few for the gallery. The unfinished floors in the centre were covered with pulp mill felt. The centre was still badly in need of a new roof; the loggers of MB's Sarita Division generously donated cedar blocks, then arrived to split the shakes on site, and then installed the new roof.

An application to the Leon & Thea Koerner Foundation for an arts library grant was successful, enabling the purchase of new art-related books valued at $500. Word spread about the library, and donations of art books poured in. The pottery group and the creative writers turned over their libraries. The centre now had a growing arts library. An application to Canada Council for the Book Donation Program was also successful; two hundred new books arrived under this program, and all were available to the general public. Volunteer librarian May Weeden came in once a week to keep everything in order.

In January 1978, I wrote a fictional piece for the *Alberni Valley Times* newspaper's weekend edition, *Spectrum*, entitled "Arts on Strike." The story was about a community that didn't care what happened to the arts. The artists eventually all go on strike, and so on. Strikes were something Port Alberni residents could relate to. The newspaper gave the story top billing and had its cartoonist do a full-page illustration to go with it.

Also about this time the Adopt a Tree project was initiated as another way of raising money. With a donation to the centre, a group or individual could have a plaque with their name placed at the base of one of the Rollin Art Centre trees. With sixty-six trees on the property, I thought the project would be a winner. Letters were sent to every service organization in town asking for a donation. The first year the Adopt a Tree project realized $2,000, and the project was repeated over two or three years. City council was a little skeptical when I cheekily appeared before them asking for a donation to one of their own trees; they chose the monkey puzzle tree!

As a result of the "Arts on Strike" article and the Adopt a Tree project, an invitation arrived to speak to the local Rotary Club luncheon. Did my speech influence their decision? I don't know, but the club announced the Rollin Art Centre would be its project for the year 1978. The club paid to have a beautiful carved wooden door installed for the entrance and a stairway built to the upstairs gallery at a cost of $7,000. With this support the building neared completion.

Another Canada Works grant for another year enabled the painting to be finished and new programs to begin. With $28,000, we hired three men: a project manager, a gardener, and a labourer.

One of the most unusual and memorable CAC fundraising events was the Bizarre Bazaar. It was held in the Rollin Art Centre, which was not quite ready to accommodate the large number of people who turned out for the event and to have their teacup read. With no sink or plumbing in the kitchen, the bathtub was put to good use. Backbreaking work for the volunteers! The venue for this successful event changed the next year. The CAC also sponsored a few gourmet dinners that were a lot of fun but more hard work by volunteers.

In 1978 the Captain Cook Bicentennial Celebrations, called Summer of Discovery, sponsored by the Alberni–Clayoquot Regional District Community Events Committee, of which I was a member, made the Rollin Art Centre a lively place with convention kits, banners, poster competitions, and more. About half of my time was devoted to making this celebration a success using the centre as a base. Port Alberni's Captain

Cook was John Andrews, a former teacher turned real estate salesman and musical theatre director. With his English accent, navy background, and theatrical experience, he made a perfect ambassador for Port Alberni—complete with a Captain Cook costume.

In March he arrived unannounced at a luncheon in the Empress Hotel in Victoria being hosted by Travel Industry minister Grace McCarthy. She was caught a little off guard when Andrews strode through the media scrum, introducing himself in a booming voice as "Captain James Cook from Port Alberni," then bent over and kissed the minister's hand. While the CBC cameras rolled, Andrews ad-libbed his way through a few minutes of small talk with the minister before being led off to meet the provincial government's own Captain Cook.

In May 1978, the centre faced another summer without any paid personnel. Tom Fielding, director of the BC Arts Division of the provincial government assured of some help in the fall if we could get local support for the summer. Peter Dutton, a friend in the hotel business and also an associate on the Captain Cook Committee, had once told me to call him if I ever needed help. This was no time for pride, so I called and related the problem. He thought he could get some financial assistance for the summer. At the next meeting of the Captain Cook Committee of the Regional District he presented facts and figures showing how the Rollin Art Centre had supported the committee. He requested the centre be given a grant of $2,000 for summer employment, and the committee agreed.

The Summer School of the Arts, held at the centre in August, featured J. Ward-Harris and William Featherston, both well-known British Columbia visual artists. Ward-Harris was the first artist-in-residence. Featherston said when he arrived in town he had asked the way to the Rollin Art Centre, only to be met with a blank stare. "What art centre?" he was asked. It was obvious we still had work to do to establish the Rollin Art Centre in the mind of the community. A garden market was held weekly during July and August, and a maritime exhibition was scheduled for Vancouver Island artists.

The mounting of the first art exhibition in the Rollin Art Centre in November was a milestone for the CAC. Local wildlife artist Allan Wright exhibited his work. Wright was noted for his fine bird paintings. He was especially pleased to exhibit there, as he had been a piano student of Ellen Rollin. Until this time local artists had shown their work in the lounge at Echo Centre; now there was a dedicated gallery with a calendar of regular exhibits.

The gallery was booked solid for the next year. Local craftspeople sold their work from a small craft outlet in the centre, and the building was used almost every evening of the week by CAC-affiliated groups. The Rollin Art Centre was like a seedling newly planted in Port Alberni; all it needed was nurturing.

In 1979, I was appointed to the British Columbia Arts Board for a three-year term, replacing outgoing member Jim Swan from Nanaimo. Meg Scoffield, who had replaced Laura Evans as editor of *Tawasi*, now took over administrative duties at the Rollin Art Centre, and did a wonderful job of bringing fresh ideas and new blood into the organization. Margita Hartman became CAC president. Both women moved the centre forward in a new direction with the board's assistance and with the help of a generous donation from Helen and Armour Ford. This enabled the transformation of the gardens and the building of the bandstand, a replica of the city's earliest bandstand. The Fords were made Patrons of the Rollin Art Centre in 1979.

Several decades later, the Rollin Art Centre is still operating. As well as serving the needs of artists in the community, it is a popular venue for outdoor weddings and known for its "Tea in the Garden" served during the summer months. The garden features a concrete balustrade and classical fountain designed by artist and craftsman Peter Szachiv. There is also a Japanese garden, a gift from Abashiri, Port Alberni's twin city in Japan. Rocks were shipped from Japan and a gardener came from Abashiri to oversee the entire creation.

The beautiful gardens, still tended by volunteers, transformed the Rollin Art Centre and made it inviting for residents and visitors alike. Fred Rollin would have been happy to see his property used in this way for the enjoyment of the community.

A VISIT FROM PRIME MINISTER TRUDEAU

While we negotiated the Rollin Art Centre lease, the CAC sponsored the first Youth Festival of the Arts, a month-long celebration held April 25 to June 5, 1977. This was an effort to focus public attention on children in the arts. Such a festival had never been done before, and to my knowledge this was the only one of its kind in the province. Schools and community organizations were approached for funding and support.

The list compiled of all activities in the community involving children in the arts was impressive. It included dance lessons, music instruction, speech arts, Parks and Recreation programs, and school programs related to the arts; Port Alberni was indeed fortunate in this regard. School District 70 board of trustees and school principals gave their support, as long as it wouldn't interfere with schoolwork. Schools and community organizations involving children in the arts were invited to contribute their arts event to the festival. There were quite a few events relating to the performing arts but few for the visual arts, so a poster contest and a visual art exhibition for all of School District 70 was held, and the Art Gallery of Greater Victoria was invited to bring an exhibition to tour the schools during the festival. Nick Tuele, extension officer with the gallery, set up the shows from the gallery's collection and did an excellent job of presenting these to the young people.

Member CAC groups got involved. The Alberni Valley Creative Writers sponsored a writing contest with prizes; the Pottery Association sponsored a pottery contest; the Alberni

District Historical Society volunteered a history essay contest entitled "My Heritage." The Alberni Valley Art Group held a children's paint-in; the Port Alberni Highland Dance Association held a Scottish Ceilidh, an evening of music and dance; and the Gymnastic Academy gave its first public performance in Mt. Klitsa School gymnasium. Music teachers sponsored a school choral workshop that culminated with a mass choir concert at ADSS, one of the most thrilling events of the festival with hundreds of children singing before a packed house.

There were some schools without a music program and little or no art program. Principals apologized for this shortcoming. The first Youth Festival of the Arts had only one musical theatre event—Wood Elementary School choir, directed by Doreen Langmead, presented *Oliver!* But four years later there were eight musical theatre events! The school board hired two new music teachers, splitting their time between four schools that previously had no music program. As a result, there were now two additional school choirs and two more school bands. These were remarkable improvements, and the influence of these two teachers had a tremendous impact on the size of the festival the next year.

Radio station CJAV and the *Alberni Valley Times* gave free publicity to the events, with speech arts pupils reading the advertising on the radio; a worthwhile experience for all concerned. The festival had cost about $300 in printing costs for the program but countless volunteer hours overall. To see the schools get behind the festival, and see the community turn out for the events, made all the hard work worthwhile.

The highlight of this first Youth Festival of the Arts was the appearance of the prime minister of Canada, Pierre Elliott Trudeau, when he participated in the closing ceremonies. Canadians had a love-hate relationship with Trudeau; he was either their crown prince or detached professor. He was known for his wisecracks and sharp, memorable lines, delivered in a vigorous style. His marriage to Margaret Sinclair and the birth of their three children were kept in the background. He considered his family life separate from his public role, and it was generally known that Margaret did not like being in the public eye and would much rather her husband retire to family life.

The closing ceremonies event of the Youth Festival held in Glenwood Centre on June 5, 1977, included a massed choir of 350 children, the children's drama group, and the Ucluelet ukulele band. The children of School District 70 saw their prime minister up close for the first time as he presented prizes for contests in art and writing. An audience of four thousand people attended the event.

Trudeau's visit to the west coast was a stroke of luck for the Youth Festival. The first mention that he would be visiting British Columbia in May and June had come in a CJAV radio interview with Comox–Alberni MP Hugh Anderson. There was no indication he was coming to Vancouver Island, but Powell River on the nearby Sunshine Coast was one of his destinations. Margaret and their three children—Justin, Michel, and Sacha—would accompany him. As I listened to the broadcast I heard our MP remark, "If anyone has an event to which the prime minister could attend at this time, please contact me and I will pass it on." The dates mentioned coincided with the closing ceremonies of the Youth Festival of the Arts. How wonderful it would be, I thought, to have the prime minister and his family at this event! I immediately called Hugh Anderson's office and told him about the Youth Festival of the Arts and said the CAC would be honoured if Trudeau attended and presented prizes to the children. Anderson was delighted and thought the event was a perfect fit. He promised to pass it on.

When the first call came to my home from the Prime Minister's Office in Ottawa, I was shocked and surprised. But his secretary immediately put me at ease. She wanted details of the festival. The closing ceremonies had been booked for ADSS auditorium, a venue that could seat only one thousand people.

It wasn't clear to me at this stage that Trudeau would come. Days later another call came, this time from Hugh Anderson advising me that the prime minister would be pleased to attend the closing ceremonies. My heart skipped a beat at the good news.

I had gone ahead and made this arrangement without first getting approval from the CAC executive. Never in my wildest dreams did I think there would be any opposition to having the prime minister come to Port Alberni to attend a CAC event. The town had never had a visit from a sitting PM; this would be the first. Politics hadn't entered into the debate—yet! I called a meeting of the executive to give them my exciting news. Their reaction confused and surprised me. While some favoured the visit, a good number were against. I argued, how could you not want the prime minister to participate in your event? Very reluctantly they gave approval to proceed with the arrangements.

There were several more calls from Trudeau's secretary, and one from Trudeau himself. His telephone call to my home came unexpectedly; one of my children answered the phone. I was working downstairs when I heard this yell: "Mum, the prime minister is on the phone!" The conversation with Trudeau has remained with me. He asked several questions—why did Port Alberni want a visit from him, what was the political climate, what were the economic conditions? He also wanted to know about the city. I told him that Port Alberni had never had a visit from a sitting prime minister, and that we on the west coast felt quite remote from Ottawa. We talked about the Youth Festival of the Arts and how it was an effort to promote the arts in schools. Trudeau was an easy man to talk to, and we had an enjoyable talk.

I had given little thought to the ramifications of ensuring the prime minister's safety while visiting the city. City council was informed, and when an advanced team from Trudeau's office came to town to outline the route and the location, among other things, I was invited to a joint meeting of council and Trudeau's advance people. By this time I had changed the venue of the closing ceremonies from the ADSS auditorium to Glenwood Centre, a much larger facility. Mayor Howard McLean chaired the meeting held in Echo Centre. I planned to leave it up to city council and the mayor to make the arrangements with the PM's team—until I heard them say that Prime Minister Trudeau would make a speech to the audience then leave before the children's concert started. Immediately I was on my feet protesting. There was no way, I told them, that the PM would speak then leave, not with hundreds of children waiting anxiously to perform and get their prizes. I argued that no one could possibly expect them to sit still long enough to listen to a long political speech.

From the end of the table, I could feel Mayor McLean's eyes on me. I was sure he was thinking, "How could she embarrass us like this." The advance team did not intimidate me, though! This was a Youth Festival of the Arts event and the CAC would have a say in the order of proceedings. They reluctantly agreed.

The day of the event, June 5, was a glorious sunny afternoon. Trudeau and his entourage flew in by helicopter from Powell River directly to Glenwood Centre. Margaret and the children didn't come—Margaret was not feeling well, I was told. There was disappointment all around that his family would not be coming; everyone had especially looked forward to seeing the children. Glenwood Centre was packed with an estimated four thousand people. Some were lined up at the back of the hall and outside. The children's choir—four hundred children assembled from school choirs within School District 70—sat anxiously on bleachers waiting to perform. The stage was set with chairs for the dignitaries.

Foolishly I had assumed that Hugh Anderson would be the Master of Ceremonies, and introduce Prime Minister Trudeau. Not so! Anderson told me I should do it because I knew all about the festival. When I explained I had never spoken into a microphone before in my life, I was quickly given some instruction, all of which was an absolute blur to me as I was so nervous. But it was too late to find someone more suitable and experienced in public speaking. As I anxiously waited at the stage entrance, suddenly there was a small commotion at the door and in walked Trudeau. My first thought was, "He is so much shorter than I thought"—having only seen him on television. I quickly introduced myself, and we talked like old friends. He was pleased when he looked around, commenting on the large crowd inside and outside Glenwood Centre and what a beautiful day it was.

And so the closing ceremonies began with members of the press milling around the front of the stage snapping photos at will. I took the microphone and apologized for my inexperience, then got on with the job of introducing our young performers. The choir was wonderful, and the look on the children's faces when they received their prizes from the PM was very rewarding. Trudeau's speech was politely received; then it was all over, and people began to leave. As I turned to thank him for being with us, he grabbed my head and pulled me toward him, planting a big kiss on my cheek. Then he was gone, back in the helicopter and flying off to meet his family. The polished politician, and hundreds of charming children, overshadowed my small participation in the event.

At the 1978 Youth Festival of the Arts, MP Hugh Anderson sponsored a writing contest for junior and senior secondary schools and awarded the prizes on behalf of the prime minister. The festival lasted three years.

CAC-SPONSORED EVENTS

Another event initiated by the CAC during my term as president was Folkfest. The Victoria newspaper gave lots of coverage to the event held there, and I thought this was something our community might endorse with so many multicultural organizations in town. However, before being considered for the event, the Victoria Folkfest Society had to be convinced that our CAC could handle it. Since we had just sponsored the successful Youth Festival of the Arts, I assured them this was an event that would be welcomed and supported by the community. The Folkfest organization accepted our application, and as co-sponsor would supply us with posters and promotional material. It would also permit the use the Folkfest symbol, the dancing woman.

All the affiliated groups agreed this was something they would enjoy, and the CAC agreed to be the sponsor. Louise Robasco, from the large Italian community, was a staunch supporter and worked tirelessly on the event for many years. We chose Glenwood Centre as a venue for the event. It was large enough to accommodate ethnic booths and had a stage for performances.

After planning the event throughout the year as chairman, I discovered I could not be present on that day as my family was gathering in Kingston, Ontario, to celebrate my parents' fiftieth wedding anniversary. Lillian Weedmark graciously agreed to stand in for me. The first Folkfest celebration held in Port Alberni was on July 1, 1977.

Following the parade and the singing of "O Canada," a giant cake was cut and the celebrations began. Dance and music groups performed and there were samples of food from around the world served from group-sponsored booths around the hall. It was a huge success and gave Port Alberni another way to celebrate Canada Day. Folkfest continues with an independent committee, Port Alberni Folkfest Multicultural Society, that was formed under Winston Joseph, who, along with the "Mayor of Folkfest" Bob Forbes, has kept the event alive.

There were many other memorable events sponsored by the CAC, including the Heritage Festival held in Echo Centre that resulted in the beautiful Heritage Quilt now proudly displayed in the Rollin Art Centre. I also worked with the Outreach

Committee of the Emily Carr College of Art in Vancouver, bringing exhibits to Port Alberni, and in 1978 I joined the Community Events Committee of the Alberni–Clayoquot Regional District which was trying to promote tourism in the region. I designed placemats and banners and a calendar of events for the entire region, and organized the 5k Paper Chase.

Somehow I still found time to paint. I had three successful solo exhibitions at Echo Centre, but my greatest pleasure was having an exhibition of my work displayed in the Rollin Art Centre.

In 1979 the CAC presented me with a honorary life membership. That same year I joined the British Columbia Arts Board representing Vancouver Island. Membership on this prestigious board, which oversaw all the arts funding in the province, was a challenge for it meant time away from family. While there were only four or five meetings a year, these usually lasted several days. However, I considered my presence there would be good for our CAC, for Port Alberni, and for Vancouver Island. Dr. Peter Smith, dean of fine arts at the University of Victoria, was chairman of the board. Members included Professor Norman Young, of the Frederic Wood Theatre at UBC; Maxine Dewdney, from the Trail and District CAC; Mary Chen, a recreation commissioner from Prince George; John Springer, Vancouver Board of Trade; Daryl Duhamel, an artist from Kelowna; Susan LePage, Vancouver CAC; and Douglas Talney, UBC music department. Others were Barry Moore, Dawson Creek; Ronald Longstafe, Vancouver; Dr. Eric Gunn, Kitimat; Murray Mackie, Chilliwack; Gordon Smith, West Vancouver; and Michael Wiggins, Port Hardy. We were a diverse group with knowledge and skill in all aspects of the arts. It was an honour to be appointed and to work with such distinguished board members.

The three years on the board were rewarding and gave me an opportunity to visit different communities in the province and learn about their art programs, which were always in need of funding. During that time I was appointed to a three-member committee that studied visual arts in the province. I was also named regional chairman of the Arts Board, bringing a voice to regional concerns. As a member of that board I happily used my influence to speak or write on behalf of art students from Vancouver Island who wished to further their studies at the Banff School of Fine Arts, Emily Carr School of Arts, or other art institutions across the country.

{ *chapter seven* }

SUGAR IN THE FRIDGE; MICE ON THE TABLE

In March 1981 my life took a different turn when I began working for the *Alberni Valley Times* as a junior reporter. I had submitted weekly news copy related to the arts in the community and province for several years before publisher Ron Nelson asked if I would like to work full-time for the newspaper. With my knowledge of the community he thought I would be a good addition to the newsroom. I loved writing, and it seemed like a good opportunity and a chance to write about subjects holding my interest.

The newspaper office was on Fourth Avenue, in the floodplain area of town, across from beautiful Dry Creek Park. The building was small but efficient, with the newsroom, advertising, and administration in front, the print shop at the back, and the composing room and darkroom located between the two. In 1981, the staff included the editor, a full-time photographer, a sports writer, and three reporters. I was the only woman in the newsroom. I was inspired, though, by other women who had worked for the newspaper at various times, including former editor Meg Trebett and news reporter Ruth Roberts, both of whom I knew and admired.

I loved working at the newspaper. I loved the smell of newsprint just off the press, and the anticipation of the first quick look at the front page, checking for mistakes, and the satisfaction of knowing it was a job well done. Soon the newspaper would be on doorsteps around the city, and delivered throughout the valley and across island. Every day was a new high for me!

The *Alberni Valley Times* was owned by Conrad Black as part of Sterling Newspapers Ltd., British Columbia's largest community newspaper chain. Sterling was unique in that it published a handful of dailies, and at that time 80 percent of its three hundred BC employees were unionized. Our paper was unionized under the Graphic Communications International Union, with Denis Houle the shop steward. Everyone in the newsroom and print shop was union, except for the editor, Rob Diotte.

When Sterling moved into the province in 1971 it gained a reputation for penny pinching and for instituting what became known as the "three-man newsroom, and two of them sell ads." Arthur Weeks was Sterling's general manager. Occasionally there were visits from Conrad Black's right-hand man, David Radler. The only time we heard from Black himself was when someone had won an award or was retiring; they might get a signed letter of commendation for their work with the newspaper.

In my first year with the paper Radler congratulated me on being a runner-up in the Jack Wasserman Memorial Award, an award given annually to a reporter with no more than three years' experience. Our editor had submitted three feature series that I'd written. The series on air pollution in the Alberni Valley was later picked up and followed up on by the CBC. Another series was on DES (the hormone diethylstilbestrol), an artificial hormone prescribed to pregnant women between 1941 and 1971 to prevent miscarriage. Medical research showed that many daughters born to women who had been prescribed the drug later developed cancer of the vagina or cervix. The third series was about the Port Alberni and District Association for the Mentally Handicapped.

The awards were given on May 19, 1982, at the Vancouver Press Club. I was excited to be there with the other reporters receiving an award. The winner was Ray Masleck of the *Trail Daily Times*, for a series on shady real estate transactions in his community. Second place was Jerry Collins of the Vancouver *Province* for stories on the lack of juvenile detention facilities in BC. The two men were introduced along with their academic credentials at college and university. When it came to me (I was getting an honorary mention), I was introduced as "the middle-aged housewife from Port Alberni." I was surprised to get the recognition, and have laughed about my credentials ever since.

One particular visit from Radler and Weeks was very strange indeed. Everyone was asked to attend a lunch hour meeting to hear Radler talk about the future of the newspaper. All were assembled in the backroom listening intently to him speak, thinking there must be some major announcement coming. He rambled on and on for about half an hour about economics and the situation in the newspaper business. After ten minutes the faces around the room had that glazed-over look. There was no announcement, and we were all left wondering what it had all been about.

More recently everyone in the news business watched in shock when Black and Radler's sale of Hollinger International in 2003 landed both in a Chicago courtroom. Radler, charged with mail and wire fraud, pleaded guilty to one count of mail fraud. He cut a deal to pay back millions of pounds of what the Securities and Exchange Commission called "ill-gotten gains," in return for serving his sentence in Canada. He served only ten months of a twenty-nine-month sentence. Meanwhile, his partner Black went to prison in the US for supposedly looting his own company, charges he fought hard against. He served his sentence and has since been released from prison and is now back in Canada. The two men had been in business together for over forty years. Radler was once president of Ravelston Corporation, a privately owned corporation owned by Black and Radler to control their former newspaper empire. Ravelston owned Argus Corporation, which in turn controlled Chicago-based Hollinger International.[1]

NEWS STORIES THAT MADE HEADLINES

A small room adjacent to the newsroom housed a gigantic computer that carried Canadian Press news on provincial and national stories, a service for which the newspaper paid a fee. The machine had to be turned off on Fridays and turned on again every Sunday night to get copy for the Monday paper. The teletype machine in the newsroom gave a constant printout of news items coming from Toronto; most we didn't use, but to other news stories we added local content. When a particularly important story came across the wire, a bell rang alerting the newsroom of a major story coming in.

On March 30, 1981, I had only been working for the paper a few weeks when bells began ringing. The editor rushed to the wire service and read that US president Ronald Reagan had been shot after a speaking engagement outside a Washington, DC, hotel. He and three others were shot and wounded by John Hinckley Jr. Fortunately Reagan quickly recovered. Hinckley was found not guilty by reason of insanity. Bells rang again on May 13, 1981, when there was an assassination attempt on the life of Pope John Paul II in St. Peter's Square in Vatican City.

One big story we almost missed, or at least didn't pay much attention to in the beginning, was Rick Hansen's "Man in Motion" world tour. Everyone still remembered the Terry Fox Marathon of Hope that had ended so tragically just the year before in Thunder Bay, when cancer spread to the young man's lungs. Now here was another young man with a disability trying to do what seemed impossible.

Hansen was born in Port Alberni on August 26, 1957. He grew up in Williams Lake, but some of his family still lived in the area. In a car accident at age fifteen, he sustained a spinal cord injury that paralyzed him from the waist down. Undaunted, he continued his education and became the first student with a physical disability to graduate from UBC.

One morning in March 1985, his uncle came into the newsroom to tell us how his nephew was planning to tour the world in a wheelchair. While his uncle was very positive about the outcome, we were a little skeptical. We duly took note but did little in the beginning to promote the epic journey. It wasn't until Hansen was into his second year of the trek around the world that everyone began to sit up and take notice as his story caught on internationally. Hansen completed his incredible journey on May 22, 1987, after logging more than 40,000 kilometres (25,000 miles) through thirty-four countries on four continents in twenty-six months. As he wheeled into Oakridge Mall in Vancouver on that day before cheering crowds, he had raised over $26 million for spinal cord injury research.

The newspaper ran several stories that involved children of the Alberni Valley. When four-year-old Chad Dwolinsky couldn't get all the money he needed from the provincial medical service for heart surgery at the Mayo Clinic, valley residents opened their wallets and within days had donated $24,000 to the young boy and the Alberni Valley Open Heart Society. His plight had touched a raw nerve with the city then suffering through a deep recession. A year later, Chad had fully recovered from the delicate heart surgery and was well enough to lead the first Open Heart Society's walkathon in Port Alberni.

Young Travis Baker was inspired by Steve Fonyo's attempt to run across Canada to complete what Terry Fox had been unable to accomplish. Fonyo, a young man with a disability, started his Journey for Lives marathon on March 31, 1984, and completed his run on May 29, 1985; he had raised over $14 million. Travis was an ardent supporter of the marathoner and did his own run to raise money in Port Alberni for the Cancer Society. As a result he was given the opportunity to travel to Vancouver to welcome Fonyo's return home at BC Place Stadium. Along with his mother Elverna, they travelled with acting mayor Don Whyte in his magnificent Lincoln Continental. I accompanied them to cover the event for the newspaper.

When Fonyo arrived in the stadium the crowd cheered. Travis got down to the ringside seats and was able to see his hero take a run around the stadium. It was a day he would not soon forget, and a memorable day for those accompanying him.

THE DAILY GRIND

I learned to write on a computer on my first day at the newspaper; until then I had typed all copy on a typewriter. Next I learned to forward my copy to the editor's computer for editing. My first assignment had been a regular school board meeting. The report was written four times before I learned how to send it electronically to the editor. I kept punching the wrong key! The story got more concise with each rewrite, but after the third attempt to "send" failed, I screamed.

Jean Illman, the receptionist in the front office, heard my cries of frustration—and laughed. She assured me things would get better. The front office staff was very supportive. They included circulation manager Art Toms; later John Richardson stepped into this position when Art retired. Olga Kanigan was the office manager and secretary to the publisher.

I always marvelled at the skill of the editor, Rob Diotte, who could take my raw copy and turn it into something worthy of a front page. Rob then lived in Nanaimo and travelled back and forth each day, until the day his car left the road and plunged into Cameron Lake. Shortly after, he and wife Lille moved to Port Alberni. Rob was a good teacher and I learned a lot from him. If I didn't know how to begin to write a column, he would prompt, "Tell me what happened last night." After I had briefly explained the highlights, it was clear what the story would be.

The editor sorted through a mountain of mail each morning, with most ending up in the garbage. Rob's experience and intuition enabled him to decide what went into the paper. There were lots of press releases from government; public relations people; religious, business, health and education officials; and a few oddballs. He also had to listen to what the publisher wanted. It was not always an easy task!

Rob also wrote the headlines, one of which gained international attention and was even mentioned in the British magazine *Punch* after publisher Nigel Hannaford sent it in. The headline read: "The cause of the flooding was too much rain." It was one of those gems that somehow slipped past the editing process.

Sports editor Carl Vesterback was an all-round good guy, a likeable, tall and gangly man with long blond hair, who loved playing basketball. As sports editor he reported on a wide variety of sports—all except golf, because, as he explained, "It isn't a sport!" He refused to cover the game even when there was a major tournament event in town. This left the onus on our golfing enthusiast, advertising staff member Knox Coupland, to submit copy.

Photographer Roy Snikkers was the son of visual artist Rie Snikkers and photographer Anton Snikkers, both well-known personalities in town. Roy did some amazing work with the camera, and very patiently taught me the rudiments of photography and the intricacies of the darkroom. I loved this aspect of covering the news. During a slow news day, the editor would ask Roy to go shoot some "aw" shots. Obviously these were photos that when the subscriber opened the newspaper, they would exclaim "a-a-a-w." Usually the photos were of cute little children, or animals, or picturesque moments in the city. In the summer months, Roy always managed to find some lovely young woman clad in a bikini on the beach at Paper Mill Dam or Sproat Lake Park, and that photo filled the front-page hole for another day. Roy eventually left the newspaper, leaving it up to the reporters to supply the front-page photo. I was always on the lookout for a good photo. Our family dog, a little West Highland terrier named MacTavish, sometimes filled the void.

There were many people who worked for the *AV Times* who never saw their name in print but who worked diligently to put out one of the best community newspapers on Vancouver Island. The advertising department staff included Bill Arnst, Knox Coupland, Carol Boxrud, Mame Schroeder, and Stan Osiel. The typesetters were Joyce Unger, Marg Croteau, and Mildred Nelson. The composing room staff included Ron Attenbury, Patrick Jones, Des Howarth, and Doug Petsul. The backroom boys who actually printed the newspaper were Sandy Stewart, Denis Houle, and Mike Lyle.

When I first started work, there was no kitchen as such for coffee breaks or lunches, only a refrigerator and a table with a coffee pot and sugar nearby. One day I went for a morning coffee and found a message Scotch-taped to the wall: "Sugar in the fridge: mice on the table." I loved this little gem but it also got me thinking about the topsy-turvy world we live in. Not everything or every place is what we expect, and sometimes it is the opposite. Of course, being close to Dry Creek we did get visits from a few furry friends. Later, when renovations were made to the building and the interior reconfigured, staff got a much-needed lunchroom.

When publisher Ron Nelson died suddenly on a trip to Vancouver, everyone was shocked. Loveable Ron always spoke up for his newspaper and staff, and represented us in many community organizations. Nine months later, Nigel Hannaford took over as publisher; he had previously been with the St. Fort John newspaper. With his soft English accent, Nigel introduced himself to each staff member, getting to know them personally. He had a love for everything military.

A lot of reporters passed through the newsroom while I was there, including Gavin Wilson, Jim Leahy, Marcus Davies, Shelly Browne, and Angela Wirtz. There were also many college and summer students who worked during the summer months. One young man only worked a few days; we discovered he was high on drugs during most of that time. But most of the young people were eager to learn and find work in the newspaper industry. The *Times* also gave school class tours of the facility, and there were the usual cheque presentations to record and photograph, perhaps mundane but so important in a small community.

Community columnists were a vital part of the newspaper. Rodney Wade, a Maquinna Elementary schoolteacher, was one of the *Alberni Valley Times'* most successful columnists. He wrote about local politics, issues of the day, or anything that caught his interest. Rodney's reputation was solid. He was regarded as an authority on the 1964 tsunami, for he had done what no one had thought of doing—he interviewed and recorded the experiences of residents who had suffered through that dreadful night. On each anniversary, when the outside media came calling for a story about the event, they were usually diverted to Rodney. Over the years he picked up an award or two from his long-standing knowledge of the city. He wrote:

> *A good reporter does not start with an opinion or point of view about a problem or issue. Yes, he may have unconscious bias—but that is true of everyone. It is a self-cancelling common denominator. A good reporter asks questions and then, when a large body of information has been assembled, seeks an angle or point of view from which to write honestly.*[2]

There were other columnists of note. Keitha Adams, whose father, the Rev. Frank Edwin Pitts, had been the school principal at the Alberni Residential School, wrote a weekly inspirational column. Keitha had strong ties to the community. After the Second World War, she organized language classes for newcomers in town to help them adjust to their new life in Canada. She was also the first president of the Alberni District Museum and Historical Society. And schoolteacher Winston Joseph's columns were always upbeat; he wrote about many subjects, always with a positive theme. There could not have been a more optimistic person in town.

One of Nigel Hannaford's most innovative ideas as a publisher was a letters-to-the-editor dinner. The newsroom staff shook their heads in disbelief when he made the proposal. The thought of all those readers who had an axe to grind about the newsroom, or some other subject, being in the same room together gave us cause for concern. When he further suggested that the newsroom staff should do the serving, we all groaned.

Despite our obvious opposition to such an idea, Nigel went ahead and invited all letter-writers to join him and newsroom staff at a dinner in the Timberlodge Motel. We were indeed skeptical about these dinners, but we all grew to enjoy the happy exchange of ideas and personalities. Guest speakers were brought in to entertain and educate. Prizes were awarded for the best letter, most thought-provoking letter, and so on.

One guest speaker who got a lot of attention and whom everyone enjoyed hearing was Dr. Tomorrow, Frank Ogden, from Vancouver. He challenged our thoughts about the future, about the world, education, science, and technology. He said, "You can't predict the future but you can prepare for it." Ogden lived on a houseboat in the Vancouver harbour, furnished with all his high-tech toys such as computers, faxes, modems, televisions, video machines, and other gizmos. He found a way to turn his interest in the future into a thriving business.

Mornings at the newspaper belonged to that day's paper—"putting it to bed," as they say in the industry. Afternoons were for writing or researching a story. I loved the excitement of putting out a newspaper, learning about photography, and processing film in the dark room. I even enjoyed the mundane stuff readers thought little about, such as weather reports or stock market updates, and I grew to appreciate the way the backroom staff skilfully pasted everything together. At the time, I thought there must be printer's ink in my veins!

The job introduced me to many community leaders and issues of the day. There were highlights and lowlights, but always lights! Over the years, I was assigned to school board, city hall, and regional district meetings, as well as to many of the town's social events. Staff also covered the Wednesday morning sessions for first offenders at the courthouse. Crown Counsel Steve Stirling oversaw the proceedings; he always had a busy court docket before Judge McLeod.

In the early 1980s, with enough staff there was time to research some of the larger stories such as air pollution, unemployment, social programming, even alcoholism, and delve into the many reports that came across the editor's desk. I particularly enjoyed meeting the old-timers of the Alberni Valley and sharing their stories with our newspaper's readers.

There was always a story to be written about the forest industry—obviously, considering the city's economic life revolved around MacMillan Bloedel Ltd. I wrote about the shrinking forest base, the changes in the industry, and the fact that if you were under forty and employed in the industry the chances were you would be forced to move out of the community to find work in another industry. In my interview with the province's chief forester Bill Young he was optimistically guarded about the future of the industry. He quipped, "The Arabs may have oil but BC has trees."[3] In his opinion, there was no question which was the most valuable resource in the long haul. There was also a full feature on the history of MB in Port Alberni, as well as many stories about the people who worked in the industry, from labour leaders, loggers, and mill workers to the unemployed. Everyone had an opinion about the forest industry.

All hell would break lose if we made a mistake on history. Our keen community watchdog in that regard was historian Dorrit McLeod. She had once worked for the newspaper so was not bashful about setting the record straight or telling us, in no uncertain terms, to "get the facts right!" When we saw all five-feet-two-inches of her storming through the newsroom door, we knew we were in trouble. We learned quickly to check and double-check facts, but occasionally something slipped through by mistake. When I first met Dorrit she was president of the Alberni District Historical Society, and I got to know her when she dropped into the Rollin Art Centre to see how the renovations were progressing. We shared the same interests in history and in the community, and over the years we grew to enjoy each other's company.

When I started working for the newspaper, little did I know I had stepped into a job that would involve recording one of the deepest recessions the town had ever experienced.

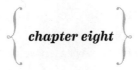

chapter eight

THE RECESSION HITS

In 1972 Port Alberni was the seventh-largest city in the province with the largest integrated forest production complex in Canada; it ranked among the top ten cities in Canada in per capita income. MacMillan Bloedel and related service industries employed most of the town residents. Mills stretched along the waterfront at the head of the Alberni Inlet. One mill fed another in order to get the best use out of the trees. Logs of a higher quality were manufactured into plywood, lumber, and shingles; small logs, sawdust, and trimmings provided raw material for pulp, newsprint, and linerboard.

MB's most important asset, other than its workers, was its timber resource, considered the best in Canada. The mills were supplied with softwood logs from forests that MB owned or managed under its two tree farm licences on the west coast, TFL 21 and 22 (later amalgamated into TFL 44), and its own Tree Farm 19. These assured the company of a steady supply of raw material.

At the peak of its operations in the Alberni Valley in 1981, MB had a total of 5,600 hourly and staff employees with a gross payroll of $157 million. The population of the Valley had grown to thirty thousand. The Alberni Plywood plant had 660 employees, the Alberni Pacific Division 600, the Somass Division 1,180, the Alberni Pulp and Paper Mill 1,350. The remaining MB employees were employed in logging at Franklin River, Ash, Kennedy Lake, Cous, Cameron, Taylor, Estevan, and Cypre.

As the Port Alberni mills were all located on the waterfront, shipping was completely incorporated with production. Deep-sea freighters berthed and loaded beside the mills. The port was the third largest in the province and kept the port manager, Captain Don Brooks, busy with more than two hundred ships calling in annually to carry products to markets in Great Britain, Europe, and Asia as well as the United States, South America, and Australia. It was not unusual to see one freighter sitting out in Stamp Harbour while another loaded at the Assembly Dock and another at the pulp mill.

The forest industry was very good for the City of Port Alberni coffers as it benefited from MB's business and property taxes. In 1953 the company paid $62,636; by 1973 this figure had grown to over $2 million. The 1979 property taxes were $5,903,940 and business taxes $628,098. The company's share of taxes amounted to 50 percent of the total collected by the city.

LOSSES AT MB

In the mid-1970s there was a financial downturn in MB fortunes due to transportation losses, but an even greater loss was that of the company founder. Harvey Reginald MacMillan died on February 9, 1976, at his home on Hudson Street in Vancouver, at the grand age of ninety-one. H.R. was a giant in the forest industry. He once told a friend:

> *God is very wise. When a man has lived a long while and has learned a great deal about how to do things, God arranges to take him away. It is a good rule.*[1]

Hundreds attended his funeral. All the company offices were closed for the afternoon. There was a sadness felt throughout the industry, particularly in Port Alberni where he had been a familiar face and staunch supporter of an integrated forest system.

Shortly after H.R.'s death the company announced the first loss in MB history. The Canadian Transport Company's losses for the year were greater than had been forecast. The CTC was founded in 1924 to transport MB products by chartering ships owned by others. Through ship brokers, the CTC chartered a vessel of a suitable size for the amount of lumber being sold and arranged to have it take on cargo in Port Alberni, Vancouver, or Chemainus. Instead of the $17 million loss CTC had estimated earlier, it was now $32 million. Dennis W. Timmis, who had been president and CEO for three years, offered his resignation. J. Ernest Richardson became chairman and acting president until a new chairman could be recruited. In September 1976, C. Calvert Knudsen filled the position of CEO; he was from Tacoma, Washington, and had been senior vice-president of Weyerhaeuser Company.

By fall of the next year things were starting to turn around and the company edged into the black. Knudsen's first order of business had been to breathe new life into the company. Some mills were obsolete, and others were plagued by high production costs. There was also an atmosphere of doubt and low morale in the company. Knudsen set out to change this, and he did it by reorganizing management. The product groups were reduced to four: building materials, under John St. C. Ross, who had joined the company in 1962; pulp and paper, under Ray V. Smith, who joined MB sales in 1957; linerboard and packaging, under H.V. Townsend, who was responsible for building MB's container organization; and raw materials under James H. Lawson, who had completed his work as acting head of the transportation group.[2]

Many of the Weyerhaeuser methods of long-range planning were adopted into MB. The company fleet of vessels was cut back, and there was some belt-tightening at the regional level. Every cost had to be justified.

Good news was announced for the Port Alberni mills in July 1978. Alberni Pacific Division would have its seventy-four-year-old sawmill replaced with a new $50 million mill, and the company would modernize the Alberni Plywood plant at a cost of $20 million. Another $63 million was earmarked for Powell River. Alberni Plywood got a complete upgrade of all its equipment, making it competitive with other plywood mills. These mills had been designed for an era when logs entering the mill were bigger and large timbers were in much greater demand overseas. But markets had changed and the profitability of such sawmills had declined. Change was needed if they were to survive. The plans were to build a new highly computerized mill on the site of the old sawmill. The following year, a $23.4 million program was announced to modernize and speed up three newsprint machines at the pulp mill. These announcements were good news for Port Alberni.

In the east, meanwhile, the corporate giants of industry were eyeing MB with thoughts of a takeover. The first to come calling was the giant Canadian Pacific Investments whose chairman, Ian Sinclair, was told by Premier Bill Bennett, "BC is not for sale,"[3] and quickly squashed any plans for a takeover. Bennett had cut short his holiday to reject any shift of ownership that would cause MB to lose its BC identity. The government had the right to cancel a company's forest management licence if there was any change in ownership without prior government approval. Port Alberni may have breathed a big sigh of relief, but the door had been opened a crack for a future takeover.

In December 1978, MB lost another giant in the industry—W.J. VanDusen, who died at age eighty-nine. He had joined MacMillan as manager in 1919, and became a member of the board serving until his retirement in 1969. The two men made a successful team for over half a century. Like H.R., when VanDusen saw an opportunity, he took advantage of it. In his retirement he devoted his time to serving as chairman of the Vancouver Foundation and other charities. In 1970 he donated land to the City of Vancouver that became the VanDusen Botanical Gardens. Former chairman B.M. Hoffmeister was quoted as saying,

> H.R. was the ideas man, and it was VanDusen's role to refine the idea, look at them from every possible angle, and to make sure they would work.[4]

The company was now BC's largest public corporation, with assets ranked second only to the BC Telephone Company and with holdings in Britain, Continental Europe, and Pine Hill, Alabama. Its forest resources were one of the world's largest under private management.

A recession began late in 1979 after the US Federal Reserve Board announced a policy that permitted interest rates to climb or fall in reaction to market demand. It grew as there was a dramatic decline in housing starts in the US. Two million housing starts a year in the US meant sawmill prosperity in BC, whereas a decline to one million meant hard times in the BC mills. The Canadian economy, inextricably linked to its largest trading partner, braced for the fallout from the turmoil in the US. Within a year US housing starts dropped below one million. They also declined in Canada, Britain, and Continental Europe. In Japan they plunged to the lowest level in fourteen years—just as the new Alberni Pacific Division sawmill began producing lumber specially cut for the Japanese market.

Calvert Knudsen became chairman of MB in April 1980, retaining his position as chief executive officer with a salary of $419,898.[5] He expressed optimism about the company's performance, predicting that MB would become stronger and more competitive because of its strengths and resources. A year later his salary was reduced to $381,441.

In 1981, Noranda announced it had succeeded in amassing 49 percent of MB shares. This was the biggest takeover in Canadian history. Five Noranda representatives joined MB's board of directors. Adam Zimmerman became vice-chairman; he was also Noranda's executive vice-president. He said, "Compared with Noranda, MacMillan Bloedel's head office was top-heavy beyond belief. They had vice-presidents for everything."[6] Zimmerman counted on MB assets to see the company through this rough period.

Both the new computer-age sawmill in Port Alberni and the newsprint mill at Powell River generated profits, and the company expanded its Alabama Pine Hill linerboard mill. Within a few months, Noranda found itself in a takeover bid by the giant Brascade Resources Inc. This resulted in Brascade owning 42 percent of Noranda's shares, and added to the complexity of companies connected to MB ownership.[7] Control of MB now shifted to eastern Canada, where both Noranda and Brascade were based. H.R. would have been horrified that his once proud company was now run by the kind of people he described as "never having had rain in their lunch buckets."[8]

British Columbia's economy was harder hit than any other province and the downturn more prolonged. From 1981 to 1984, employment in the province fell by 79,000 with losses of 3,100 in forestry, 10,400 in mining, 23,600 in construction, and 37,700 in manufacturing. Jobs in the forest industry dropped by more than 8 percent and cut deep into the service sector.[9]

STRIKES AND PROTESTS

The year 1981 in the Alberni Valley was one of strikes and protests. The term "Recession City" was coined as the community suffered through one of the longest strike periods in recent history. First the Insurance Corporation of British Columbia closed its doors. Then BC Telephone employees joined their colleagues in twenty other cities across the province by occupying their offices. Soon they were out on the picket line. Then the Canadian Union of Postal Workers brought mail to a halt while local members of the Hotel, Restaurant, Culinary and Bartenders Union turned taps dry. Most critically, the forest industry ground to a halt. The unions involved were the Office and Technical Employees Union (OTEU), the IWA, the International Brotherhood of Electrical Workers (IBEW), and the two CPU locals 686 and 592. The librarians of the Vancouver Island Regional Library decided to join the ranks on the picket lines and were joined by the staff members of the Canadian Union of Public Employees.

The strike in the forest sector began in July when the small OTEU struck Alberni Pulp and Paper. This small union was like "the mouse that roared" for it kept local mills at a standstill and heralded the start of a lengthy strike. About 2,100 local IWA members joined the strike of 7,000 other members across the province. MB locked out the plywood plant and the sawmills in an effort, the union said, to put pressure on the OTEU. With MB's net earnings down by 73 percent in the second quarter of 1981, the situation did not look good for the company—or for Port Alberni.

The ten-week strike affected everyone in the town. It kept most workers off their job. Earl Foxcroft, president of IWA Local 1-85, blamed MB for people being unemployed. He claimed that children were going to school without proper clothing or school supplies. "It's blackmail," he charged when speaking to the partisan Port Alberni District Labour Council. He claimed the sawmills and plywood plant were locked out to pressure the OTEU into a settlement. Foxcroft advocated taking away MB's licence to TFL 21 unless it started to take out the timber.

> We can very well start these operations ourselves—we don't need MB. Every plywood plant in the province is working except ours. MB said they were concerned about the market conditions, but there were market

conditions for other plants in the province. The mayor should be calling on the minister to get this community working again.[10]

Foxcroft wanted action from city council. But there was little council could do except write to the labour minister.

OTEU shop steward Kevin Anderson said although his union was small it had tried to get a settlement and had negotiated throughout the year. There had been a vote to reject the company's offer and a strike vote of about 98 percent, and so they were still on the picket lines.

President of the labour council Walter Behn felt it was a sorry day for labour in Port Alberni:

There is not much to look forward to and with oil and gasoline prices increasing many will find it difficult to heat their homes and also the high interest rates are hurting everyone plus the whole uncertainty of the labour future.[11]

In September, ten weeks into the strike, feelings were strained and an air of quiet desperation had taken hold. Even the fall celebrations of the Salmon Festival and Fall Fair gave only a brief respite from the economic situation rapidly bringing the city, not just the mills, to a standstill. Small businesses, contractors, truckers, and stores in the Alberni Mall were hurting. Then amazingly, within days, the OTEU strike was settled and the long hot summer of labour unrest was over.

The Alberni Valley had been hit hard by the recession. Appearing on the popular Jack Webster show in 1982, Knudsen said, "The industry is in tough shape, nothing is moving." He told Webster and his TV audience that the company had switched from restraint to survival.

In the last 14 months we have taken 1,100 people out of salaried positions. That is a 20 per cent reduction.

> *Unemployment amongst our workers changes weekly from 2,500 to 10,000. But there is some indication there will be improved economic activity in the U.S. within the next three to six months. This will only happen in Canada when interest rates start to come down. We are going to avert going broke.*[12]

Knudsen predicted that it would be two or three years before things would return to normal in the forest industry. To weather the storm, the forest industry asked hourly employees for a wage rollback of the 1982 contract, from a 13 percent wage increase to 6 percent for the contract year. MB put its Vancouver head office up for sale at a price of $75 million, then rented space in the building for its reduced workforce. Knudsen predicted that the lumber industry would go nowhere until the US housing situation improved.

In 1982 MB regionalized its operations. Where before individual plant managers fought for their own operation at the board level, decisions were now made at a regional level. There were now three regional business units: Alberni, Powell River, and Nanaimo. The latter included the Chemainus sawmill, the Fraser River mills, and the Harmac mill in Nanaimo. Each region was an integrated unit, responsible for harvesting its own timber and for converting that timber into end products in its own mills. Bob Findlay, manager of Harmac in Nanaimo, became the manager of the Alberni region.

It seemed at first this was just another cyclical turn and MB would bounce back as before, but this was something quite different. The company was in survival mode. Employees had salary cuts and deferrals; there were layoffs and extensive downtime; staffing levels were reduced, capital expenditure programs deferred, and proposals for new projects gathered dust on office shelves. Company shareholders suffered dividend cuts and mill inventories were under strict control. One could only speculate what H.R. would have thought or done about the dire situation now facing the company he helped to build—it had a new face and it was a stranger to many.

Calvert Knudsen was an outspoken man and respected on the subject of economics, but even he did not foresee the slump in the US housing market or the world economy, and its effect on the forest industry. He said at the time that MB has the best and most extensive forest base in the province. Those may have been comforting words to some, but to others they were small solace.

In 1982 the Chemainus sawmill closed and 682 jobs were lost; machines were also closed in Powell River with a loss of 400 jobs. A year later, the job losses continued with the closure of the Vancouver Plywood mill and the loss of another 400 jobs.

Port Alberni had its own share of job losses. Almost seventeen hundred hourly workers in the Port Alberni mills were laid off according to seniority. The same could not be said for the salaried workers, some only a few years from retirement and sporting the company's twenty-five-year gold watch. They were called into the manager's office, informed that they were to be let go, told to gather up their belongings, and then were escorted from the building and driven home. This abrupt departure from the mill was devastating and demoralizing. For those nearing retirement, in order to qualify for full pension their age and years of service had to total eighty. If they were short this number, the loss was considerable. The resentment still lingers for some who felt bitter about how they were treated when terminated.

For the hourly workers it was death by a thousand cuts. After being laid off, if they felt there was a chance for a callback, the uncertainty contributed to a daily emotional roller coaster. Some waited and waited. Men took over domestic duties while their wives started working full-time. In order to get severance benefits, the worker had to be laid off for eighteen consecutive months, and once severance pay was accepted, seniority was lost. If a worker returned to his job for a day, he had to wait another eighteen months for severance pay. If he did not answer the callback, he lost his position in the union and forfeited his chance to be rehired at the mill full-time. One worker described unemployment like being in a black tunnel with no light at the end.

If there was a bright side to the forestry cutbacks, it was the mini baby boom at West Coast General Hospital in 1982.

As the fortunes in the forest industry go, so goes Port Alberni. The town had suffered through many ups and downs in its history, but the downturn in the 1980s was different and more profound. There was a standing joke that if you were going to be unemployed then Port Alberni was the place to be with its excellent fishing, hunting, and great outdoors. But this was no joke! There had never before been a soup kitchen to dispense food for unemployed workers or a centre specifically set up to help and offer advice. For Sale signs went up on houses around town as people left to find jobs in other places.

Many lost their homes. Forty percent of the mortgages initiated by one bank in the first six months of 1981 failed and the houses were repossessed. The courts were so backlogged that repossessions took eighteen months to process. The bank owned so many houses that it was reluctant to evict the former owners because it did not want to leave so many houses vacant. Eviction was often unnecessary anyway; those who were unable to continue making payments, and unable to sell their homes, simply walked away.

The Port Alberni unemployed workers joined forces to create the Organization of Unemployed Workers (OUW), an offshoot of the Alberni District Labour Council unemployment committee that consisted of Don Lloyd, George McKnight, and Dave Crosby. In March 1982, an Unemployed Action Centre was established at Victoria Quay as a self-help centre, in a building recently vacated by the United Native Nations Clothesline store. Prior to this, the group had been working out of the basement of the IWA Hall. The OUW rent was partially funded by the B.C. Federation of Labour. The local group was also affiliated with the seven-member B.C. Coalition of Unemployed Workers.

Port Alberni was not alone in this recession, of course; thirty-three similar centres were established around the province. But Port Alberni's Action Centre was the first and blazed the way for others. Dave Crosby was the first chairman. Crosby, like many others, didn't think unemployment would happen to him. He had been working at Somass Division since 1977. But after the forestry strike of 1981, he never got back to work. He kept hoping, though. It wasn't until December 1983 that reality sunk in—when he was terminated from MB because his rights of recall had expired.[13]

As one OUW member put it, "We are struggling and bungling our way through to break ground." Soon organizers were gathering information about unemployment insurance, social assistance, medical and dental coverage, mortgages, and numerous other conditions affecting the unemployed. Collecting resource material was a slow and tedious grind. As well, the Action Centre supplied lunch each day and started a food bank. It also supplied clothing, jokingly called "the OUW boutique." The soup kitchen became a way to survive the early 1980s in many communities.

Mayor Paul Reitsma did not endear himself to the OUW by making derogatory remarks about the group on an open-line radio broadcast. This evoked stormy encounters at city council meetings in January 1983 when members packed the council chamber. Reitsma was ill for one meeting, out of town for another; he generally avoided any face-to-face confrontation. Aldermen Joe Stanhope, Gillian Trumper, Walter Behn, Art Wynans, and Ken Hoffmann disassociated themselves from the mayor's remark. Only alderman Len Nelson seemed to waffle when he placed a motion on the agenda asking for an apology for the OUW members, then later withdrew it. Don Lloyd of the OUW assured council his group played a very necessary role for the unemployed. "They are not receiving charity, they are receiving assistance from their brothers and sisters in the community ... it is not their fault that they do not have a job."[14] Lloyd predicted the struggle had just begun and the spirit and determination along with the numbers would continue to grow.

Mayor Reitsma was in fact in Victoria lobbying for a second crossing of Rogers Creek at Tenth Avenue. The November election had shown that residents by a large majority supported such a crossing. When the mayor heard what had happened in council, he said the controversy was between him and three members of the OUW. "I was in Victoria looking for jobs and funding for the Alberni Valley."[15] He denied he was avoiding them.

The Port Alberni OUW planned a massive public protest demonstration on the steps of the provincial legislature on April 9 with five other workers associations from Campbell River, Nanaimo, Victoria, and the Lower Mainland's OUW. They hoped for five thousand people, possibly the biggest rally ever by the unemployed in BC. There were five major items on their agenda: welfare reform, a moratorium on evictions and foreclosures, an end to the restraint programs that allegedly were undermining government services, support for labour against contract concessions and wage controls, and shorter hours of work as an answer to technological change and high unemployment.

For five days they trekked to Victoria. Many had blisters when they arrived after having completed the march of over a hundred kilometres (sixty-two miles). A thundershower on the Pat Bay Highway drenched but did not dampen their enthusiasm for the cause. People rushed outdoors and to windows as the chanting trekkers, armed with placards and escorted by police, trudged their last two miles down Douglas Street to be met by a small group of Victoria's Unemployed Workers Union. When the marchers heard the election writ had been dropped Thursday they all shouted for joy.

The *Alberni Valley Times* sent reporter Gavin Wilson down to get a first-hand account of the protest. Hundreds carrying placards demonstrated at the provincial legislature on April 9, 1983, chanting "we want work" and "jobs, not welfare" and demanding an end to high unemployment. The number of demonstrators—about three thousand—was not as large as first anticipated; the islanders were also disappointed that only a few people had come over from the mainland, deciding to hold a Vancouver rally rather than having the expense of the ferry and bussing protesters to the island. But it was still one of the largest protests in recent years. With a provincial election about a month away, the crowd railed against Bill Bennett's Social Credit government and called for a Dave Barrett NDP victory. The NDP was challenged to work with the unemployed to create meaningful, long-term jobs at union pay rates and under safe conditions. "We want lasting jobs, not ones that use the desperation of people," said Bill Massey, another member of the Port Alberni's OUW. "We can't afford to wait any longer, it's been two years now."[16]

Massey said the trek had been fun, "but it was hard, and emotional. It built up a spirit of solidarity that won't be easy for us to forget." The trek had made headlines in newspapers and television across the country. The unemployment situation was a subject the general public could relate to. The national unemployment figures were at an all-time high of 1,658,000 in March, according to Statistics Canada, but this didn't include those who had given up looking for work because there were no jobs available. In the Alberni Valley, MB stated that eighteen hundred woodworkers would never return to work even with the recovery of the economy.

Perhaps it was inevitable the group would become political. Crosby made a run for alderman in the November 1983 election, and while his political aspiration failed he had succeeded in drawing public attention to the problems of the unemployed. The OUW continued to lean heavily on government to get action. Poverty was something unemployed people were becoming more and more familiar with.

BEING UNEMPLOYED: AN EMOTIONAL ROLLER COASTER

Losing their job took workers on a ride from shock to despair. Stories began to surface in the community about employees arriving at work in the morning and being told they no longer had a job. Many were devastated and hurt, which led to drinking and the breakup of families. For older workers there were shattered dreams marred by financial insecurity. Hardest hit were those aged fifteen to twenty-four, though, with nearly one in four unemployed. Parents had difficulty understanding why this young person was still hanging around the house and not out looking for a job. The old advice of "go home to mother" didn't hold true anymore; chances were that both parents were unemployed too.

Alderman Gillian Trumper showed concern about the unemployment rate among young people who had left school in the past two or three years. She pointed out that besides being unable to find work they were ineligible for unemployment insurance benefits and often couldn't collect welfare.

Many unemployed workers felt exploited by MB and placed the blame there, then realized that the recession was happening not only in Port Alberni; it was being felt internationally around the industrialized world. With BC's economy export-oriented, the province was hard hit. Resource revenues dropped from a high of about $1.6 billion in 1980 to $570 million. This was a recession the government could not spend its way out of.

The Ministry of Human Resources office in Port Alberni was a busy place. Some jokingly called it the only growth industry in town. Parking in the area was limited and the office was a hive of activity. There were now two district supervisors taking care of 2,600 claims registered in the area, and an estimated five thousand people on assistance; the office bulged at the seams. Each claim could include a husband, wife, and a number of eligible young adults. The office didn't feel the impact until the summer and fall of 1982 when unemployment benefits ran out. Terry McFadden, who had worked as a supervisor with the Ministry of Human Resources for fifteen years, said he had never seen anything like it. There was enough work for two offices.

Gus Barrett, manager of the local Canada Employment Centre, described the unemployment situation as "horrendous. It began in the winter of 1981 and there was such a backlog of claims, some had to be sent to other centres to be processed." In 1984 there were two thousand active claims. During the previous three years the federal government had paid out $56.97 million on UI in Port Alberni alone. Add to that another $5.6 million for 170 job creation projects giving short-term employment to over a thousand people. Barrett's staff of five counsellors and twenty-six support staff were hard-pressed to keep up with the demand. He said:

We just got to the point in the first year where we were trying to work our way out of the backlog but it was like climbing up only to be hit on the head and brought down again. It is a real downer and there is never any light at the end of the tunnel.[17]

The prospect of finding work in Port Alberni was almost impossible. For years people had relied on the forest industry to supply jobs, but this was no longer possible. Other forces were also at work as the forest industry became more automated; less labour was needed as the industry became more productive through the use of new technology. The new, modern sawmills of the future would employ fewer workers, and the outlook seemed grim for high school or university students who would no longer find work on the green chain on weekends or summer holidays.

Those workers who had spent a lifetime working in the woods or in a sawmill were now being advised to train to operate computers or work in tourism and the service industries, all lower-paid jobs. Many looked for new job training at North Island College in Port Alberni, where enrollment had increased and there were long waiting lists for vocational courses. Welding, driver training, and air brakes courses all had full waiting lists. The college initiated a course for welders hoping to find work building the new "fast ferries," a fleet of catamaran-type vessels operated by BC Ferries from 1999 to 2000. Unfortunately the new ferries were not popular with the public; they were eventually withdrawn from service and sold in 2003 for $19.4 million. Building the ferries in BC was an NDP initiative to support the province's shipbuilding industry.

The longer a person was unemployed the more difficult it was to get hired. Workers and their families began leaving town searching for work in other communities. Someone erected a sign at the outskirts of town that said, "Will the last person leaving turn off the lights."

When MB began hiring students for summer employment, the OUW took action by setting up a picket line at the company regional headquarters on Sixth Avenue. They argued that unemployed family breadwinners should be hired before students, and further added that some of the students were sons of MB management staff. The picket line was up long enough to get the point across.

COMMUNITY SUPPORT

The food bank became a way of life for many. Ministry of Human Resources supervisor Terry McFadden didn't seem to think there was anything so unusual about referring people to the food bank or the Salvation Army for grocery hampers.

In 1983 Reverend Bill and Katie Stobbe opened up the Bread of Life soup kitchen on Third Avenue under the auspices of the Bethel Church. The couple had moved up to Port Alberni from Ucluelet where they had operated church camps and a bible school for west coast Natives. For the next four years, they baked, boiled, and stewed food from the Third Avenue soup kitchen, cooking a hot lunch for Port Alberni's poor and unemployed.

Volunteers who staffed the kitchen described the mammoth shopping, preparation, and serving responsibilities they shared with the couple. About a thousand men, women, and children a month were served from this modest kitchen. The generosity of the community came through with donations of cash and food. Once a local farmer donated the bones from a whole cow, which kept Katie in soup stock for a year. The eighteen litres (five gallons) of fresh milk donated by McKinnon's Dairy three times a week helped round out the hearty lunches. Bill and Katie had eight children of their own. They retired in 1987.

Some community-minded residents tried to help the unemployed find work or start a new business. Cecile McKinnon was the driving force behind the Alberni Valley Cottage Industry Society. The group tried to get people off social assistance and unemployment insurance. Society funding came from bingo games, while MB and the unions provided support. MB supplied plywood for the group's first job of renovating the old firehall. The unemployed workers also cleared trails in the area, picked up bags of garbage, and assisted with the BC Summer Games.

McKinnon was a former Liberal Party candidate and outspoken in getting people back to work. She once turned the table on B.C. Federation of Labour president Jim Kinnaird when he came to Port Alberni in April 1982. Kinnaird was on a speaking tour of the province with other executive members, warning workers of the government's intentions of imposing wage and price controls again. He was speaking before a labour audience in the IWA Hall when McKinnon asked: "Why can't labour and management work together for the benefit of the entire country?" She called for a "revival of the Canadian spirit."[18]

Kinnaird blamed the lack of co-operation on the heads of business and government. The crowd applauded when he added that companies such as BC Tel and MB reap "massive profits" year after year but do not share them with workers.

Throughout these tough times, Port Alberni was portrayed to the outside world as a town with a large number of unemployed workers from a depressed forest industry; there was little mention of the communal sharing and individual triumphs. The OUW brought public attention to the needs of many of the town's residents, proving that when trouble arrives people have the ability to pull together. Some argued the group was "too political," but in order to effect some change the OUW had to deal with government and that meant politics.

In spite of the recession, the city was determined to move ahead. It was not sitting still letting things happen. There were people working very hard to move it toward greater independence from its past as a one-industry town. But they had difficult statistics to deal with.

In 1986 the population of the city dropped from 19,892 to 18,241.[19] All through the 1970s the city was ranked with the top ten cities in Canada in per capita income; in 1979 it was ranked seventh. By 1981, its ranking had dropped to number forty, and in 1987 it had sunk to eighty-ninth.

Port Alberni Mayor Les Hammer sits in a vintage car that once belonged to Arthur E. Waterhouse, the first mayor of the city.
COURTESY OF ALBERNI VALLEY MUSEUM

Mayor Fred Bishop with chain of office.
COURTESY OF ALBERNI VALLEY MUSEUM

Opening of the Alberni Valley Museum extension on March 24, 1983, with (L–R) MLA Bob Skelly, museum director John Mitchell, Helen Ford, Keitha Adams, and Mayor Paul Reitsma. COURTESY OF ALBERNI VALLEY MUSEUM

Harry (Cougar) Brown. COURTESY OF ALBERNI VALLEY MUSEUM

H.R. MacMillan presents 2-Spot to the City of Port Alberni on July 24, 1954, at the corner of Redford Street and Third Avenue. Sharing the platform were (L–R) MLA John Squires, Ernie G. Shorter, Port Alberni Mayor Loran Jordan, Alderman Fred Weaver, and Joe Johannson. COURTESY OF ALBERNI VALLEY MUSEUM

Women who worked to preserve history: (L–R) Sue Watson, Gen Joyce, Dorrit MacLeod, Helen Ford, and Keitha Adams, all past presidents of the Alberni District Historical Society. JAN PETERSON PHOTO

George McKnight. COURTESY OF ALBERNI VALLEY MUSEUM

MLA Bob Skelly. COURTESY OF ALBERNI VALLEY MUSEUM

Freighter at Assembly Dock with the Alberni Pacific and Plywood divisions in the background. COURTESY OF ALBERNI VALLEY MUSEUM

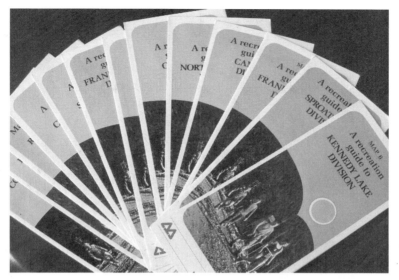

Guide maps for each MacMillan Bloedel division. JAN PETERSON PHOTO

A winter view going over "the hump" on Highway 4: Mount Arrowsmith, the highest mountain (1,819 m) on southern Vancouver Island.
COURTESY OF ALBERNI VALLEY MUSEUM

TOP LEFT *George Watts, Tseshaht Band manager, 1977.* COURTESY OF ALBERNI VALLEY MUSEUM TOP RIGHT *Adam Shewish, hereditary chief of the Tseshaht Band.* PHOTOGRAPHER BOB SODERLUND. COURTESY OF ALBERNI VALLEY MUSEUM

The Mill Stones monument was erected in front of the pulp mill by Bloedel, Stewart & Welch to commemorate the first pulp mill built at Alberni in 1891. The grinding stones were originally from an old dismantled paper mill in Scotland. JAN PETERSON PHOTO

Poster of film Every 12 Seconds, *showing Wolfgang Zimmerman and Sven Frederickson.* JAN PETERSON PHOTO

Mass arrest on August 9, 1993, at the Kennedy River Bridge blockade on West Main logging road. IMAGE COURTESY OF FRIENDS OF CLAYOQUOT SOUND

MacMillan Bloedel's commemorative mugs. JAN PETERSON PHOTO

Alberni Harbour Quay, showing clock tower with observation deck and New Zealand sculpture carved during Expo '86. The Quay is the hub of the harbour with small shops, a gallery, and the popular Donut Coffee Shop.
JAN PETERSON PHOTO

Dr. George Clutesi with artist Nuri Mohammed at the opening of her exhibition in the Alberni Valley Museum. JAN PETERSON PHOTO

One of the village homes at the McLean Mill. JAN PETERSON PHOTO

Parks and Recreation Clown College graduation in 1982. JAN PETERSON PHOTO

Welcoming the restored No. 7 Alberni Pacific Railway engine at the train station. JAN PETERSON PHOTO

The Alberni Valley Times *newsroom: sports editor Carl Vesterback, reporters Gavin Wilson and Jan Peterson, editor Rob Diotte.* ALBERNI VALLEY TIMES PHOTO

Peter Szachiv with the author at the opening of his exhibition in the Alberni Valley Museum in June 1983.
JAN PETERSON PHOTO

Trevor Jones with his brother Vance and mother, Bonnie. IMAGE COURTESY OF TREVOR JONES

Kitsuksis Creek looking quiet and peaceful, with Beaufort Range mountains in the background. The popular walking dyke circling Kitsuksis Creek was built to prevent severe flooding of the Somass River and Kitsuksis Creek. JAN PETERSON PHOTO

Community leaders visiting Expo during Vancouver Island Regional Week at the BC Pavilion. L–R: Cowichan-Malahat MLA Barbara Wallace, North Island MLA Colin Gabelmann, Port Alberni Mayor Gillian Trumper, regional committee member Jan Peterson of Port Alberni, Oak Bay MLA Brian Smith, regional producer Sally Glover, Saanich MLA Hugh Curtis. BC GOV'T/EXPO '86 PHOTO

Premier Bennett at the opening of the Plaza of Nations at Expo '86.
JAN PETERSON PHOTO

AC2 Pat Cummings School of Dance Funshine Dancers performed "Logger's Stomp" at Expo '86. Clockwise from back left: Kelly Dolan, Nadia Guerra, Kathy Booker, Kim Parket, Pam Donald, Ericka Netzer, Corinne Craig, Eleanor Peterson. IMAGE COURTESY OF ALISON COWAN.

Pat and Barry Miller.
IMAGE COURTESY
OF BARRY MILLER

From MB Journal *July 1999, MacMillan Bloedel CEO Tom Stephens and Weyerhaeuser CEO Steve Rogel shake hands upon announcing the merger of the two companies.* JAN PETERSON PHOTO

Naesgaard Farm Market on River Road is a popular spot for locals and visitors alike looking for locally grown fresh produce. JAN PETERSON PHOTO

Wayne Coulson, CEO and president of Coulson Group of Companies and the youngest son of Cliff and May Coulson. IMAGE COURTESY OF COULSON GROUP

Coulson Aircrane Martin Mars C-FLYL (top), with its state-of-the-art command and control lead-in aircraft, and the C-FIRW, a Sikorsky S76 twin-engine helicopter. IMAGE COURTESY OF COULSON GROUP

{ *chapter nine* }

FIGHTING BACK

Port Alberni, a proud and big-hearted city that gave so much to charities, was going through a dramatic turn of events that brought residents from the affluent seventies into survival mode. The outside media had a field day. Provincial and national newscasts portrayed the city in decline. It was easy to film a going-out-of-business sale or a boarded-up window. Other communities around the country had gone through a similar recession, but it seemed big news when it happened in Port Alberni. Residents did not look kindly on the unfortunate publicity, feeling that the media only touched the surface of what was really happening in the Alberni Valley.

It was not all bad news. Port Alberni began digging in and fighting back. As the saying goes, "Good things happen to cities in the worst of times." Granted, there were bankruptcies and several businesses had closed their doors; some consolidated while others centralized in bigger cities such as Nanaimo. However, new businesses opened up. And real estate sold well during this period; a waterfront lot at Sproat

Lake with 36 metres (120 feet) of beachfront on Stirling Arm Crescent sold for $69,000.

There were larger developments as well. Health Minister Jim Nielsen opened the Fir Park Village senior intermediate care facility, which housed sixty-seven people and gave employment to nearly seventy staff. The $4 million Alberni Harbour Quay development enhanced tourism in the city when completed; the project included a forestry museum, shops, restaurants, an art gallery, and a children's playground, and gave residents access to the beautiful waterfront. A new Teleglobe building was constructed near the Alberni Plywood plant, and architect plans were unveiled for a new courthouse for the city on Fourth Avenue.

FAMILY BUSINESSES

One of the good-news stories during this time was in agriculture. Many of the farms in the valley were in the Beaver Creek area. At about 35.6 hectares (88 acres) these were not large farms, but they did produce crops, vegetables, and dairy products for the local market.

Beaver Creek farmer Ivor Rage had just completed an expansion of three thousand square metres (thirty thousand square feet) of greenhouses for growing cucumbers. Rage happily took the title of the "King of Cukes" as his product was shipped daily to Victoria. He had tried a number of crops after buying the farm in 1961, but always returned to cucumbers. Originally he used plastic greenhouses but found that direct light made the cucumbers bitter, so he built new greenhouses. Like many farmers he faced challenges but somehow managed to overcome them. He was proud that his two sons worked on the family farm, which employed about forty people.

In 1980 Thomas and Karen Naesgaard, with their daughter, Anita, and sons, Helge, Ernest, Asker, and Robert, started a small market from a hut located along River Road, selling strawberries, corn, and other produce from their farm nearby. Robert was a well-known cyclist who represented Canada in international competition. Naesgaard's strawberries and corn, when in season, were much sought after throughout the region. Naesgaard Market has since blossomed into a thriving business and a popular shopping destination for residents year round. The attractive rustic barn-like market captures the interest of summer visitors en route to the west coast, and the market has added pottery, crafts, and garden items to its inventory. Farm produce is also shipped to other locations on Vancouver Island.

The Hertel family has processed meat in the valley since 1967. Initially Paul Hertel built a small abattoir on his farm on Bland Road, but it was his son, Tom, who founded the business known today using an original pork sausage recipe created by his family's ancestors in Europe and brought to the valley in the early 1930s. Four generations later, Hertel Meats is known for its variety of delicious meat products sold throughout the Island and the Lower Mainland.

Lyle Price of Port Potato Farm also sold his produce across Vancouver Island. The farm produced some of the best potatoes on the island. They were washed, graded, packaged, and distributed from the Price farm south of the city near Cox Lake.

When Allan and Cecile McKinnon arrived in the valley in 1956 they started a dairy farm business, McKinnon's Dairy. Cecile came from a large family in Saskatchewan and trained as a hairdresser before she married Allan, a dairy farmer, in 1945. They had eight children: Mary, Henri, Fred, Cecilia, Theresa, Helen, Alice, and Joseph. Together the family built up the business to include an ice cream market.

Bob Cole started his business of Port Boat House in 1980. He loved boats and he loved fishing, so he put the two together to create a profitable business. He was born in Port Alberni and raised at Sproat Lake, and today is still one of the city's biggest boosters. Cole put the economic situation this way: "Let's face it, if you are unemployed this is the best place to be in the country. We have lakes to swim in, rivers to fish and mountains to hike. It is a great place to be unemployed."[1]

These were all good indicators that family businesses were not sitting back waiting for the forest industry to get back on its feet. The fishing industry also continued to do business on the west coast, to Port Alberni's benefit.

Port Alberni's prized possession was its deep-sea harbour with three deep-sea berths and a storage area of 6.8 hectares (17 acres) capable of handling lumber, pulp, newsprint, plywood, and logs while awaiting shipment to world ports. The harbour was also home to the west coast fishing fleet. During the 1970s and 1980s there were about 120 large seiners and 250 gillnetters fishing in Barkley Sound. It was one of the largest fishing industries on Vancouver Island and many in the fleet used Port Alberni as their base. Later, when they didn't bring their catch into Port Alberni—that was sold to the big packers—they restocked and had repairs done when in port.

The fleet had been coming into the harbour for years. Bill Patenaude, of Woodward's, always welcomed and looked forward to it. Related businesses did well at this time. There was a spin-off effect at local hotels and beer parlours as the fishermen's families travelled from all parts of the province to visit with them.

The fleet pulling out of the harbour as they headed to the fishing grounds was an amazing sight. They fished Monday to Wednesday, then returned to Port Alberni on Thursday. Some of the vessels docked in the Ucluelet harbour.

THE POLITICS OF THE RECESSION

Everyone was concerned about the unemployment in the forest industry, so when NDP opposition leader Dave Barrett visited Port Alberni in October 1982 there was some anticipation about what he might say about the situation. Before an evening meeting at Echo Centre, he toured the city, visiting Alberni Pacific

Division, and then met with the Alberni Valley Chamber of Commerce. This had been a busy day for the former premier but it didn't show when he spoke to the crowd that night. Barrett was a dynamic and forceful speaker, and straightforward in his presentation. He was speaking to the converted when he talked about the high unemployment in the town.

> *I get fed up when workers are told to tighten their belts when there are 14 millionaires in the Social Credit government who have never lost anything. I am fed up with the doom and gloom coming from provincial and federal politicians. I am fed up with the cuts in health care and education.*[2]

He said the only limitation for the 22 million Canadians "is the psychology. I am not afraid of the future. Canadians have a major role to play on the world stage. This is no time for despair. Together we can build a better BC."

Barrett gave enough promises to fight an election on, but the fact that there was no election coming up didn't seem to bother him. He reminded the audience that every program he had introduced during his tenure as premier was still there. He estimated the current recession would last another three years.

On a personal note, he talked about his mother who was seventy-six years young. As an immigrant, she had worked hard and had raised "three wonderful children" with the whole purpose of making a better life for them. She now questioned her son Dave why she had to worry about the same things for her grandchildren.

A DAY OF DISCOVERY

While everyone recognized that the forest industry was cyclical and Port Alberni had seen its share of recessions over the years, it was now a year after the 1981 strike and downturn in the forest industry and the area still had not recovered. This was something new! Community leaders were so concerned they decided to meet in Port Alberni for a one-day conference called "The Day of Discovery." The Economic Development Commission of the Alberni–Clayoquot Regional District sponsored the conference hosted by its officer Ken Hutcheson. Over a hundred delegates met to examine the various economic elements that do, or could, contribute to economic diversification, and to develop a plan of action.

The keynote speaker was Chris Dobrzanski, international economist with the Bank of British Columbia. He warned that the economic policies of Ottawa and Washington would make any kind of economic growth difficult. He predicted the forest industry would remain the area's largest employer, with its greatest opportunities in the underlying worldwide demand for housing. "The cyclical changes in the lumber market can be reduced," he said. "The key remains in the flexibility of mills to switch products."[3]

This was a day of discovery for everyone, including the special conference guests from the various ministries and governments who found that the Alberni–Clayoquot region was not about to give up, but would fight for renewed growth and vitality. Ideas were thrown in, accepted, or rejected. Strengths and weaknesses were analyzed, individually and collectively.

What the delegates discovered was that as the region looked ahead there needed to be planning for growth in tourism, fishing, agriculture, a specialized wood products industry, and specialty manufacturing. The potential was here and now.

Tourism held the greatest potential for the region, but an overall plan was needed. Delegates recommended the immediate formation of a task force to study this as a second industry. A full-time tourism officer could insert a professional approach to this development. The area had good accommodation, a convention centre, the Pacific Rim and Strathcona parks, offshore diving, and a natural environment on its doorstep. The popular and historic MV *Lady Rose*, which carried mail, passengers, and cargo to the west coast, had an international reputation for its scenic route. There was first-class sports fishing and boating, and an abundance of artists and craftspeople. But most of all, the delegates agreed, the biggest resource to support a tourism industry was the people.

There was a large consensus of opinion that the area's biggest plus was the deep-sea port and the opportunities that existed for offshore development. Servicing oil rigs was discussed. The conference also decided there was a need for a processing plant to customize fish processing, and there was potential for ocean ranching though there was no government policy for dealing with this.

Agriculture was listed as the fourth-largest area of economic base following forestry, fishing, and tourism. Some of the original homesteads settled by farmers still existed in the Alberni Valley, and there were presently fifteen full-time farmers producing between $5 and $6 million worth of wholesale produce, including celery, strawberries, cucumbers, and potatoes. Most of the produce was transported to Victoria.

Opportunities related to forestry were also identified. The abundance of raw material could be utilized in wood-processing industries. Furniture production was an obvious choice. Decorative wood products, boat building, shakes, firewood, and packaged shingles for supermarkets were only a few of the many suggestions put forth. Local NDP MLA Bob Skelly proposed a wood thermal power plant be located in Port Alberni. This had received endorsement from Port Alberni City Council, and the suggestion had been forwarded to the minister of energy, mines and petroleum resources, the Hon. Robert H. McClelland. But no one held his or her breath waiting for approval.

Specialty manufacturing also had potential, with a marketing company established to promote small cottage industries.

The delegates recommended that government regulations should be reassessed in light of the current economic conditions existing in the region, and more specialized government offices, such as branches of the Ministry of Agriculture and Ministry of Labour, should be located in the area.

At the close of the think-tank conference, Alex Tunner, head of Operations Management Division of British Columbia Research, gave concluding remarks: "A lot of vigour has taken place today. It will now be up to the economic development officer to come up with some strategy and take all the pieces of the jigsaw, the big vat of ideas that were fermenting today, and put them together in a coherent way."

At the end of the day, Chris Dobrzanski's prediction that the forest industry would remain the area's largest employer, and that the key was flexibility of the mills to switch products, left many feeling there might still be a future in forestry but that there were other avenues to pursue toward renewed prosperity.

The Port Alberni and District Labour Council countered with its own Day of Reality workshop. It concluded that legislation should be passed to ensure that TFLs provided productive forests in perpetuity.

HURTING THE KIDS

The repercussion of the economy's downturn was felt throughout the community, but no organization felt it more than School District 70, which included the west coast communities of Tofino, Ucluelet, and Bamfield. The year 1982 was like a spring storm, a very emotional time for all concerned. Within ten years district school enrollment had dropped from 9,000 students in 1971 to 7,196.[4] The decline in population combined with the government's restraint program was the death knell for five rural schools.

The decision was not easy. In March 1982 the school board met to try to reduce its 1982 operating budget by $315,554 and limit its 1983 budget to a 12 percent increase over 1982, as dictated by the provincial government's new restraint program.

Education Minister Brian Smith said he did not know who had leaked the document outlining the new education finance formula.

Shortly after, two bills were introduced in the legislature that had great significance to school boards. They received first reading on April 13. Bill 27 was the Education (Interim) Finance Act, which provided the legislative authority for the new finance formula. Bill 28 was the Compensation Stabilization Act, containing the restraint legislation. Gary Begin, president of the B.C. School Trustees Association, called the Education (Interim) Finance Act "a threat to democracy, which had the potential to devastate local autonomy of education."[5]

When the school board met to discuss the ramifications of the new legislation Bob Moss, superintendent of district schools, said, "This was the toughest board meeting I have ever attended."[6] Trustee Jim Spencer pointed out there was a crisis and there was no short-term answer when faced with declining enrollment, increased staff costs, mandated programs, expanded services, energy costs, and inflation. After everyone had had their say about the situation, west coast trustee Mabel Klee, as the school board chairman, had the final word. She said the most economical method of cutting costs was to close schools. It was a sound and realistic step in trying times.[7]

A prepared press release stated that the five elementary schools would close effective June 30, 1982. The board found it had no alternative. "It is cheaper to have 500 students in one building than have 200 in a smaller building," Moss said. The elimination of small elementary schools also meant the loss of teaching and support staff. Pupils enrolled in the schools would be accommodated in larger elementary schools that had empty classrooms because of the decrease in population. Wood and Gill schools had three empty rooms in each, for example, while Eighth Avenue School had five empty classrooms.

The small rural schools—G.W. Gray, River Bend, Faber, Maebelle, and C.T. Hilton School—were mothballed or transformed to another use, their equipment used in other schools. The teachers and principals were assigned to other schools.

Special public meetings were held to allow parents to discuss their concerns with the school board. Paul Richardson, president of the Alberni District Teachers Association, predicted the entire education system would suffer. At meeting after meeting angry and frustrated parents lashed out at the school board; some openly cried. Trustees Bob Hoadley and Gary Swann attended the first of the five public meetings, and they seemed as frustrated with the provincial government as the parents were with the school board. "Why does it have to be the kids that suffer?" one parent asked. "If we don't close the schools there will have to be more teacher cuts," was the reply. It was estimated there would be twenty-seven fewer teaching positions the following year. Trustee Gary Swann reacted:

> *I sense some frustrations and anger from you, but we are just the middle people. Write to the Ministry of Education if you care enough. Your taxes will be going up $10 more. I think the taxpayer would pay the increased costs just to keep the schools open. Because of the new formula we no longer have MB to rely on, we have lost our industrial base.*[8]

Some perceived the school district administration as top-heavy and suggested eliminating some of those positions. The answer came at the next meeting. One position at the administrative level was eliminated, along with the speech pathologist, the driver-training program, and the skating program. Two positions with the Native curriculum development and seven teacher aides were gone, as were twenty-eight teaching positions. The Native Indian Education Awareness Society protested the cuts it viewed as a threat to Native education.

When Premier Bill Bennett called an election for May 5, 1983, he ran on a conservative restraint program that led his Social Credit Party to a resounding victory. In July, Finance

Minister Hugh Curtis delivered his budget speech. After his speech he introduced twenty-six pieces of legislation directed at changing the social contract in British Columbia. The extent of the program shocked everyone. Included in the legislative package was the Public Sector Restraint Act, which allowed the government to terminate employees without cause to decrease the size of the public service.

For School District 70 the most contentious part of the measure was the Education Interim Finance Amendment Act, which gave the government power to supervise the budgets and expenditures of school districts and to fire unco-operative boards. Of the shocked school boards around the province, seventeen joined forces to fight the bill. SD 70 trustees reluctantly decided to comply.

Trustees were criticized for not taking a stand with the seventeen other school districts that had voted against the government restraint program. Trustee Jim Spencer said he would write a letter to Victoria to protest. Trustee Rosemarie Buchanan angrily denounced the government: "We should all tell Bennett to go to hell with this . . . [T]his board should have stayed with the other seventeen boards." Buchanan was the only trustee to vote against the school closures. The board's letter to the government was later released to the public; it protested the unilateral action taken by the government causing services to be removed and suggested this was an erosion of local autonomy.

Superintendent Bob Moss stood his ground, and while he listened patiently and courteously to the parents' concerns, he knew the action was needed to reduce the budget as mandated by Victoria. For a time it seemed the decision to close the schools might be deferred, but this was not to be. The school closure campaign moved on to Victoria. Seven parents, including Hugh Morrison and Allan Wright, met with Minister of Education Brian Smith and local MLA Bob Skelly and presented them with petitions signed by over two thousand people. Smith told them it was his ministry's policy not to interfere with local school board decisions.

A few weeks later Smith officially confirmed the closure of the elementary schools effective July 1, 1982. The declining enrollment and the government restraint program when combined had effectively closed the five schools. By summer all had been boarded up or were to be utilized by community organizations. Everyone in town felt the loss.

Bob Moss gave a big sigh of relief. It had been a gruelling two months, but he concluded, "It ended satisfactorily from my point of view."[9] He expected school boundaries to be redrawn. Mabel Klee praised the school board staff and guaranteed the quality of education equally for every child in the district.

OPERATION SOLIDARITY

Premier Bennett explained his restraint program as a result of the international recession that had hit British Columbia hard, especially in its resource revenues which had dropped from $1.6 billion in 1980 to $570 million. Plus, the province was paying $180 million in interest on last year's debt.

The government strategy was designed to lower the cost of doing business and send a signal to investors that the province was putting its house in order and was a good place to do business. Great ideals, but many people were affected. The price of tobacco went up, sales tax was increased from 6 to 7 percent, the Human Rights Commission and the rentalsman position were dissolved, and rent control was eliminated. Before long there was a groundswell of opposition to the restraint program.

There were other bills that alarmed the labour movement. BC's 200,000-member civil service was cut by 25 percent, Bill 2 gutted the BCGEU collective agreement, and Bill 3 allowed for the firing of public servants without cause after their collective agreement lapsed on October 31.

Art Kube, president of the B.C. Federation of Labour, was quick to talk about a general strike and plan action against the legislation. The program named "Operation Solidarity" surprisingly brought together trade union leaders and community activists who had not always seen eye to eye. This gave the movement strength and purpose.

On July 24, 1983, BC Place Stadium in Vancouver was packed with twenty thousand people for a rally. Four days later, more than 25,000 marchers protested on the grounds of the legislature in Victoria. The local labour council decided to join the protest in Victoria. This advertisement appeared July 26:

> *The Port Alberni & District Labour Council, in conjunction with the B.C. Federation of Labour is sponsoring a rally and demonstration to protest the budget and removal of human rights in British Columbia, on Wednesday, July 27, 1983 at 3:00 p.m. on the steps of the Legislative Building, Victoria, B.C. Free buses will be leaving the I.W.A. Hall, 4904 Montrose Street at 10:00 a.m. July 27, 1983.*[10]

In the legislature, the NDP filibustered debate on every one of the government bills. Protest marches were held around the province. The government decided on closure. It was a controversial move to stop debate in the house. Kube pressed for a general strike. Throughout the summer, the province was in turmoil. Then 35,000 members of the BC Government Employees Union (BCGEU) hit the bricks on October 31 when their contract ran out. A week later teachers went on strike. Bus, ferry, and transportation workers followed.

Even more strikes loomed ahead. In November Jack Munro, president of the IWA, got involved. If the IWA's forty thousand members joined the other strikers, this would have led to a general strike, and union members would have lost a paycheque right in the middle of the biggest recession in recent history. Munro was in a difficult position for he was already in talks between the IWA and the forest industry, but his union executive urged him to get involved and try to stop a general strike. The BCGEU had settled, but rotating strikes by teachers continued throughout the province. No one was backing down; there needed to be a face-saving solution.

Big Jack opened discussions with the government, then flew to Kelowna to meet privately with Premier Bennett. After a few hours the two men reached a deal. Munro phoned the B.C. Federation of Labour's offices to get agreement to proceed; they voted unanimously to accept the agreement. There were some within the labour movement who thought that Munro had sold them out in Kelowna. Munro thought that Kube should never have been made president of the B.C. Federation of Labour, a job he inherited when Jim Kinnaird passed away suddenly in February 1983.

The province gave a big sigh of relief; the summer of discontent was over. But the forest industry, and Port Alberni, were about to be challenged on another front entirely.

{ *chapter ten* }

FORESTRY IN THE HOT SEAT

In 1983 the forest industry in Port Alberni was hit by one of British Columbia's major environmental stories of the decade. The problem had simmered since 1979 when MB announced plans to log on Meares Island in Clayoquot Sound as a winter show. The plan initiated major opposition on the west coast. The island lies adjacent to the village of Tofino, whose residents relied on Meares Island as a source of area water. Opitsaht village on the island is home of the Tia-o-qui-aht First Nation, a member of the Nuu-chah-nulth Tribal Council.

MEARES ISLAND LOGGING

When rumours circulated in Tofino in September 1979 that Meares Island was about to be logged, a coalition formed to fight the project. It was named the Friends of Clayoquot Sound (FOCS) and was headed by Harry Tieleman, a local businessman who operated Happy Harry's Fish and Chips in Tofino. The island was included in logging plans for both MB and BC Forest Products. In December that year, MB submitted for public display its five-year plan to log the island. According to law, the plan had to be displayed for thirty days. This was just enough time to rally forces in opposition to the logging. The province's chief forester Bill Young decided that an integrated resources management plan should be undertaken and he wanted public input.

The Meares Island planning team, chaired by district forest manager Russ Campbell, began studying the environmental impact of logging the island. Since Tofino's water supply originated on the island, the village had a vested interest in what happened there. An alternate source of water might have been Kennedy Lake, but the cost of getting the water to Tofino was prohibitive. Pacific Rim National Park Reserve opposed any activity that would have a negative impact on the environment or would detract from a visitor's enjoyment of the coastal landscape. No one wanted to see another giant clearcut like the "black hole," as it was known locally—an area logged twenty years earlier and replanted several times. This ugly blight on the landscape became a lightning rod for every argument made about clearcutting.

Alberni NDP MLA Bob Skelly requested a moratorium on logging on Meares Island and called for a public enquiry under the Environment and Land Use Act. This request was ignored by Social Credit Minister of Forest Tom Waterland, who wisely did not want to interfere with the planning process already underway.

The FOCS was the most vocal of the groups concerned, making an emotional appeal for the preservation of the island. But it seemed everyone had a stake in its future. The controversy over logging Meares Island gathered steam as picture-postcard scenes were shown on television screens across Canada. Campbell soon had a stack of submissions two feet high and more than 130 letters from across Canada. Most wanted the island left untouched; others voiced concern about the domestic water supply.

This small west coast island was going to be studied from one end to the other. As the study gathered steam, some questioned the future of the forest industry on the coast. Could it withstand the erosion of the existing land base in the interests of conservation or any of the other outstanding reasons being advanced to trim cutting rights? Already there were planning teams at work in Haida Gwaii, Tahsis, and now on Meares Island.

MB was often asked why it took the Meares Island wood supply so seriously, considering it only represented 3 percent of MB's total resources in the region. Company forester and economist Noel Brett-Davies explained that Meares was only one of three hundred areas in BC where the right of MB to log was being challenged, so it was an important symbol. The dwindling land base had some concerned about the future of the forest industry in the whole province, not just on the west coast.

In March 1983 MB quit the Meares Island planning team and suggested that any effort to tie up the trees through a deferral plan might result in the company taking the BC government to court. The company could not agree with any of the three options on the table: deferral, partial preservation, or total preservation. Campbell assured everyone that the planning team could continue without MB.

MB also made a good argument for harvesting the mature timber:

> *This is the most attractive undeveloped timber unit available to Kennedy Lake Division of logging during the winter months, January to April. Related to Alberni Pacific Division this would mean nine per cent of the 1983-planned production of 780,500 cubic metres. The total preservation of Meares would be a loss not only to the forest companies but also to the province.*[1]

The company estimated that total preservation could cost the province as much as $25 million in lost taxes and royalties, and MB would have to be compensated for the loss of part of its TFL. The twenty-six jobs that would be lost in the Kennedy Lake Logging Division currently generated $939,000 annually in wages and benefits.

This was serious. When the planning process began, the economy had slowed in the province due to the recession. Everyone in the Alberni–Clayoquot region was feeling the recession by 1983, with logging in decline and, more important to Tofino, fishing also in a downturn. If there was a bright spot it was that employment in tourist-related businesses had slightly increased—probably due to all the publicity around Meares Island.

The controversy heated up on June 2, 1983, at a public meeting held in Wickaninnish Elementary School in Ucluelet. Campbell described it as emotionally "highly charged." Three hundred people debated the logging project that had divided the two villages of Tofino and Ucluelet. The FOCS presented a twelve thousand–name petition opposing the logging. But the village council of Ucluelet, home of many of the loggers, favoured the plan. For three hours the people of Tofino argued with the loggers of Ucluelet. The meeting almost got out of hand but was brought under control by chairman Henry Nedergard, president of the Port Alberni and District Labour Council. The meeting ended with a vote overwhelmingly favouring a motion proposed by MLA Bob Skelly—that a logging moratorium on Meares Island should be continued for a time period established by consultation between all parties.

On July 4, just as the province announced its budget for the year, the Meares Island planning team forwarded its draft report to chief forester Bill Young. The report did nothing to resolve the differences between MB and those opposed to logging. The decision was now in the hands of the province.

By the summer of 1983, the mood in the whole province had soured. It would be remembered as the summer of discontent, with thousands rallying across the province to vent their anger with the government's restraint policies. The worldwide recession had played havoc in BC. Premier Bennett had tried to grapple with conditions never experienced before: declining prices for export products, high inflation, falling government revenues, and soaring unemployment rates. The term coined by economists was "stagflation" but it did not begin to describe the depth of the crisis.

From 1982 to 1984, employment in BC fell by 79,000, with losses of 3,100 in forestry, 10,400 in mining, 23,600 in construction, and 37,700 in manufacturing. Nearly half of the manufacturing decline was in the forest industry.[2] Between 1981 and 1985, almost 20 percent of British Columbians lost jobs that would not be replaced.[3]

In November 1983 the provincial cabinet approved a partial preservation plan for Meares Island. The Environmental and Land Use Committee (ELUC) released details of its decision. Eight hundred hectares (1,976 acres) of the island visible to the north of Tofino would be under a log-deferral for ten years, at which time the cabinet would again sit down and assess the area. The deferred portion contained the village's drinking water supply and answered concerns for the aesthetic view line for tourists and local residents. The area to be logged would be landscaped to protect the intrinsic sightlines.[4] Skelly was not happy with the partial preservation plan and asked Ombudsman Karl Friedman to investigate the decision.

In January 1984 Mr. Justice Reginald Gibbs of the British Columbia Supreme Court heard from the Ahousaht and Clayoquot bands who had filed a suit asking for a court order to prevent MB from logging Meares Island, where the bands had two hundred members. They asked the court to declare the TFL as void because, in light of their aboriginal claim, the government never had the authority to issue permits.[5]

The same court also heard from MB's lawyer Duncan Shaw, who stated that twenty thousand people were employed directly and indirectly by the forest industry on Vancouver Island but that these jobs could be in trouble if the Native bands succeeded in stopping MB from logging while their aboriginal claims were being decided by the courts. Shaw argued that if the bands were successful on Meares Island, it could lead other bands with claims to about 40 percent of Vancouver Island to seek similar injunctions, and this could shut down logging and sawmill operations. He said the implications were so enormous as to be inconceivable from the province's point of view. He named BC Forest Products and Tahsis Company as other major forest companies working on disputed land on Vancouver Island.

This application for an injunction to stop logging was allowed to proceed. It was the first of several lawsuits that would tie up the courts for years.

Meanwhile, Tofino's major concern about its water supply from Meares Island was resolved when the city received an $11 million grant for a much-needed water and sewer project. Tourism seemed for the first time to be an alternative to logging and fishing, with the possibility of developing this into a viable industry.

The Meares Island issue was brought before Port Alberni City Council on March 12, 1984 by MB regional forester Norm Godfrey, who expressed concern for the loss of this valuable forest resource to the company. He warned, "The loss of fibre for existing mill capacity is critical, especially over the longer term. The end result could result in permanent mill shutdowns."[6] Godfrey estimated there would be a loss of 130 man-years of jobs, and Kennedy Lake Division would lose one-half of its existing winter show. These were dire warnings for city council trying to manage affairs during the economic slowdown.

Spiked trees, threats of vandalism, protests—Tofino was hopping mad. Logging was scheduled to start in September

1984 near Heelboom Bay on Meares Island. Tofino surgeon Ron Aspinall, who opposed logging, put the fear into every logger and mill worker in Port Alberni with his rumoured threats of spiked trees. Henry Nedergard, the safety director for the IWA Local 1-85 in Port Alberni, tried to quell those fears. He found it hard to believe that anyone would spike the trees knowing that this would pose a serious hazard to loggers. Port Alberni mill workers processing the logs would also be at risk if undetected spikes damaged the equipment.

MB was fighting for a precedent. It wasn't just for the value of the trees but for the legal right to log, and it intended to go ahead with its plan anyway. An RCMP investigation found that steel spikes had indeed been driven into at least thirty first-growth trees, but it doubted the persons responsible would be caught. Paul Varga, manager of Kennedy Lake Logging Division, confirmed that employees using metal detectors had found spikes.

In October 1984, the Port Alberni IWA Local 1-95 voted to support MB's plan to log Meares, but the union decided not to battle environmentalists in order to work nor would it interfere with any demonstration. The union expected the law to protect the loggers.[7] In Victoria, meanwhile, Skelly stepped into the top job with the NDP following a leadership race to replace leader Dave Barrett.

MB sent an information leaflet into all the homes of residents in the Alberni–Clayoquot Regional District. The company estimated 240 jobs would be lost forever if Meares were not logged. This was broken down into 26 logging jobs, 29 in the plants in Port Alberni, 25 in converting plant jobs elsewhere on Vancouver Island, plus another 160 indirect jobs. Logging of Meares Island, already postponed several times, was now scheduled to begin in the winter of 1985–86.

The worst fear of protesters was realized when MB received official approval on November 16, 1984, to begin logging Meares Island. Russ Campbell said the cutting permits and all the necessary documentation was complete and MB could now move on to the island.

A few days later, logging crews were on their way. The island protest had reached a critical stage and environmental groups tried to generate as much publicity as possible. Could MB afford to lose the public relations battle? Could it afford hundreds of arrests in the woods? Could it tolerate children lying in the mud trying to save a tree? The environmentalists didn't think so. Port Alberni workers, who had a lot at stake, waited patiently for the west coast to settle down.

Meares Island became a land claims issue when the Ahousahts and Clayoquots claimed their people had never given up aboriginal title to the island, and their lawsuit launched earlier sought an injunction to stop all logging until the case could be heard before the court. Finally, on January 11, 1985, Mr. Justice Reginald Gibbs ruled that the Crown and Parliament were sovereign, even on Meares Island. Lawyers for the bands had failed to convince the judge that they had sovereignty on the island, which co-existed with the Crown. The environmentalists' lawyer appealed the decision. But Gibbs expressed little sympathy with the FOCS, stating its protest had no standing in law.

George Watts had promised that the Nuu-chah-nulth Tribal Council would save Meares Island. Watts had been involved in tribal politics for half of his life, and he vowed that Native people were not going to be taken advantage of on Meares. He said:

> *Non-Indian people made one mistake with us—they educated us, and we are not going to stand for it anymore. The pressure is boiling up in Native communities and things are going to blow pretty soon. Meares Island is a small part of the country—too much wealth in too few hands.*[8]

Until now MB's executives had been quiet on the subject of Meares, leaving it to regional managers to explain the company position. But the situation had reached a dangerous level, and they now felt the need to speak out. MB senior vice-president Bob Findlay went on the hot seat in the televised *Vancouver Show*, putting the Alberni region front and centre in the controversy. He released a strongly worded statement charging activists with using Meares as the first step in a campaign to stop logging completely. He said:

> *It's naïve to believe this debate is simply over our plan to log one per cent of Meares Island a year. We know that activists are planning to block logging on such islands as Flores and Nootka, north of Meares. If they are successful in blocking MB on Meares, every logging operation from Prince Rupert to Prince George and from Kelowna to Cranbrook could be hit with similar claims and opposition. I wish people would sit up and take notice before this thing strangles the economy of this province.*[9]

Findlay told *Vancouver Sun* columnist Marjorie Nichols that a legal solution could resolve the escalating controversy. He refused repeatedly to finger the provincial government for its position denying the legitimacy of land claims. When challenged about MB's sale of raw logs in the face of the expressed need to log Meares, he explained that the Alberni region must manufacture its own logs, and it was not economical to bring logs from the east coast of the island to the Alberni Inlet.

The company newsletter, the *MB Journal*, refuted some misconceptions about the island. It had been logged before, for one thing: as far back as 1905, and again in 1957, and again in 1972. The Sutton Mill, one of the first sawmills on BC's coast, was located on the island. Another fact surfaced about a noticeably logged area on Lone Cone's southwest face, visible from Tofino, that was attributed to Native logging during the mid-1950s.

In March 1985, the decision by the B.C. Court of Appeal sent shock waves throughout the forest industry. In a 3–2 decision, it overturned a ruling by B.C. Supreme Court Justice Reginald Gibbs that had given MB the right to log Meares. It ruled that MB could not begin logging Meares until the Native land claims were resolved. It was only a small victory because it only dealt with the injunction against logging, but it showed that the legal system must be more sensitive to what Natives were saying. MB said it would appeal the decision to the Supreme Court of Canada.

The opponents of logging on the island were jubilant with the court decision, but the IWA leader, Jack Munro, who never minced words, said on the Jack Webster show in March 1985 that the ruling was "a bloody disaster" for the forest industry. He blamed media attention focused on "kooky environmentalists" for blowing the Meares dispute "out of proportion."[10]

The next day MB chairman Adam Zimmerman met with George Watts to discuss the dispute. The informal meeting was a get-to-know-you session. Earlier Watts had gone before the House of Commons standing committee on fisheries and forestry, telling it that Natives would be satisfied with a land claims settlement giving them about 5 percent of Canada's natural resources. Watts planned to visit Zimmerman again in Toronto to continue their discussion.

MB took aim at the provincial Social Credit government, stating it should settle the land claims. MB's vice-president and chief forester Grant Ainscough said that MB disliked being painted the villain over Meares Island. The company wanted the BC government to get busy settling Native land claims. He urged bands to better organize their positions when dealing with companies like MB on forestry issues. He encouraged bands with multi-million-dollar oil revenues and other resources to lend their experience and expertise to impoverished bands.

Would this tiny island on the west coast of Vancouver Island be the key to a settlement of aboriginal land claims? For George Watts, chairman of the Nuu-chah-nulth Tribal Council, the fight for Meares Island had become his raison d'etre. He said:

We might get everything we want, but if we have to live in a world of tension for the rest of our lives, and we have to sentence our children to smart-ass remarks from white people because of a settlement, then what did we get for our kids? If we win Meares, other tribal groups in the province will go to the premier and say: "Mr. Premier, if you're not going to negotiate with us, we'll go to the courts too."[11]

Watts knew that when the case reached the Supreme Court of Canada, a ruling in favour of the Meares Island Natives could change the face of the province. Native bands claimed aboriginal title to almost half of Vancouver Island, a timber supply area that employed more than 28,000 people and supported manufacturing plants built at a cost of more than $1 billion. Similar claims covered large areas elsewhere in the province. The federal government accepted the claims for negotiation, although the BC government always told the Natives: "Your dispute is with Ottawa and not us." At the heart of the case was the question of aboriginal title: Who lawfully owned the land?

MB was in a difficult position. Meares Island had been in the public eye for over a year, and from a public relations viewpoint it had been a disaster for MB. The sight on television of Adam Zimmerman, president of Noranda Mines Ltd. and chairman of MB (of which Noranda owned 49 percent), holding forth from his Toronto highrise headquarters on the future of a small island almost five thousand kilometres away in BC was especially insensitive and guaranteed to provoke local wrath. The PR was bad. If MB wanted to speak on Meares, it should have been Ray Smith, president and CEO, as he lived and worked in Vancouver and was more in tune with local sensitivities.

Some accused MB of corporate arrogance. It was a battle the forest company couldn't hope to win in the age of television and a savvy news media. Images of Native elders teaching youngsters how to steam clams over an open fire, or Natives carving traditional canoes from huge cedar logs, or a flotilla of small boats blockading loggers with chain saws, or women singing protest songs in the rain, all these scenes, accompanied by sympathetic commentary, were aired on the evening news across Canada. The optics were bad—and offensive to the MB executives, especially when a carefully positioned shot only showed the back of a protester's head as he hammered a big eight-inch metal spike into a tree. There were some who likened this protest to that of the East Coast seal hunt, where protesters painted the fur of baby seals to make them valueless.

Those who worked in the forest industry felt they were in the middle of a storm between MB and the environmentalists. In Port Alberni, the good feeling they once had about working in the woods was being challenged every day they went to work.

A DANGEROUS PROFESSION

Some working in the forestry industry were being challenged in other ways as well. The recession hit everyone in a different way. Being unemployed was bad; being unemployed and disabled was devastating. Working in the forest industry can be a dangerous profession. One of the most tragic stories to emerge during this difficult time of the recession was that of Wolfgang Zimmerman and Sven Fredrickson, two employees of MB's Sproat Lake Division. They lodged a complaint with the BC Human Rights Commission for "being denied continued employment." Zimmerman, age twenty-five, a paraplegic, and Fredrickson, age sixty, a quadriplegic, claimed that MB had treated them unfairly by placing them on "indefinite layoff."[12] The basis of their claim was that finding employment, as compared with able-bodied men, would be almost impossible. Their case set a precedent for all disabled workers in BC and was the first of its kind originating from the Alberni Valley.

Zimmerman had come to Canada from Germany in 1976 and went to work for MB, planting trees for three months. In June 1977 he was working with a forestry crew doing roadside work, brushing and clearing trees along the road edges, when an alder tree barber-chaired and damaged his spinal cord. "Barber-chairing" is a term used to describe a sudden splitting of the tree as the result of insufficient undercutting. The young man was whipped on the back and thrown in the air, fracturing two vertebrae causing spinal damage. He had only been on the roadside job one week, had received no prior training and was unsupervised at the time of the accident. Married only one year to Heidi, he wondered whether he was going to live:

> *I found that being in a wheelchair is literally hell on earth, especially when everything you did was centred around your physical well-being. The turning point for me was when we went shopping for the first time and I was in a wheelchair. It was unbearable being so restricted, so limited. The following Monday I went to GF Strong Rehabilitation Centre and said, 'From now on, that wheelchair is staying at the centre.'*[13]

The important factor in his recovery was the support given by family and friends. Heidi stayed in Vancouver while he underwent therapy. Before long the wheelchair was gone—a testimony to the young man's tenacity. Zimmerman now wore leg braces from the knee down and walked with a cane.

Fredrickson had become a quadriplegic in 1975 as the result of a logging accident. He had been a logger all his life. He graduated from forestry at UBC in 1951 and two years later went to work for MB. He was a member of the logging camp safety committee and known to be a cautious man. On the day of his accident, he picked up the crew, drove to the worksite, and dropped a dozen or so trees. By 10:30 that morning he was paralyzed from the armpits down. The tree he was cutting had swung around with such force that it snapped his head forward, breaking his spinal cord.

Few can imagine the agonies a big man like Fredrickson went through adjusting to life in a wheelchair. It also affected his family life. Two years after the accident his wife passed away as a result of the stress. His home had to be renovated to accommodate a wheelchair. A wheelchair kitchen was installed, and Workers Compensation Board built a ramp to the front door. Yet his movement was still limited; no more hunting or fishing like he used to do on weekends. Now he needed a full-time attendant whose salary came from his WCB Disability Pension; Fredrickson carried his own medical insurance. Without these services he would have been in an intermediate care home.

Both men worked at Sproat Lake Division where a program called Jobs for the Needy was initiated, a project that ensured work for those with a disability. They were not included in the program, however, because everyone thought they were being taken care of.

In 1980 Sproat Lake Division asked Fredrickson to come back to work. He was unsure he could do the job and was a little reluctant to accept the position, but agreed to go back on a thirty-day trial basis. To his surprise and delight they kept him on. He loved working.

Zimmerman's story was similar. A year after rehabilitation at GF Strong Rehabilitation Centre in Vancouver, his future prospect for employment was discussed with MB. In March 1978, a new forestry operations recordkeeping system was introduced in all MB woodlands operations and the divisional forester saw an opportunity to employ him. So Zimmerman began work again in the office while taking courses at North Island College. He did his job so well he was offered a similar job doing administrative work in the office.

Both men continued to work successfully for two years until MB was hit by the recession. In September 1982, Zimmerman was advised he would be working for only ten more days, just enough time to allow him to clean up the backlog from the spring program. He was placed on the indefinite layoff list and told that salaried staff would carry out his duties. It was a similar situation with Fredrickson.

There is no doubt the economy was a factor in the layoffs. Sproat Lake Division hourly workers were reduced from 435 to 230, and the workload was drastically reduced. But an irritant for Zimmerman and Fredrickson was the fact that their jobs were still being carried out by able-bodied staff.

The two men mounted a campaign that went to Premier Bill Bennett's office, to the office of the opposition NDP leader Dave Barrett, and to Calvert Knudsen, chairman of MB. When local MLA Bob Skelly approached regional manager Bob Findlay about their situation, Findlay said he expected the government to provide a safety net.

A letter to the editor of the *Alberni Valley Times* from Nick Bos, IWA first vice-president, expressed the dismay of employees at Sproat Division over the company's treatment of the two disabled employees being laid off:

> *The economy and the takeover by Noranda has had an effect on everyone. These guys are like a cancer on MB. It would have been better if they had been killed. Then they could have forgotten about them. Since 1950, 10 people from the Sproat Lake Division have been killed. We now have a hard time remembering their names. There were 48 deaths this year in BC's forest industry and the industry hasn't been working full-time, one-third. Sven and Wolfgang should be allowed to do their job, even if it is only a few days here and there.*[13]

Fredrickson was offered a settlement of $14,000 for early retirement. He felt insulted. "This money couldn't even buy me a van which would cost $17,000."[14] He hired a lawyer to make an assessment of the case with the possibility of a lawsuit. Zimmerman called Mike McCardell, a well-known reporter who covered human-interest stories for BCTV News. The news program had dozens of repercussions. Eventually the premier's office intervened and Zimmerman got a commitment from MB that he would be employed.

As a result of their fight and with the help of the Human Rights Commission, both men managed to bring their cases to a satisfactory conclusion. (In July 1983 the province abolished the Human Rights Commission.) Zimmerman reached a settlement and went to work at the Kennedy Lake Division while continuing studies at North Island College, eventually graduating from the business administration program. In 1986 the CBC *Journal* shot a half-hour documentary with him titled *Insult to Injury* about the challenges faced by people injured at work.

Fredrickson received a written contract that stated he would have a part-time job with MB until his retirement. This meant he would now receive all benefits until there was a job available.

Zimmerman and Fredrickson had seen the face of the disabled forestry worker and decided to do something about it. They helped in founding the Disabled Forestry Workers Foundation of Canada, along with Peter Lawrie of MB; Earl Foxcroft, former president of IWA Local 1-85; and Brian Payne of the Canadian Paperworkers Union. Before long they had established the National Institute of Industrial Disability Management and Research at North Island College.

With funding help from MB, Associated Film produced a one-hour documentary titled *Every 12 Seconds,* a grim reference to the frequency of disabling industrial injuries in Canada. Zimmerman was the executive producer; he hoped the film would dispel the "it won't happen to me" attitude of most workers. Some money earned from the film paid for construction of a centre for the disabled in Port Alberni. The centre offered education and counselling to anyone disabled in a traumatic accident, something that Zimmerman knew about first-hand. On June 25, 1992, he received the Order of BC at Government

House in Victoria. The award recognized his advocacy work on behalf of the disabled.

In October 18, 1994, when North Island College officially opened its new Port Alberni campus, the renamed National Institute of Disability Management and Research opened its new facility adjacent to the college, with another $2 million in an endowment fund—$1 million each from the federal and the provincial governments. The institute would train management in industry and would focus on adapting the workplace to maintain employment for disabled workers.

Ray Smith, chairman of MB, admitted his company had made a mistake in 1982 when the two injured forestry workers were overlooked during the downturn as jobs around the Alberni Valley were falling by the way. "It was wrong to let them go," said Smith. He called them "trench fighters," crediting their lobbying with getting them re-employed by the company.

{ *chapter eleven* }

THE FLOODPLAIN DILEMMA

Port Alberni City Council faced another difficult situation in 1983. To comprehend the problem, it is necessary to understand the destruction of the 1964 tsunami that devastated the lower parts of Alberni and Port Alberni, and the corrective measures that were taken afterwards to alleviate flooding on the Somass River Delta.

Following the 8.5 earthquake in Alaska on March 27, 1964, a tidal wave raced down the west coast of the Pacific Ocean at speeds up to 720 kilometres (447 miles) an hour. Four hours later, around midnight, while residents of the Albernis slept, water silently crept up the sides of Alberni Inlet into Stamp Harbour and up the Somass River, covering all the low-lying streets and the cars parked there. Within twenty-two hours, there were a total of thirteen wave cycles. Only three were significant, and only two caused damage. But what damage.

The old town of Alberni, sitting at the mouth of the Somass River, was hardest hit. Fortunately there were no deaths, and only a few minor injuries were recorded among the 694 people displaced by the wave. However, there were 375 properties damaged and 55 washed away. The Water Rights Branch conducted a study shortly after, recommending River Road be raised and Kitsuksis Creek dyked, and the unprotected land along the Somass River purchased for parks and marina purposes. These improvements, it was considered, would provide flood protection.

In 1969 dykes were constructed but the city was unable to purchase the land because of financial limitations. For the next twenty years the picturesque area on the western edge of the city where the first settlers had farmed was prone to periodic flooding and became a source of consternation for city councillors and the provincial government.

The problem lay in the geographic configuration of the river and creeks. The Stamp-Somass River watershed drains into the Alberni Inlet. Lugrin Creek has two main branches, which both drain into Kitsuksis Creek via two culverts equipped with flap gates. During high tide, the flap gates closed and water backed up in Lugrin Creek, flooding the area.

With the mid-1970s already turbulent years for local politicians, city council was reluctant to make crucial decisions regarding the floodplain. Some residents requested permission to develop their property, but the city engineer advised city council against it. Meanwhile, the provincial government dragged its heals on yet another study; it had already borne the cost of previous studies in 1959, 1964, and 1978.

Following severe flooding in other areas of BC, the province asked all municipalities and regional districts to enact zoning bylaws. The Port Alberni zoning bylaw already had the provision that the floor level of any "habitable room" be no less than 3.2 metres (10.5 feet). This standard had been adopted following the 1964 tidal wave; it was based on local knowledge of high flood levels, not on any scientific data.

Since the high-water mark of the Somass River was 1.4 metres (4.5 feet) and the province wanted regulations on buildings at 3 metres (10 feet) above the high-water level, city council had no recourse but to recommend the bylaw be 4.4 metres (14.5 feet). The city said this was too restrictive, and suggested it should conform to the flood protective works. What ensued was a reduction to 3.6 metres (12 feet) for subdivisions that had already registered their building plans. Anything new would have to wait for another study. Some residents raised their house anyway because of the constant flooding.

Another city bylaw dictated that no fill be allowed in the area west of Kitsuksis Creek. Those residents who still wanted to develop their properties were refused by city council, which started an ongoing battle. In 1977, six hundred homeowners signed a petition protesting their tax assessment. They were successful in getting a 25 percent reduction, though only for a year.

Taxes in the floodplain, and the price of homes there, were similar to those in other areas of the city. But there was no sewage system in the floodplain. Still, people enjoyed living there. Some described it as "almost country," and it was a desirable area for young families. The small bungalows situated in the rural setting yet close to town seemed the ideal place to begin married life and raise a family. With a small farm located behind the area giving it an almost rural setting, residents could see many fruit trees and the occasional chicken or cow in the summer. Being close to the Somass River, the land was ideal for gardening and a beautiful place in the summertime. During the winter, however, at high tide, many unsuspecting new homeowners were stunned to open their door one morning and find water up to their doorstep and the entire street flooded.

Flooding occurred almost every winter during heavy rainfall. In March 1981 floodplain residents jammed city council chambers demanding sewage service for their area. Spokesman Ernie Rusel, who worked for the Port Alberni Fire Department and lived in the area, presented council with a petition signed by residents. He told council they were tired of being treated as "second-class citizens." But council said it was morally obliged to refuse the sewage system petition until the city-provincial tidal wave study had been completed. Residents were getting tired of waiting for studies; they wanted something done now about the problem and began pressuring city council. They considered taking the city to court.

The flooding only seemed to worsen each year. The situation reached a crisis on February 11, 1983, when record rainfall swamped the floodplain in knee-deep water. Resident Trevor Jones's septic field backed up into his bathtub; in fact, the entire neighbourhood went without toilets for a day. Complaints were made to the health inspector for the area. MLA Bob Skelly was contacted, as were Mayor Paul Reitsma and members of city council. Residents felt no one was listening to their concerns. Alderman Walter Behn introduced a motion asking the Ministry of Environment to require real estate agents to inform prospective buyers of the flooding problems. But he quickly withdrew the motion when residents complained their area would be geographically referred to as the "floodplain," which would lead to deterioration in property values.

Area residents decided to take action by forming the Lugrin Flood Association (LFA). The LFA hired a private engineering firm from Vancouver and together they mapped and walked the entire creek from end to end for about a week. The cost of the report was close to $80,000, money the LFA did not recoup. It was this report that was eventually used by the government to make improvements.

The 150 members of the LFA asked the Vancouver law firm of Russell and DuMoulin to investigate solutions and possible legal proceedings. In April 1983 LFA president Trevor Jones, whose bathtub had been flooded by sewage two months earlier, presented city manager Jim Sawyer with a letter of intent notifying the city of an impending lawsuit. "It is about time we took a stand," said Jones. "The only answer for us is court. There's too much at stake for everyone here."[1] Jones, thirty-five, married with two sons, worked as a provincial park ranger and had just moved back to Port Alberni in 1981 and bought a house in the floodplain. His mother, Bonnie Jones, worked for the city before retirement and lived in the area. Trevor Jones recalled:

> There was a terrible human side to the problem with people losing their homes, and divorces etc., which made me work even harder for my friends and neighbours that I grew up with.[2]

The LFA sought damages for the February 11 flooding; no dollar figure was put on the damages. This was not a class action suit, as only LFA members would benefit from a favourable decision.

Chief Justice Allan McEachern presided at a pre-trial hearing held in Nanaimo Supreme Court in September 13, 1983. Earlier in the day the 150 members assembled at Nanaimo Civic Arena and made a protest march to the historic courthouse on Front Street. CJAV radio station sent along Ike Paterson to cover the event. Surprised at the large turnout, he wondered out loud who Trevor Jones was and remarked that he had never seen such organization. I was representing the *Alberni Valley Times*. Extra chairs were brought in to accommodate the overflow crowd. When he saw the crowd the judge joked, "I didn't know you were having a big party."

Bill Berandino, representing the LFA, gave a short history of the sequence of events leading to the flooding. The City of Port Alberni's lawyer Bill Beckingham said the arguments that the city failed to help and failed in the design were not substantiated. He said it was important to find out whether the residents had moved into the area knowing of the flooding and had done nothing to protect themselves. His comment caused some laughter in the courtroom while people, obviously annoyed, shuffled in their seats. "They could have put up sand bags, or something," Beckingham continued flippantly.

Beckingham was a well-known lawyer in Port Alberni with his own law firm, Beckingham & Company. His record of service to the community was well known; he was a former school board trustee, president of the Alberni Valley Chamber of Commerce, and had served on the Port Alberni Harbour Commission.

The lawyer for the province, Don Clancy, supported Beckingham in his arguments. McEachern promised an early trial date.

In the meantime, Port Alberni City Council did its best to avoid the floodplain issue. But more and more it was drawn into open debate. Trevor Jones believes he lost his job with the government because of his involvement. In October, he decided to run for alderman in the city. On advice from Beckingham, returning officer George Wiley, who was also the city clerk, refused to accept his nomination paper and affidavit for election. Wiley stated that a section of the Municipal Act states that those who have a "disputed account" with a municipality are not allowed to run.

At the October 3 council meeting, Jones asked to speak about his eligibility, but before he got to the podium, Mayor Paul Reitsma read a prepared statement disassociating council from the decision making and leaving Jones to pursue the ruling before the courts. Jones argued he had done nothing but try to help some people find a solution to their problem. If he was denied he vowed to launch a lawsuit against the city. Reitsma suggested that Jones's difference of opinion was with the returning officer. Jones planned to ask a judge to rule on that decision. "Appearances before council are for people who want to address council on urgent and important matters," Reitsma declared.

There was more flooding on November 15, and once again the LFA threatened a new lawsuit. Their previous trial date was set for April 15, 1984.

On November 18, Jones and some of his supporters were in the audience at a city council meeting. He felt good about the decision made that day by the courts to allow his name on the ballot for alderman.[3] Helping with his campaign was the city's deputy fire chief Ernie Rusel. They both had stated openly that they supported Alderman Gillian Trumper for mayor. When the city manager made the standard announcement before the opening of the council meeting, "All rise for the mayor and alderman," the first person to appear was Trumper, followed by other aldermen. Rusel smiled, made a slight bow and with a sweep of his hand whispered, "Your honour." Trumper blushed and smiled, a little embarrassed. Those in the council chambers didn't miss the implications. Mayor Reitsma was last to arrive in chambers and may have wondered why everyone was smiling when he turned around to deliver his short prayer. The entry procession of aldermen and mayor into council chambers was normal, but on that Monday night there were other overtones.

Another lawsuit was filed for damages for thirty-seven plaintiffs flooded during November 1983. Jones showed his frustration when he said, "Some people in Port Alberni still do not understand what the LFA is fighting for. Our problem is with Lugrin Creek, and we will not stop until the problem is rectified."[4]

Residents in the area were angry and didn't look forward to another two or three months of winter. There could be more lawsuits. The record rainfall total for November was about 300 millimetres (11.8 inches), already surpassing the average total for a typical November.

At the November 1983 civic election, Gillian Trumper was elected as the new mayor of Port Alberni, defeating Paul Reitsma. Jones had the satisfaction of running in the election, though he did not get elected.

In February 1984 city council hired an independent engineer to investigate and advise on the Lugrin Creek flooding. Allan M. McCrae would act as an expert witness during the trial due to begin in the Port Alberni Law Courts in April. The cost would be shared equally between the city and the province.

Just days before the lawsuit was due to go to trial, the LFA agreed to a settlement with the city and the province over the flooding in the Lugrin Creek area. There were no celebrations, only cautious optimism. The trial was adjourned for six months to give time for the terms of the settlement to be met. This could mean as much as $300,000 would be allocated to solving the flooding problem. The city would contribute $200,000 while the province gave $100,000, and the Crown agreed to pay up to $50,000 toward legal costs and apply for federal funds to finance work in the area. In return, the LFA gave up claims to damages. It would have to make up the difference in its legal costs.

This was a bittersweet victory for the people along Lugrin Creek. Their problem of flooding would now be corrected, but it had cost them financially. Jones called it a victory. Before the project was completed the costs had escalated to $450,000 and the city went to the province seeking additional funds. During the first storm in January 1986 there were no reports of flooding even though 71.5 millimetres (2.8 inches) of rain fell, breaking a record set in 1959.

Jones tried once again in November 1984 to run for alderman and was again rejected by the voters. He subsequently moved to Mackenzie to work in the sawmill, and now lives in retirement on Vancouver Island.

{ *chapter twelve* }

A YEAR OF CELEBRATION

THE FORESTRY CAPITAL OF CANADA

There was a certain irony about the City of Port Alberni being named Forestry Capital of Canada in 1986. For the previous five years MB had been fighting off protests from environmentalists as it tried to log Meares Island as a winter show for the Kennedy Lake Logging Division. What happened on the west coast had dire ramifications in Port Alberni where the logs were processed, and the city was smarting from the bad press MB and the forestry industry were receiving. Mill workers feared they might find a spike in the logs they were processing, and loggers saw their job diminished by bad publicity. Residents had difficulty feeling sympathy for the environmentalists as they passed through town on their way to the protests on the west coast. So everyone hoped that perhaps good publicity from being named the Forestry Capital of Canada would counteract the negative feelings about the town.

Port Alberni City Council charged ahead with a full year of activities. MB was foremost in all the accolades and events, but this was the year of Expo and the big fair in Vancouver perhaps overshadowed the city's celebration.

Alderman Joe Stanhope, chairman of the Port Alberni Forestry Capital Committee, welcomed visitors to the area in the souvenir edition brochure inviting them to look at the miles of regenerated forests:

> *Visitors to this area can see the majesty and grandeur of our virgin forests in Cathedral Grove at MacMillan Park and the vastness of the rain forest on the outer West Coast. Some of these trees were growing when Christopher Columbus discovered America in 1492.*
>
> *Visitors to the Port Alberni area can also see miles of thriving groves of regenerated forests. Modern logging can be seen as well as the finished finest products being shipped around the world from modern converting plants located here in Port Alberni. Our future depends on reforestation and we are confident that with continued care, this new forest will provide succeeding generations with a livelihood.*[1]

Joining Stanhope on the committee were Mayor Gillian Trumper and aldermen John Bathurst, Bud Schroeder, Don Whyte, Nita Jack, and Walter Behn. MLA Bob Skelly sent his congratulations on the designation. He hoped the recognition would result in greater priority being given to maintaining a highly productive forestland base and a healthy, diversified forest industry, which would provide jobs and economic benefits for years to come. MP Ted Schellenberg also offered best wishes and continued success. In the House of Commons, he said, "I express the hope that National Forestry Week will create 'a tidal wave' of support for our number one industry. Our forests are our future."

There was even a message from Minister of State (Forestry) Gerald S. Merrithew, who wrote:

> The community of Port Alberni typifies the hundreds of communities throughout the province, and the rest of Canada, which rely upon the forests as the mainstay of their economy, and whose citizens enjoy the bountiful pleasures the forests can in turn provide them for recreation and relaxation. Forest land is without question the most valuable natural resource held by the Canadian people.[2]

Merrithew recognized that forestry was the undisputed top resource in the province, and that one out of every four persons derived their income from the forest sector.

MB conducted tours into the forest for visitors and locals alike. Each area had a marker showing when it was planted. Mayor Trumper planted MB's 60 millionth seedling in the Alberni region, a fact that ended up on some prized coffee mugs. The company promised to plant its 63 millionth tree. After her tree planting experience, the mayor was presented with a yellow "Boss Logger" hard hat at a council meeting; this was her second one, the first being given by BC Hydro during the construction phase of Alberni Harbour Quay.

Minister of Forest J.H. Heinrich pointed to change within the forest industry in his statement of congratulations.

> Changes will continue to be made in the future. Forestry is a dynamic science as are the sciences associated with wood conversion. So also, will legislation and policies change to meet ever-increasing and complex social and economic demands placed upon the resource.[3]

A regional resource map was drawn showing attractions in the area, including the J.V. Clyne Bird Sanctuary, the Baeria Rock seabird colony, Stamp Falls Park and the fish ladders, and Robertson Creek Fish Hatchery, plus all the parks and trails. The map depicted a recreational paradise.

No one mentioned Meares Island. No one mentioned the trials or the conflict. No one from the Nuu-chah-nulth Tribal Council spoke about land claims. For the time being, the subject of Meares Island was before the courts and out of the public eye. Everyone was happy to accept the accolades being offered the city for the present. Town boosters thought it was time to show Alberni Valley pride in the forest industry that had been the economic driving force in the region for 126 years.

Social community events did well during Forestry Week in April. The IWA sponsored a Logger's Stomp dance in the Canadian Italian Centre; there was a Miss Port Alberni Pageant and ball and a Golden Oldies dance. All these events sold out. The town was clearly ready to celebrate! But in the summer of 1986, the news headline was the big fair in Vancouver.

CONTRIBUTING TO EXPO '86

Premier Bill Bennett welcomed the world to Expo '86, a showcase of transportation, technology, culture, and people. Prince Charles and Lady Diana opened the event in the new BC Place Stadium. For the average British Columbian, however, it was businessman-tycoon Jimmy Pattison who would be remembered for welcoming them at the gate every day with his broad smile putting a positive face on the event.

Pattison said later that he was only one of the people who helped put on the Exposition. "There have been 96 Expo Committees formed in the small towns of British Columbia. There have been literally hundreds of projects of which Expo has been the catalyst. If there are heroes of this Exposition, they are the volunteers and the people of the small towns of British Columbia who've supported us from day one."[4]

Communities throughout the province became part of the Expo celebration. Visitors to Port Alberni were welcomed at the top of the hump with flags and an Expo garden. For weeks residents had watched with anticipation as the giant mound of dirt became a beautiful garden. The city had a hard time keeping the flags on the pole, though, and several were taken as souvenirs. Port Alberni also hosted an exchange master carver from New Zealand. During the summer he carved at the Alberni Harbour Quay, amazing all with his skill.

Close to seventy thousand people packed BC Place Stadium on opening day May 2. Most of Port Alberni City Council attended, and another hundred residents of the city were given tickets courtesy of MLA Bob Skelly. Each MLA in the province had received a hundred tickets for their communities. Mayor Trumper joined dignitaries at the opening reception at the Pan Pacific Hotel. Alice Chiko, who had made a bid for the Social Credit Party in the last election, was invited to cruise with the royals from Nanaimo to Vancouver on board the *Queen of the North*. Another hundred people were invited on the cruise.

My invitation to the opening ceremony, embossed with the provincial coat of arms, came in the mail. It stated what we were to wear: men in business suits, ladies in an afternoon dress. Audrey's Ladies Wear in North Port did roaring business getting women suitably attired.

There was so much to see and do at the fair it required several visits to see all the pavilions. Fifty-four countries from around the world and provinces from across Canada opened pavilions, buildings, and tents. There were lineups everywhere, but no one seemed to mind, as there was always something to talk about while waiting to get into an exhibit.

At the start of the fair the weather did not co-operate, and it wasn't until July that the sun came out and then stayed until Expo ended on October 13. A record one-day visitor count was 341,806. The event originally estimated to attract 14 million reached 22 million.

The Expo Centre bandstand during the day became a nightclub in the evening. Via Rail turned a working train station into a showcase for rail transport. Everyone saw, and could ride, the new SkyTrain that was being proposed for Vancouver.

The food at Expo was a cultural feast. No one will forget Port Alberni's own "Cod Father" as he wooed visitors with his delicious smoked salmon products, and fish and chips. Alderman Joe Stanhope delivered about 113 kilograms (250 pounds) of Port Alberni salmon on August 19 for a barbecue at Stanley Park, courtesy of the city and held for those working in the pavilions. Stanhope ended up filleting and cooking some of the fish himself.

Logger's Sports, and the Boom Boat Ballet of choreographed marine tugboats, showcased the rough and tumble side of the forest industry. In the evening fireworks across the harbour brought the day to an end in spectacular fashion.

PORT ALBERNI'S PRIDE

Steam Expo was a chance for everyone to get involved in the thrill of the rails. Port Alberni's Western Vancouver Island Industrial Heritage Society display was a big hit. The heritage group took the old logging engine 2-Spot and various pieces of forestry equipment to Vancouver to be part of the event. The venerated old engine was cleaned, greased, and painted in preparation for the show. Then two weeks before the opening, it was loaded onto an E & N Railway freight flatcar heading for Nanaimo and a ferry to Vancouver.

The opening day of Steam Expo was May 23, 1986. Steam locomotives from across the country took part in the Grand Parade of Steam, and 2-Spot was there chugging away carrying with it all the pride of the Alberni Valley. Leading the way was Vancouver's Royal Hudson steam train.

Port Alberni music schoolteacher Barry Miller, an avid train enthusiast, wrote about that memorable parade:

> *Then came 2-Spot with her bell clanging and whistle shrilling in the gentle breeze flowing from Burrard Inlet. Smoke belched and steam hissed as 2-Spot emerged*

from under the overpass and put on a display that had the crowd breaking into enthusiastic applause. In the cab, grinning from ear to ear, were engineers Mark Mosher and Dick Grandy, firemen Dave Lowe and Clem Rousseau.

Upon reaching Cardero Street, Mark Mosher told me that the last half hour had been one of the greatest moments of his entire life. Dick Grandy was for the first time in his life almost speechless and tears flowed from his eyes. He had not slept in over 40 hours due to the pressure and excitement of getting ready for this moment.[5]

Taking their place as conductors were Ken Rutherford, Irvin McIntyre, Rick Lord, and Barry Miller. The firemen were Dave Lowe, Darcy Windsor, Clem Rousseau, Hugh Grist, and Doug Wilson. Hundreds stood in line to view the Port Alberni display of the 2-Spot, a steam donkey, a Hayes Logging truck, and a Wee McGregor saw. Local contractor "Soup" Campbell erected an A-Frame loader on the site to transfer logs from the truck to the skeleton car. Society president David Lowe was thrilled his group's participation at Expo had made everyone in the city proud.

Port Alberni's talented musicians and dancers had an opportunity to perform on the Expo stage as part of the regional representation from around the province. Coordinating the performers from the central island region was a busy time for me, organizing the adjudication while still working full-time at the newspaper. Meg Scoffield helped coordinate the judging in ADSS auditorium in the spring while I was in surgery at the hospital. At the Plaza of Nations, the Funshine Dancers from the Pat Cummings School of Dance performed "Logger's Stomp," with original music and choreography showcasing loggers working in the woods and the spirit of the forest industry. Almost four thousand people watched these young dancers take to the stage lighting up their performance with enthusiasm and pride.

Expo gave everyone in the province an opportunity to celebrate, and for a brief few months to forget the recession of the past few years and the trouble in the forest industry. The Expo legacy is still enjoyed today with Science World, Canada Place (formerly the Canada Pavilion), BC Place Stadium, SkyTrain, and the annual dragon boat races in False Creek.

TWINNING WITH JAPAN

The year 1986 was also the year of the "twinning" of the cities of Port Alberni and Abashiri, a city of forty thousand people in northeastern Hokkaido, Japan. A delegation from Abashiri had visited Port Alberni in October 1985, receiving a warm welcome and an introductory tour of the city. After visiting the west coast of the island they returned to Port Alberni for a Thanksgiving dinner at the home of Mayor Gillian Trumper. This preliminary visit did much to cement relations with Abashiri, and an exchange visit was to be arranged for the next year.

A delegation subsequently was scheduled to visit Abashiri in February, with School District 70 trustees Jim Spencer and Linda Derkach joining Mayor Gillian Trumper and Alderman Walter Behn. This Japanese trip, however, created a dilemma for the city. Mayor Trumper wanted to present a city flag to Abashiri in return for receiving one from that city. The city flag had been debated for years without any decision being made. It had been discussed under former mayor Paul Reitsma, with aldermen Len Nelson and Ken Hoffmann on the flag committee.

Now the pressure was on. There was a note of quiet desperation as the councillors tried to decide between two designs. One was an enlarged city logo—four green stylized trees radiating from a central point and enclosed by a black circle, all on a white background. The other design was identical except it replaced the black border with a gold border. Both examples hung limply from the coat rack in the committee room. The councillors showed no enthusiasm for either one.

Alderman Joe Stanhope threw a wrench into the debate by questioning the possible inconsistency between the flag and the city logo. The logo was just being registered but was already on city trucks, for example. If the gold-bordered design was chosen for the flag, would the city have to change all the logos on the trucks to match? Would the gold ring stand out? Mayor Trumper expressed her concern. Alderman Bud Schroeder declared, "We need a flag," and moved approval of the gold-bordered design. His motion carried, with dissenting votes from Stanhope and Alderman Nita Jack. Now the flag could be produced in readiness for the Abashiri trip in February.

But the story of the flag did not end there. A few weeks later the subject arose again. Mayor Trumper produced the newly designed flag, which no one liked; she felt she could not present it to Abashiri. Could another flag be produced with the black instead of gold trim by the weekend when they were to leave for Japan? She was assured it was possible. And it was done. When the mayor came into the newsroom to show us the new flag, she was happy and said she would be proud to present it to the mayor of Abashiri. So ended the great flag debate!

The official twinning ceremony and signing took place in Port Alberni on May 22. The Japanese visitors returned home with gifts from the city of ninety kilos (two hundred pounds) of salmon from the Smokehouse. The vacuum-packed salmon was sent to Japan to see how marketable it would be over there and how well it travelled.

For the past two decades plus, there have been many visits back and forth between the two sister cities, making important cultural contributions to each other and strengthening the bond between Canada and Japan. The twinning has also benefited 820 Abashiri students and 400 Port Alberni students who have crossed the Pacific on cultural exchanges.

A YEAR OF POLITICAL CHANGE

Halfway through the Expo '86 fair, Premier Bennett announced he was retiring. Instantly, Bill Vander Zalm was thrust into the spotlight. He easily won the leadership race at a conference in Whistler. Even before that, "Vandermania" was sweeping the province. With his wife, Lillian, wearing her stylish sixties headband, Vander Zalm flashed smiles, kissed babies, shook hands, and generally swept away all opposition with his charm and charisma. On a campaign stop in Port Alberni, an organ had been set up in the centre court of the Port Alberni Mall. Hundreds milled about while George McKnight, a known socialist, happily played "Tiptoe through the Tulips" before the huge crowd. Everyone wanted a photo taken with Vander Zalm.

Unfortunately, within a few years Premier Vander Zalm would be embroiled in a conflict-of-interest controversy over the sale of his Fantasy Gardens theme park in Richmond. The problem arose when the Taiwanese buyer, Tan Yu, was provided with VIP treatment and lunch with the Lieutenant-Governor prior to the sale. Although Vander Zalm claimed that control over the theme park was his wife's responsibility, the case went before the BC Supreme Court and resulted in his resignation. Rita Johnston succeeded him in 1991.

When the year 1986 drew to a close, a few people wondered whether anyone remembered that Port Alberni had been designated Forestry Capital of Canada. During the year, alderman John Bathurst had replaced Joe Stanhope as chairman of the committee. But a woodworkers strike put an end to any mention of the honour bestowed by the Canadian Forestry Association. Mayor Trumper wanted to end the year on a high note and suggested a "walkway of trees" to honour past city mayors. The suggestion was received politely, but no one took up the challenge. It had been a busy year.

{ *chapter thirteen* }

INTERVIEWS OF NOTE

During the eighties, while working for the *Alberni Valley Times*, I interviewed many people. Most were local, but occasionally there were people of note who were visiting on holiday or to fish, like Jack Webster, or who came on a book tour, like Stu Keate. Meeting these two seasoned journalists was an honour. I was also privileged to meet and interview a few aging cougar hunters, their lives linked to these beautiful wild cats. Almost every area of Vancouver Island had its own cougar hunter; they were vital to the safety of the community.

NOT JUST A PAPERBOY

When I interviewed him in 1981, Stu Keate, the former editor of the *Vancouver Sun*, reminisced about the early days of Port Alberni. His presence at North Island College, then in the old Smith Memorial School, was for a Paper Festival event celebrating the ninetieth anniversary of the first paper mill in Port Alberni.

Keate had just published his memoir, *Paper Boy*. His amazing career had started with the Vancouver *Province* and the Toronto *Star*. After the Second World War he worked for *Time* magazine, first in New York and then in Montreal. Later he became publisher of the Victoria *Times* before moving to the *Vancouver Sun*. In 1974 he was elected to the Canadian Newspaper Hall of Fame, and in 1976 he was named an officer of the Order of Canada.

Now retired from the newspaper business, Keate had spent the past few years writing his memoirs. His doctor had advised him to keep busy in his retirement. Since he had started in journalism as a writer, drifting later into administration, he was curious to find out if he could still write stuff people would read. With forty-five years of journalism to his credit one would have thought he would have no trouble getting it published.

The rough draft of *Paper Boy* was sent to McClelland & Stewart to see whether they were interested in publishing it. Jack McClelland replied that while he liked the idea of the book, he wanted it rewritten with considerations to such questions as "What is the significance of the *Globe and Mail* in Canadian journalism?" The question didn't excite Keate enough to answer it. A second publisher also rejected the book. Finally, it was accepted by Clarke, Irwin & Company. Keate told me that his greatest satisfaction with the book was the proof he could do it—produce 100,000 words that people would read.

He found the challenge of critics, whirlwind tours, talk shows, and bookstore receptions fascinating. Of hearing himself introduced on a TV station as "a man who goes back to the earliest days of the press in Canada," he said, "This reminded me of the fellow who approached me on the street in Vancouver, just before I retired, put out his hand and said, 'Didn't you used to be Stu Keate?'"

Keate was no stranger to Port Alberni, particularly Sproat Lake, where he spent many summers, starting in 1920. The dominant recollection for him was "the majestic stand of timber, virtually unspoiled, and it appeared to be one giant forest all the way from Nanaimo to the valley. Something like Cathedral Grove is today, but wilder." His family connection began even earlier, in 1907, when his parents spent their honeymoon at Klitsa Lodge, on Sproat Lake.

> They made the journey in a stagecoach driven by Jack Burke, who became a great friend. I recall my mother telling me that at one point in their conquest of the summit, passengers had to debark and help push the coach over the top. The lodge, situated on the end of the peninsula, presented a bit of a transportation problem for incoming guests. There was no road. What they did was unload their bags near Bishop's Landing on Faber Road, then ring a bell or fire a shotgun, which would summons a boat from Klitsa Lodge.[1]

He recalled some of the colourful characters at Sproat Lake. One was Cornelius Vanderbilt Jr., who bought the island opposite Klitsa Lodge as a gift for his wife and "stormed around the lake in a high-powered boat, flying the Stars and Stripes. Vanderbilt was fond of wearing a red bandana on his head and filing stories to the *New York Post* about his life among the wild Indians of Vancouver Island."

Another character he recalled was Hilmer Weiner:

> ... he was by far, the most formidable figure at our end of the Lake. Weiner was either Swedish or German, I have heard him described as both, immensely talented —a cabinet-maker, boat builder, house contractor and creator of superb violins which he fashioned entirely from local elements, even to the stain which he boiled up from salal. I will never forget the smell of the boiling salal.

The Weiner legend has become part of Sproat Lake history. In September 1944, at 2:30 a.m. a violent explosion shook the Weiner property. The house and buildings went up in a fireball. The blast was heard throughout the valley, Keate recalled.

Some people struggled out of bed and were amazed at what they saw. But there evolved a mystery, which remains, unsolved to this day. Where was Weiner? Who touched off the conflagration? Some suggested he might have drowned in the muddy waters of Weiner Bay.

The RCMP searched and even had the area bulldozed and found no trace of Weiner. A search of the outbuildings turned up a few chips, which indicated a case of arson. Keate said the case remained a great mystery. "In 1946 when I was working for *Time Magazine* in New York, I submitted an article on the strange disappearance of Hilmer Weiner to an outdoor magazine. I received a letter from the editor saying he liked the story but 'it had no ending.' If Weiner turned up, they would publish the piece."

Keate's father, William Lewis Keate—Louie to his friends—was a timber broker who bought and sold logs and timberlands. When his father had a deal on, his mother would tell the children, "Be quiet tonight, boys." If successful, there was new clothing for everyone and bills got paid; if the deal collapsed, belts were tightened.

Keate remembered being cheered once when his father sold some Rockefeller forest on Barkley Sound in the Port Alberni area. He said the buyers were the Bloedel people and they paid $1 million.

"'Isn't that great?' I said to my mother when she told us the good news. 'Now Dad will have $100,000 for his commission.'" Keate told me his mother smiled wanly before replying, "Yes, it's great, except that he owes $94,000."

THE PEOPLE'S ADVOCATE

For more than twenty years of open-line talk on radio and on television, Jack Webster played the people's advocate for a generation of British Columbians. Nicknamed the Oatmeal Savage, referring to his Scottish upbringing, he took on countless politicians, grilled labour leaders, and challenged businessmen. Interviews were like using a surgeon's scalpel: he could pick and probe people's brains, and he goaded and delighted in seeing his guests squirm before live television audiences. There could not have been a more recognizable personality in British Columbia, nor one more loved.

My interview with Jack Webster was on a summer day in July 1985. He had just caught six fish and was a happy man, all smiles as he milled about the crowd gathered at Alberni Harbour Quay. Webster was the guest of Bruce Thomson of Alberni Pacific Charters and his fishing guide was Gary Knapp. Thomson had written inviting him to visit and offering a fishing trip.

When I met Webster at the waterfront location, he was laughing and joking as cameras clicked. He introduced his two grandsons, Duncan and Angus Troup, who were on holiday from Edinburgh University in Scotland. Webster was a father of four, a grandfather of nine, and a devoted husband. It was just a few months after his wife, Margaret, had died after forty-six years of marriage.

When one Scot meets another Scot, the first thing that happens is you identify the location of the accent. With Webster there was no doubt; the thick twang of his Glasgow upbringing was evident instantly.

"Where're ye from?" he asked me, recognizing another Scot.

"Strathaven," said I.

"Oh, isn't that where the man with the crooked legs and crooked stick came from?" he asked.

"You mean Sir Harry Lauder?"

"That's him."

Sir Harry was a well-known entertainer-personality from my home town. He was a singer and songwriter who performed in full Highland dress with kilt, sporran, and tam o'shanter and always with a twisted walking stick, which became his trademark.

Later in the interview I asked Jack, "What do you think of Port Alberni?"

Webster replied that, judging by different news reports, he thought we were in trouble. "But just look around. This is fantastic," as he waved his hand at the beautiful waterfront just teeming with tourists on this warm and sunny July day.

Someone yelled at him, "Why don't you do a TV show from here?"

"Not a bad idea," Webster responded, adding he would consider coming back to do a show during the spring run in September.

Ted Smith, from Smith's General Store at the Quay, pushed a large ice cream cone into his hand. I joked to him about his Pritikin diet. "I know, I shouldn't be eatin' this," he said as his tongue lapped away and the ice cream dripped down the side of the waffle cone. He told me he had lost thirty pounds since starting the diet.

"Is he a Socred?" he asked of Smith.

"Yes," I replied.

"I thought so." Webster nodded as if pleased with himself for having guessed correctly.

Webster had been called many things over the years—Oatmeal Savage, Haggis McBagpipe, the Mouth that Roared, and some unmentionables. His gruff, probing mind and sharp tongue had grilled many a politician and left them spent. He loved putting guests on the spot before the cameras. But there was another side of Webster—on this day, I found a warm, friendly, engaging man, "Grandpa" to Douglas and Angus.

He said he had joined the Glasgow *Evening News* fifty-three years ago, but despite his long experience in the print media he enjoyed television the best. Webster came to Vancouver in 1947, and eventually became city editor of the *Vancouver Sun*. He quit the newspaper in 1953 in a dispute over overtime. Later he joined Radio CJOR and made his mark becoming one of the best known open-liners in the business. He joined BCTV in 1978, where television viewers watched his thick, grey eyebrows rise and his facial expressions change by the minute. "They can also see the twinkle in your eye, Jack," I joked. He laughed, loving every minute of the attention. Webster told me, "I will be back on the air on September 3, on BCTV at 9 a.m. prree-cisely."[2]

Following the fishing trip, Webster took a flying trip over the Alberni Valley with Greg Trenholm of Pacific Rim Airlines. His weekends were spent on his farm on Salt Spring Island until he passed away in 1999.

Webster also had another side to him; he appeared regularly on CBC's *Front Page Challenge*, an able match for another Scot, Gordon Sinclair, the crusty elder Toronto broadcaster who died in 1984 at age eighty-three. The two auld Scots, both journalists, made for memorable television commentary.

COUGAR CATCHERS

Ada Annie Lawson, also known as Cougar Annie, was one of the most interesting characters from the west coast I interviewed. Long before I met her, I had written about her life at Boat Basin, fifty-one kilometres (thirty-two miles) north of Tofino. She was a strong-willed and feisty character. Ada cleared land in the middle of the forest, a task that would challenge the pioneer spirit of the woman. She and her husband built a log cabin and began growing vegetables and raising chickens and goats on the 48 hectares (118 acres) of raw land. It took her twenty-five years to clear the land. When money was short Ada had an idea of growing and marketing dahlias, a business that grew to the point where she was shipping dahlia bulbs all over the world.

Ada became better known as Cougar Annie because of the number of cougars she had to kill to protect her goats and chickens. At one time there was a bounty on the big cats, and in 1955 she killed ten and earned herself $400. She was reported to have shot sixty-two cougars and more than eighty bears in the forty years she lived on the farm.

She married three times and gave birth to eight children. All her husbands worked the land with her, building up the nursery business. Ada also ran the Boat Basin post office from 1936 to 1971, until "the government discovered I was eighty-three and made me retire," she said.[3]

I got to meet Ada on the occasion of her ninety-sixth birthday with family and friends at West Coast General Hospital Extended Care Unit. The era of the cougar bounty huntress was passing; her memory and eyesight were fading and she had no teeth left. The years of hard work were taking their toll, but you could still feel the strong will and spirit of this grand old woman. She died in the Port Alberni hospital on April 28, 1985.

Cougar Annie was not the only cougar hunter; there were many on the island during the thirties and forties. Cougar Harold Brown earned a living hunting the big cats. My interview with him was in 1984 on the occasion of his ninety-ninth birthday. We met at his friend's apartment on Third Avenue. The room was full of friends, all there to celebrate his birthday and his long and colourful life. Many stories were told that day of his exploits, amidst choruses of raucous laughter while the old cougar hunter sat smiling in a big easy chair, obviously enjoying all the attention.

Brown was born in Washington State, and started hunting cougar for a living in 1909 in Texas. He moved to Port Alberni in the mid-1930s because, he said, there was more game there. At that time, Vancouver Island was overrun with cougars and a professional hunter could net forty dollars a kill; a non-designated hunter only got twenty dollars. The big cats were killing off the deer populations, and scaring the daylights out of parents afraid to let their children walk or play outside.

He lived south of the city in the Franklin River area in an old shack without electricity, telephone, or running water. His water came from a mountain stream nearby, and light came from Coleman lamps. A portable radio kept him in touch with the outside world. His only companions were his cougar hounds. Occasionally loggers from the Franklin River camp dropped by to make sure he was all right. When he wasn't hunting cougar, he worked in the logging during the summer. By 1951 he had bagged about two hundred cats. When the provincial government took the bounty off cougars in the mid-fifties, it put Cougar Brown and his dogs out of business.

{ *chapter fourteen* }

PEOPLE OF THE ALBERNI VALLEY

The Alberni Valley has been home to some amazing people. Their achievements—some recognized, others perhaps taken for granted—enriched the community in so many ways. Collectively they made Port Alberni a lively, exciting, friendly place to live. Most came from "away" but settled in the area and raised their children there. Perhaps it was the isolation of living in a town surrounded by forest that brought out their creative instincts and dedication to a cause. Whatever the reason, everyone benefited.

HONOURABLE CITIZENS

Each year the Kiwanis Club of Port Alberni, with its annual Citizen of the Year award, shone the limelight on one of the many individuals who worked quietly in the community making a difference in the lives of others. These are the stories of four of these recipients.

The first recipient of the award was Helen Patenaude, a familiar face around the Alberni Valley. Bill Patenaude was manager of Woodward's Department Store; the couple had three children: Valerie, Stephen, and Paul. When the Patenaudes moved to Port Alberni, Helen took her adopted community to heart. She had worked with Native people in Vancouver and became involved with the Port Alberni Friendship Centre, including serving on its board of directors and with its ladies' auxiliary. She was also a member of the Rainbow Club. She tried to help Natives spread their culture by marketing their carvings and encouraging them to be productive. As a member of the Holy Family Notre Dame Church she served on the parish council. She was elected to the school board for Smith Memorial School, an independent Catholic school in Port Alberni, and also worked with Big Brothers and the Catholic Women's League.

Helen was the first coordinator of the Port Alberni Family Guidance Association and instrumental in establishing Meals on Wheels in the area in 1972, and the Homemakers Association. For a time she also served as chairman of the Parks and Recreation Commission. She and Bill both volunteered with the Lion's Club on various projects. An advocate for strengthening family ties, she worked at the provincial level for the B.C. Council for the Family, eventually becoming president in 1980–81.

Her focus was always the institution of the family; when she saw it faltering, she single-mindedly went about doing her utmost to strengthen it. When the recession hit the community she said, "Never before has the need for a strong family base been more vitally needed and it will take each of us in our own sphere to do what we can to assist in this strengthening process."[1]

Helen was also a regular contributor to the *Alberni Valley Times*, writing articles on family life. When she died in November 1982, the Woodward's store closed to allow staff to attend her funeral. A fund was established in her name to raise money for the B.C. Council for the Family to develop videos and other materials to create awareness for strong family values.

Retired teacher Hope Porter was named Citizen of the Year in 1981 for her years working with the mentally challenged. Mayor Jim Robertson and alderman-elect Art Wynans presented the award in December 1981 during a musical theatre performance of *Fiddler on the Roof* at ADSS auditorium. The award surprised her, as she didn't feel right accepting a reward for doing something she really enjoyed.

Among her many achievements, she was involved with the Sheltered Workshop, Arrowsmith House Group Living Home for the Retarded, the Learning Place Preschool, the Infant Development Program, the Vancouver Island Training Program, and Citizen Advocacy Group. For eighteen years she also found time to work with the Pat Cummings School of Dance as a dressing room supervisor.

Twenty-five years earlier, Hope, along with Bill Brown and Howard McLean, founded the Alberni District Association of the Mentally Retarded and started a school in the basement of St. Alban's church. Later, her Beaufort School for the mentally challenged was the first in the province to be built on the same grounds as a regular school.

Her husband, Les, was supportive of her efforts. He once took a week of his holidays to help her take twenty-five mentally challenged children on a week-long camping trip.

Art Wynans praised Hope:

She took the kids everywhere ... no one was left behind, no matter how profound the handicap. She had been known to lift wheelchairs over logs, down gullies, and through uncharted woods, so that all the children could enjoy a picnic by the river.[2]

She was more than just a teacher, Wynans said; she had always been a source of hope and inspiration to the parents of mentally challenged children when they had no one to turn to. Her selfless dedication to the mentally challenged was duly honoured.

Doris Gray was another woman whose service to the community was recognized with a Citizen of the Year award, in 1982. Unable to attend the ceremony because of a serious illness, the announcement was made in the newspaper. Known as Dot to her friends, she was dedicated to the Canadian Red Cross and operated the Red Cross Loan Cupboard as a volunteer.

She and her husband, Bob, had moved to Port Alberni from Ocean Falls in 1947 and raised four children there: Robert, Brent, Grant, and Brenda. Bob worked with the city works administration. Brenda later recalled a time when a neighbour, a mother of four children, had a brain tumour. Dot went in to see if she could help. The woman was very sick, so Dot took the children home with her, and then she took the mother to hospital, where she died. Dot then found homes for the four children. "I remember waking up one night and finding a strange kid in bed beside me. The kid explained, 'Your mum said she would take care of us.'"[3] Those children, now grown, became close friends of the Gray family.

The Red Cross awarded her their prestigious Certificate of Merit in appreciation of her volunteer services to the community. To understand the scope of the job with the Loan Cupboard, consider that Dot had 561 "patients" in 1980. Each one who phoned for a piece of equipment—a wheelchair, walker, hospital bed, vaporizer, or commode, for example—became one of her patients. She took an active interest in their well-being and followed their progress toward recovery. This she managed from the lower floor of her home. She was available twenty-four hours a day. Her husband remembered once dropping her off at someone's house with a piece of equipment. She emerged three hours later—the patient had needed to talk to someone.

As well as the work with the Red Cross, Dot also coordinated the emergency lodging and food sections of the Provincial Emergency Program for the community. She was a busy woman, but still found time for her garden and for finishing antique furniture.

Dot died on December 14, 1982, a week after being chosen Citizen of the Year. Mayor Paul Reitsma said he felt privileged to have presented her with the award.

In 1983 the Citizen of the Year award was presented to Helen and Armour Ford, in recognition of their contribution to a multitude of community organizations for over twenty-five years. They received the award from Kiwanis president Egon Matheson, alderman Art Wynans, and Mayor Gillian Trumper.

The Fords were known for their donation of a 52-hectare (130-acre) property on Sproat Lake that became Fossil Provincial Park. They also willed to the regional district their home and three large lakefront lots for future recreational use.

The list of organizations the Fords gave their time to is long. It includes the Museum and Historical Society, Rollin Art Centre, West Coast General Hospital Women's Auxiliary, Kiwanis, Sproat Lake Ratepayers' Association, Port Alberni Friendship Centre, Mt. Klitsa Garden Club, and the Anglican church. They also provided scholarships for local students. The Navy League Cadet Corps was named after Armour Ford in honour of his long involvement with cadets. Armour said the award was "a great compliment. We never pictured ourselves as Citizens of the Year. We just like doing certain things. You can't sit at home."[4]

The Fords had moved to the Alberni Valley in 1958, but Helen's roots went back further. Her father, F.C. Manning, held a business interest in Sproat Lake Sawmill Ltd., located where the flying tankers were later situated. He also purchased the Fossil property, which he gave to his daughter in the 1940s. At that time, Helen was serving with the Canadian Women's

Army Corps, attaining the rank of major. She met Armour at the University of Alberta in Edmonton where they both earned degrees—she a bachelor of commerce; he a bachelor of arts and later a law degree. Armour served overseas as commander of an army artillery battery, reaching the rank of Lt. Colonel.

After moving to the Alberni area, the Fords worked quietly in all aspects of the community to make it a much richer place for everyone.

ARTISTS AND ARTISANS

When I first became involved in the local art scene, I was amazed at the number of talented artists and craftspeople who lived in the area. Editing the Community Arts Council newsletter Tawasi, and later Raincoast Arts, I got to know many of them on a personal basis. Crafts were just a hobby for some, but for others this was how they made their living—glass-blowing, pottery, weaving, carving, to name only a few of the categories. In the visual arts field the situation was similar; there were some hobbyists and some professionals. All were willing to share their talent either through an exhibition or a craft fair, or contribute to fundraising efforts for local charities. The following are some of these very talented people who called Port Alberni home.

In July 1983 I had the privilege of walking through a garden on Eighth Avenue in South Port. It was like stepping into another world. Paths wound past carefully tended rose beds, large urns made and designed by the owner were filled with flowers, and in the centre of the garden was a large fountain built to commemorate the forming of the colony of British Columbia. Instead of grass there was Irish moss; the owner explained that grass doesn't take well in the rainforest climate with its acidic soil conditions. The flowering moss looked like a beautiful soft carpet. For Canada's centennial in 1967, a wrought iron railing had been fashioned for the front porch and on it were the musical notes for the first few bars of "O Canada."

This was the garden and home of Peter Szachiv, seventy-five, a man who was born and raised in the Ukraine and graduated as a mechanical engineer. For a time he worked as a mechanic in a glass factory in Karkiev, Ukraine, before leaving that country for Belgium. After five years there he decided to come to Canada with his wife, a graduate chemical engineer. There was sadness in his voice when we talked about these early years, but he brightened up when we discussed his work in Canada. Proud of his Ukrainian heritage, he was also a proud Canadian.

The Szachivs came directly to Port Alberni, where Peter worked for a time with Souther Construction, first as a labourer and then as a carpenter. Later there was a stint at a machinist job for MB Sproat Lake Division. His wife died in 1971; their son, Boris, and grandchildren live in Surrey.

Szachiv's craftsmanship can be found in various churches in Port Alberni. He designed and built the steeple on top of St. John's Ukrainian Orthodox Church on Roger Street. A block away, in St. Mary's Orthodox Church, he made the pulpit and tabernacle, and he also did interior work in St. Alban's Church. Other church designs are located in Waterloo, Ontario, and Montreal, Quebec, as well as in Seattle, Washington.

To celebrate BC's hundredth birthday, Szachiv designed and made a mosaic tabletop featuring the dogwood and the centennial motifs in blue, white, and gold. For this he cut, ground and fitted into place about a thousand pieces of ceramic tile.

Over the years his reputation as a craftsman reached the mainland. A steady stream of visitors came not just to see his garden but also to see his musical instruments, all carefully designed and crafted. He has made balalaikas, guitars, harps, and bandores, and created a new instrument that can be played as a guitar or a mandolin. Creating musical instruments was not something he received training for; it began as a hobby.

"First it was toys then I started making musical instruments. Each time they got better," he said.[5]

When the Vancouver Symphony was in town one of the musicians played a harp designed and made by Szachiv. She dropped in to see him, then returned with other members of the symphony. Since then other musicians have come from Vancouver to see his work.

As we toured his home, we wandered down into his basement where he has three workshops: one containing about fifty machines and tools, some of which he made and designed, and others he improved or modified; another workshop with woodworking tools; and the drafting workshop where he sketches his designs and displays pictures of some of his creations. Szachiv has also created a large number of wooden items such as lamps with wooden bases and wooden-crafted lampshades, bowls, and boxes with inlaid wood patterns. Hanging on the wall was a quote: "It is not necessary to know how to do; it is necessary to want to do."

Peter Szachiv created a world of art around him—in his home, in his church, and in his community—and brought countless joy to many.

In 1983 the Alberni Valley Museum opened an exhibition of his work, *A Life of Craft*. Joan Frohn-Nielsen, of the museum advisory committee, praised the artist for his talent: "He is a rare example of the person whose vocation in one field provided the basis for an avocation in another."[6] Many of his creations are now housed in the museum. His work can also be seen at the Rollin Art Centre, where he created a concrete balustrade and classical fountain for the gardens. The Community Arts Council presented Szachiv with an Honour in the Arts Award in June 1987.

Aileen Devereux was the first recipient of the Community Arts Council Honour in the Arts Award, in 1981. Along with Bob Aller and Roy Innes, she founded the CAC in 1965.

Early memories of her life in Prince Rupert, where she was born, were not good. Needing something to give her a sense of security, Devereux turned to art. There were no encouraging words from her parents, who constantly downgraded her work. She remembered being so angry with her parents when she was six that she took down the curtains, cut them up and made a dress. This earned her her first spanking.

Tom Devereux came into her life in 1939 and they were married the following year in Vancouver, eventually moving to Port Alberni in 1944. Their marriage produced three children: Tommy, Dennis, and Julie. As with many young mothers, she felt the need to get out and meet people and have a sense of fulfillment. This prompted her to join the Alberni Valley Art Group. She took her first art lesson from Rose Colpman, a well-known local artist. Later she was inspired by the batik work of Cliff Robinson, whose work she had seen in the home of Bob Aller. She recalled:

> *I was thrilled with it and began researching the art of batik. In those days there was no public library in Port Alberni and not much information around the subject. It took me many years to master the art. The Community Arts Council awarded me a grant of $100 in 1972, which I used to take a month's course on printmaking at the Vancouver School of Art. I received first-class honours for the course. After that I was on my own learning all I could by trial and error.[7]*

Devereux mastered the art of batik and her work has been featured in many exhibitions.

Always willing to lend a helping hand, she became involved with helping an elderly gentleman, eighty-five years young, named John Halfyard. Her work with him added a new dimension to her own work. Halfyard had come to Canada from the Jersey Islands, where it was common to make dolls from paper. One he had made, the Christmas doll, was made from wrapping paper. Devereux recognized his talent and convinced him to make the dolls of more durable materials. She continued to help him in this until his death at the age of ninety-four, together amassing a total of two hundred dolls. The Cartwright Gallery on Granville Island, in Vancouver, held an exhibition of the highly regarded Halfyard dolls. Some of the prized Halfyard dolls were sent to Ottawa, while others are in the Alberni Valley Museum.

Devereux's work also touched the Friendship Centre in Port Alberni, where in the early 1970s she gave lessons in printmaking and instructed on silkscreening techniques.

Aileen Devereux's interests and talent influenced many organizations and individuals. While she continued to study and upgrade her own work, she was generous with her own time in helping others who needed lessons and encouragement to discover what they could do for themselves.

When do you stop being a teacher and become a full-time artist? In retirement, of course! Some people look forward to retirement; others are reluctant and skeptical about the future. Many are faced with deciding what to do. Marianne McClain, teacher at A.W. Neill Junior Secondary School, faced this dilemma head-on when she retired from a lifetime of teaching and decided to take the plunge into a new career as a full-time artist.

She began by holding a retrospective of watercolours and fabric designs at the Rollin Art Centre in July 1981. The exhibition of her work dated back to 1941 and included a wide range of media, colour, and techniques—a compliment to this versatile artist. On view was work done during the period when she taught at the Vancouver School of Art, when she worked with Lawren Harris of the Group of Seven, when she was custom designing fabrics for New York and Montreal, and when she prepared a brief to present to the federal government that eventually led to the Massey Commission. The future looked bright for the retired teacher-artist.

While still in high school, McClain had received instruction from Jack Shadbolt; she then graduated from the Vancouver School of Art in 1941. Her career started as an assistant teacher in the night school program. She was also a staff artist for Vancouver General Hospital and a designer for Bogards Wilson. This was followed by a three-month post-graduate period at California College of Art, where she was the third woman to attend from BC; the other two were Emily Carr and Beatrice Lenny. "I met Emily Carr in 1941 and Beatrice was a very good friend," McClain reminisced.[8]

In 1944, she was appointed assistant in the Design Department at the Vancouver School of Arts, then spent two years in London, England, adding to post-graduate studies and teaching at the Chelsea School of Art. While there, she also found time to take a music degree for teaching voice.

Returning to Vancouver, she taught art then opened her own studio of design, custom ceramics and fabrics, where designers from New York and Montreal came calling. She married William (Bill) McClain, also a teacher, and in 1960 they moved to Texas where she continued to teach art and dance at the Negro College. Bill was head of the Math Department. Another move came in 1962, this time to Michigan, following the birth of son Bradford. She now had an MA in Humanities (Art, Drama, and Music), and was a music teacher at Eastern Michigan University.

The McClains arrived in Port Alberni in 1969 and she began teaching at A.W. Neill Junior Secondary School. Since then, McClain served on many committees involving the arts and was active in theatre, staging, costume design, and directing. She was a member of Arts Action, the provincial committee on art in education, and a member of the BC Art Teachers' Association as well as the BC Drama and Music Teachers Association.

When I interviewed her in 1981 this dynamic woman was working on two major commissions. One was a ceramic sculpture entitled *Suffer the little children to come unto me* for the local Baptist Church lobby. The other was for the chapel at Shawnigan Lake School, where she was designing a ceramic font and a Raredoss curtain, a decorative screen behind the altar. There was no limit to this woman's artistic energy.

NOTABLE PROFESSIONALS

Over the years I interviewed many local businessmen and women, some in the medical field, some facing retirement, others just taking care of business, all adding to the quality of life in Port Alberni. I was interested in their background and what brought them to the city. We shared a lot of stories, and a few laughs, as we reminisced about their lives. One thing they all had in common was the love they had for the city. The following profiles present only a few of these notables.

Dr. Garnet Reynolds is better known to most of his friends as "Red." He moved to Port Alberni in 1950 and has been a practising chiropractor every since. Born in Leslie, Saskatchewan, into a family of nine brothers and one sister, his early life was spent on the family farm. He learned early that many of the old health care remedies carried a great deal of truth. He was about twenty-one years old before he saw the inside of a doctor's office, he said, because his parents always knew a remedy for whatever ailed them.

Reynolds's early education was at Foam Lake, Saskatchewan. He worked in Manitoba, Saskatchewan, and Ontario, until the war years interrupted his youth. He joined the King's Own Calgary Tank Regiment and spent the next four years overseas, taking part in the Dieppe raid in 1942. He served as a tank commander in the Sicilian and Italian campaigns. This led to a commission as a lieutenant before being discharged in 1946. He also attended the Royal Military College at Sandhurst, England. While there he found time to court and marry a young Canadian girl, Mildred Whitman, in 1942.

Returning to Canada, he enrolled at the Canadian Memorial Chiropractic College in Toronto, and was one of the first graduates in 1950. He brought his practice back west and settled in Port Alberni. Red and Mildred had four children: sons Larry, Terry, and Leslie, and daughter Rhonda. Mildred operated her own business, Reynolds' Flower Shop.

Over the years, the medical profession has not always recognized the profession of the chiropractor, but Reynolds felt he always had a good relationship with local doctors; some even referred patients to him, and he to them.

In a mill town like Port Alberni there were a great number of back injuries. Reynolds often spent time at the mills lecturing workers on the care of the back and how to avoid injury. He said, "I send most of my days adjusting spines."[9]

As the third-longest-serving chiropractor on Vancouver Island, he observed the tremendous growth of his profession through the years. When asked what made a good chiropractor, he listed these qualifications: a pleasing personality, marked by kindliness, sympathy, patience; a real desire to serve and a manner that inspires confidence; high moral character, sound judgement, and respect for professional ethics. Garnet Reynolds had all of those qualities.

Reynolds was a tireless worker, not only for his profession but also for the community. He was a charter member of the Legion Branch 450 in Toronto and held many offices in the Port Alberni Branch 55. He had thirty years of perfect attendance at the Rotary Club, was Master of the Masonic Lodge, and was an active member of St. Alban's Anglican Church, serving as a Sunday School teacher. He was president of the Junior Chamber of Commerce, chairman of the Port Alberni Harbour Commission, and also served twelve years as alderman. He was a life member of the Alberni Curling Club. Reynolds was president of the Vancouver Island Chiropractic Society and in 1975 was made a life member of the Canadian Chiropractic Association.

If a man's worth is measured by the service he gives to the community then Dr. Dick Garner is a giant among men. He came to Port Alberni in 1934 and gave fifty years of service to the community.

When I interviewed Garner with his wife, Eleanor, I found a quiet unassuming man who shied away from publicity and didn't think his life was so extraordinary. "Whatever you write make it short," he demanded. Throughout his many years working as a doctor in Port Alberni he never lost faith in the town. "It will grow and grow, even after MacMillan Bloedel has gone. There will be people all the way from Nanaimo to Port Alberni," he predicted.

To reinforce his point he told the story of a conversation he had with Prentice Bloedel, owner of the Bloedel company, prior to its merger with MacMillan in 1951. (Garner was fuzzy about the actual date of the conversation.) "If I've got to sell, is Port Alberni going to be finished?" Prentice had asked him. "I am sorry to say, I can't go on. I think it [the town] is going down," he continued, disheartened. Garner told him, "This is a nice country and not too old. There will be people all over the Island and Port Alberni will be part of it." Garner added to me, "But he sold out."

Garner was born in Ohio in 1900 and went to Europe at eighteen to fight in the First World War. He joined the United States army's 177th Infantry Rainbow Division and fought with the French under Douglas McArthur in the last battle. Garner was with the "shock troops." Only five hundred came home, he said. "We lived on horse meat," he recalled. After discharge he tackled several factory jobs, even bought a farm in Marshfield, Wisconsin.

Still not content, in 1922 he went to work for a casket company, but a year later he went back to Marshfield hauling milk. By this time he had decided he would finish school and in 1925 he went to Chicago. While studying at night school he was a driving instructor by day. In 1928 he enrolled in university on a scholarship, supplementing his income as a bodyguard to a City of Chicago alderman. About this time in his life the Chicago police picked him up. Garner explained:

> *They [the police] had found a machine gun hidden under the stairs of the house where I lived. They thought I was Dean O'Banion. He [O'Banion] was later arrested for killing 28 of Al Capone's members.*[10]

Garner said he wasn't scared at the time he was arrested; it was only later when he was released and home again that it shook him up a little. Dean O'Banion was an Irish-American mobster who was the main rival of Johnny Torrio and Al Capone during the brutal Chicago bootlegging wars of the 1920s. Members of Capone's outfit murdered him in 1924.[11]

He graduated from university in 1931 and moved to Vancouver to work at the Vancouver General Hospital. Three years later he moved to Port Alberni to join the practice of Dr. Joe Thomas. Thomas practised medicine in the Carmoor Block on Argyle Street. Their office and examining rooms were so small, "when one doctor had a patient, the other doctor walked in the hallway."

Within three years he had established his own practice. There weren't many doctors in town then. Garner recalled Drs. Allan Miller, J.C. Thomas, W.D. Higgs, C.J. Hilton, and A.D. Morgan.

About this time he met Eleanor. An operating room nurse was needed at West Coast General Hospital and Eleanor applied. She had been the night supervisor at Vancouver General Hospital. They were married in 1935 and had two children, who became Dr. Richard Wm. Garner, an orthopedic surgeon, and Dr. Susanna Lee, who taught at the University of Washington. Eleanor and Dick have four grandchildren.

Some might think it unusual for a doctor to belong to the Alberni Valley Chamber of Commerce. Garner didn't think so and was quite active. It was Chamber of Commerce members, including Garner, who helped prepare the paths of Cathedral Grove. He remembered the occasion well, and also the difficulty getting volunteers for the job. Lumberman Frank J.D. Barnjum had saved Cathedral Grove in the late 1920s, he said, but it was much later before work on the trails actually began. The government later laid out the well-travelled pathways known today.

Garner enjoyed the outdoors and liked to go fishing. He recalled Roy Taylor's dugout canoe being pulled up the Somass River to go out with his fishing buddy Alec MacDonald.

Garner's service to the community is intertwined with the activities of the Port Alberni Rotary Club, which he joined in 1940; he served as its president from 1957 to 1958. Rotarians know about community service. They passed a resolution in 1923 that stated the objectives of the club, one of which Garner knew well. It stated: What is the job that needs doing? Is there a community agency that can do the job? If so, co-operate and strengthen, don't duplicate. If not, start the ball rolling with the appropriate project, which may in time generate its own agency.

Dr. Dick Garner got the ball rolling on many projects and got the job done. Some of the many initiatives he was involved in include the River Road Park in 1949, the high school oval in the 1950s, and the establishment of Harbour Park, the location of the Sea Cadet Hall, plus the Rotary Beach House at Paper Mill Dam Park. His long years of service were recognized in 1984 when the Port Alberni Rotary Club honoured him at a special luncheon. A donation to the Rotary Foundation was made in his honour.

Archie Clouston was a chartered accountant in Port Alberni for thirty-six years before deciding to retire in 1984 in the town that anchored his professional career. At age seventy-two, he now looked forward to flying trips with his friend Harry Stirzaker, on Harry's Cessna float plane, with him as navigator.

The two friends had spent many hours flying, with trips to Alaska, northern British Columbia, and the Arctic.

Clouston had graduated in Alberta in 1942 as a chartered accountant and spent the next two years doing provincial audits in the province of Alberta. This was followed by two years with the secretary to the Department of Public Health and another two years with the income tax office in Edmonton. Bill Power, a school friend who had moved to Nanaimo, encouraged him to come to Vancouver Island, and he decided to give it a try in Port Alberni where the prospects looked good. He moved there in 1948, just as the Alberni Pulp and Paper Mill was being opened. He never regretted it, though there were the usual headaches of setting up a small business.

Clouston's first office in Port Alberni was on Third Avenue. The Woodward's store across the street had just been built and, he recalled, Woodward's comptroller, Gordon Skinner (not related to Jim Skinner), used to visit him. Skinner was a friend from Edmonton who worked for the Woodward's store in BC and Alberta.

One of the big highlights during his years in Port Alberni was the opening of the road to the west coast. He recalled:

Before that we used to travel to the west coast on the Uchuck I, or by speedboat operated by Pat Clayton on his twin engine passenger boat. It would go about thirty miles per hour which was quite fast for that time. But it burned a lot of gas.[12]

He and Marion were married in 1941, and they had two children: Linda, now living in Victoria, and Richard in Singapore.

Clouston saw the forest industry in good and bad times over the years, and he thought it was the small loggers who suffered the most. Even in the recession of the early 1980s, though, nothing was like the first depression in the 1930s, when he had just come out of high school.

There was no welfare; no UIC and people were hungry. My Dad worked through the Depression as a caretaker in an apartment building. There were five kids to support and they were all at home.

When I asked him about the 1980s recession, he said he had never seen anything like it with the number of businesses closing.

At one time small logging companies contributed about 75-80 per cent of the logs for the mills here. Now it's only a small portion. The loggers used to be awarded tree farm licenses in public working areas set aside for their use. The big companies such as B.C. Forest Products and MacMillan Bloedel Ltd bought these up. The small logging companies in the area worked out of Port Alberni and they all had sizeable crews and made a good contribution to the economy. Most have disappeared.

The ups and downs in the forest industry affected his business, but he didn't rely on that entirely. There was always local business for a good accountant.

Clouston recalled an earlier time in Port Alberni when all the talk was about amalgamation of the twin cities. The subject had been talked about for years before it actually happened he thought it should have been sooner.

There was a lot of senseless infighting going on for years between the twin cities and it was very difficult to overcome. What prevented it becoming a reality was the attitude of the North Port merchants who felt it would be detrimental to them.

There were other issues between the two Albernis:

Mail home delivery at the start was very unpopular. The traffic wasn't there for the merchants. Once I got into

> *hot water over this issue at a meeting with the North Port merchants when I advocated North Port have home delivery. South Port had already initiated it. Today they all laugh about it but it was a very serious subject then.*

The conflict with the merchants didn't hurt his business; in fact, it gained him respect. He expressed concern for small businesses. For many, he felt, business has become full of unnecessary complications in law. "Law should be simpler. This discourages a great many people." As an example, he recalled the early cablevision company that set up on the coast without any government interference and with no rules or regulations or technical requirements. "Early radio stations were much the same. Right now we are overruled. There are a lot of bureaucrats wanting jobs. Government has got out of hand. It could be decreased by as much as 75 percent and we would still have a better society."

Federal and provincial deficits also bothered him.

> *Deficit financing has been the worst possible program. All western societies are suffering from the same thing. The exception is the province of Alberta. It has been wealthy and operated on a pay-as-you-go basis and accumulated surpluses rather than deficits. This started long before the oil industry became a big factor.*

Archie Clouston now looked forward to retirement. His eyes sparkled when he talked about his flying escapades with Stirzaker. "I remember one time at Jasper, over Pyramid Lake when we became disoriented and . . . "

PAT CUMMINGS: PERSONAL REFLECTIONS

Why would a person strive to further the art of dance, work for below average salary, and give bursaries out of meagre profits to help dance students? Pat Cummings asked another dance teacher this question, and the answer was, "We feel guilty because we are doing what we want to do in [the] face of difficulties. We feel guilty because we find joy in our work and the petty hardships seem unimportant." Cummings would later point out, "Dance teachers are underpaid, misunderstood and beset by problems."[13] But she agreed with the teacher's answer.

It was in the fall of 1953 when the Pat Cummings School of Dance became a reality. The trials and tribulations Cummings went through to get her dance studio established took a toll on her health. Nearing retirement in 1983 she looked back over those years and painted a portrait many dance teachers in Canada would recognize.

This multi-talented, well-known and valued member of the community was born on a homestead in southern Saskatchewan to parents of English-Scottish origin. Her maiden name was Kemp; she was the youngest in a family of five girls and one boy. When still a preschooler she moved with her family to Winnipeg where she began her formal education, graduating from Kelvin High School. After secretarial training she worked for the advertising agents Cockfield Brown, then later with Great West Life Insurance Company.

Cummings's first dance training in ballet, tap, and musical stage was taken in Emerson, Manitoba, with Jean Wallace as her teacher. Later Mary Strom instructed her in Winnipeg. She had further training in schools in Alberta and BC, and summer schools in Seattle, Portland, Los Angeles, San Francisco, and New York. She also studied voice and piano, and was an experienced dancer, choreographer, adjudicator, and musical stage director by the mid-1940s.

She came to Port Alberni from Winnipeg in 1946 as the young bride of J. Robert (Bob) Cummings, who had just been hired by Bloedel, Stewart & Welch as sales production coordinator. The couple first lived in the army camp. Pat first taught dance in the old RCEME Hall (Royal Canadian Electrical and Mechanical Engineers) at the end of Tenth Avenue. (This building burned down in 1961.) She also taught extracurricular dance classes in the new Alberni District Secondary School when it opened in 1951. She recalled that the opening concert, in January 1952, had two dance numbers: a ballet and a tap routine. Both were well received, and she was besieged afterwards with requests to start a dance school. However, she now had two young children to consider: James Alexander and Alison Patricia. Nonetheless, she started classes at the old community hall in the fall of 1952 with thirty pupils.

> *I was still reluctant; I had been trained as a dancer, but not as a teacher and that is a big difference. We certainly couldn't afford for me to go away and take courses to learn to be a teacher. What money I had earned teaching classes in the Community Hall was mostly eaten up by pianist fees, and hall rental.*

Pupils then paid seventy-five cents a lesson and a pianist earned one dollar an hour. The hall rental was eight dollars a day. Since then wages have increased ten-fold and classes are larger, making it difficult to keep costs low. Dancing fees have increased five times.

Cummings did eventually go to Victoria and was initiated into the mystery of the children's grades of the Royal Academy of Ballet. In the fall of 1953 the Pat Cummings School of Dance became a reality.

The next few years went quickly with summers spent in Victoria and Vancouver studying and upgrading teaching techniques. During this time her students entered the Upper Island Festival for the first time and the Royal Academy of Dance examinations. Her students did well in both areas, but she sensed an undercurrent of doubt from parents because the studio facilities were so poor. The school had moved to the Carmoor Block by this time but the dance studio was far from elegant. There were no mirrored walls, waiting rooms, or classy changing rooms. The fees were still low and Cummings was loath to raise them. She had begun to see the dancing school as a "service to the community." However, the maxim "You get what you pay for" seemed to stick in parents' minds. "Many were very slow paying the $1 a lesson we then charged but eagerly paid five times as much to guest teachers from Vancouver."

In 1958, her students won the outstanding group dance award at the Upper Island Festival. "This honour we have never relinquished since," Cummings said proudly.

Over the next ten years the dance school moved up Argyle Street to the Macdonald Block, and then to the lower floor of 5029 Argyle Street. Students continued to excel, passing major exams of the Royal Academy. These exams are taken after the children's grades are completed and are designed for those wishing to follow a career in dance. One student started her own dance studio, two danced professionally in musical comedy, and one attended the National Ballet School in Toronto. Others attended the Banff School of Fine Arts, while another student, George Marshall, danced for two summers in the Butchart Gardens show in Victoria. Perhaps most important for Cummings was the fact that her daughter, Alison, became a dance teacher. She married Bill Cowan, and was a director at the school.

The year-end dance revue has always been the big event in the year for the school. In 1970, the school instituted the bursary fund to help dance students financially. All the profits from the revue were now going into the bursary fund.

In 1976, the school opened in a new building on Athol Street; it had taken twenty-three years to get out of hall rentals and into a proper dance studio facility. The question Cummings asked now (in 1983) was, could this free enterprise survive in tough economic times? The school faced property taxes of $3,000, mortgage payments, business licence fees, salaries for teachers and pianist, and other sundry items needed to run the facility. Against this was the tuition paid by nearly three hundred students, the current enrollment at the school.

> This is nothing new; people in the arts are notoriously underpaid and have no financial security in the best of times. There is no sick pay, no overtime pay, and no vacation with pay. Even when the studio closes in the summertime the taxes and upkeep go on. A dance teacher never gets ill. This is one of the biggest problems, sick or well, you have to be there. There is no substitute dancing teacher list to call.

Cummings takes great pride that in the last thirty years she has only missed a few classes, when she had to have an ear operation. This condition made teaching dance almost unbearable. There was a balance problem and the sound of tap dancers "was sheer torture."

Private dance schools have many other problems such as the collecting of fees and the competition from other non-profit organizations teaching dance in the community.

> You would wonder why anyone would become a dance teacher, or open a dance studio. The answer is that very few do, that is why it is so difficult to get good teachers in small towns like Port Alberni.

While Cummings may have complained about some of the hardships she has faced, she still felt that teaching young people and spreading the knowledge of dance was a privilege, as was finding joy and satisfaction in your work. She had few regrets about the path she chose to follow—to teach dance.

Her club affiliations included membership in the Soroptomist club. She was a Gyrette (Gyro), and as an original shareholder she holds a life membership in the Alberni Valley Curling Club. She choreographed the Logger's Stomp dance performed at Expo '86. Pat Cummings also served five years as the artistic director of the Port Alberni Theatrical Society, of which she was made an honorary member. She will forever be remembered for initiating the popular revue Funshine, trying to make light out of the rainy weather in Port Alberni.

{ *chapter fifteen* }

A CHANGING FOREST INDUSTRY

For three years anti-logging protests had simmered on the west coast. By 1988 these protests had expanded from Clayoquot Sound to the forest in Carmanah Valley, named for Carmanah Creek that crosses the West Coast Trail south of Nitinat Lake. Once the site of a former Ditidaht village at the mouth of the creek, the name Carmanah means "canoe landing in front." The watershed contained ancient Sitka spruce, western hemlock and western red cedar. Some of the cedars, including the Carmanah Giant, were estimated to be a thousand years old. Marbled Murrelet nests were found here and a number of new insect species had been discovered in the canopy.

As with Clayoquot Sound, environmentalists and loggers were at odds over Carmanah. But this conflict would be resolved quickly; MB did not need another prolonged battle over logging. In 1990 the province created Carmanah Pacific Provincial Park to preserve the lower portions of the watershed, adding the lower part of the adjacent Walbran Valley in 1995 to form Carmanah-Walbran Provincial Park.

Still, it was obvious the issue of logging on the west coast would not go away. In June 1988, the FOCS blockaded Sulphur Pass in Clayoquot Sound to halt road construction by BC Forest Products. The company just moved its crews elsewhere while it got an injunction, which led to thirty-five arrests and the conviction of several anti-logging activists for contempt of court.

In the fall of 1988, the Tofino Chamber of Commerce and Tofino District Council asked the BC government's Environment and Land Use Committee for funding to develop a regionally based Clayoquot Sound sustainable development strategy. Their proposal called for a two-year logging moratorium to allow the strategy to be developed with the emphasis on the importance of wilderness tourism.[1]

Premier Bill Vander Zalm made a much-publicized trip to the area the next year, stopping at the now infamous "Black Hole" located off the Kennedy Lake Road. While in the area he and members of his cabinet met with the mayors of Ucluelet, Port Alberni, and Tofino to inform them that Clayoquot Sound would be the focus of a land-use dispute resolution experiment, and the government wanted their co-operation. A task force was subsequently formed to develop a plan for sustainable development in the area. All agreed that the provincial government would make the final decision.

ALBERNI PLYWOOD'S DEMISE

The Port Alberni economy was dealt another blow when it was announced that the Alberni Plywood mill would close April 30, 1991, after fifty years in operation. The plant had a rich and proud history and was recognized as a world leader in the production of highest quality sanded plywood. Some men had worked their entire life in the plant, as had their children.

When the mill opened in 1941 on the shores of the Alberni Inlet, plywood was in great demand due to the war. Key men were brought in from Vancouver Plywood to staff the plant in its initial operation. There was no union at the mill in the beginning and workers were represented by a committee of employees. This lasted only a short time until the mill unionized with the IWA Local 1-85 in October 1944. Because of the war and the shortage of labour, it was one of the first plants to hire women for its workforce.

Over the years, Alberni Plywood went through several expansions to keep it relevant, modern, and productive. But in the end the economy, decline in logs, and lack of sales were deciding factors. Employees were given the opportunity to save the mill. They had to initiate a plan to make the mill profitable, but with no new capital investment the workers could not make a profit, and the mill closed. As the war in the woods raged on the west coast, the town's residents felt great sadness and unease at losing the mill. Port Alberni wondered what next! Clayoquot Sound was still simmering.

CLAYOQUOT HEATS UP

In 1991, MB obtained a BC Supreme Court injunction prohibiting anyone from deliberately interfering with its logging in Clayoquot Sound. Anti-logging activists moved to other parts of the Sound, but the injunction was extended to cover different locations within the area. In March, logging was allowed in Bulson Creek and Hesquiat Harbour, already under development, to give work to MB Kennedy Lake loggers during the committee process. One month later, a logging road bridge used by the Kennedy Lake loggers was burned, putting most of them out of work. In protest against logging in the two areas, environmentalists resigned from the process. The US-based Earth First activists conducted civil disobedience training in Tofino. Then, in defiance of the court injunction, the FOCS blocked the logging road leading to Bulson Creek; MB civil proceedings against six of the protesters resulted in convictions for contempt of court.

The provincial government took note of what was happening in Clayoquot Sound and didn't want to see the same thing happen across BC. A Commission on Resources and Environment (CORE) was appointed to resolve land-use conflicts throughout the province. The government didn't want to interfere with the existing process already underway in Clayoquot, and so excluded Clayoquot Sound from CORE.

A Western Canada Wilderness Committee (WCWC) organized a Clayoquot rally at the provincial legislature in Victoria on March 18, 1993, to put pressure on Premier Mike Harcourt's impending decision on the fate of the old-growth forest in Clayoquot Sound. The rally turned into a riot as four hundred protesters broke into the building, injuring a security guard and delaying the throne speech. All parties in the house denounced what happened, as did Harcourt who said, "I don't listen to people that use mob-scene intimidation."[2] It was an unfortunate scene that was replayed again and again on newscasts across the country because of the injury to the guard and storming of the legislature.

On April 13, 1993, Harcourt announced the Clayoquot Sound Land Use decision. It did not include Meares Island, a subject still before the BC Supreme Court. The decision permanently protected 34 percent of the Sound. Another 21 percent would be placed under special management, which allowed for some logging but protected wildlife, recreation, and scenic landscape values. The decision created one of the largest areas of protected old-growth rainforest on the west coast of North America, effectively extending Strathcona Park to the ocean.[3] One-quarter of the western side of Flores Island was protected, as well as two-thirds of Vargas Island and Blundon Island to preserve the important marine ecosystem. Soon afterwards the Western Canada Wilderness Committee, Friends of Clayoquot Sound, and the Valhalla Wilderness Society resigned from CORE to protest the government decision; they wanted more to be protected.

It was a compromise. Harcourt's decision meant that four hundred forest workers would lose their jobs and about a third of the temperate rainforest land base in Clayoquot Sound would be left untouched. It allowed limited logging in Clayoquot Sound, which provoked the environment movement to vigorous anti-government protests.

On June 2, the provincial government accepted most of CORE's recommendations. They included the formation of an independent watchdog committee, weekly government logging checks, a 40-hectare (98.8 acres) clearcut size limit, more public advisory panels, innovative logging methods, and the Sound's designation as a UNESCO Biosphere Reserve.

The response from anti-logging activists was overwhelmingly negative. On July 1, they set up what became known as the "Peace Camp"—a village of tents and trailers situated by the clearcut known as the Black Hole. In the four months it operated, over twelve thousand people visited and protested. The Australian band Midnight Oil played a benefit concert at this location.

One of the first notable visitors to the Peace Camp was Robert Kennedy Jr., who had accepted an invitation from Native leaders to visit Meares Island and support opposition to the Clayoquot decision. On July 30, 1993, Kennedy toured the area and met with them on Meares Island. He condemned the corporate destruction in the area, and said Natives should be given control of the forest resources.

Things really began heating up in the area when a community coalition supporting the Clayoquot majority option blockaded three entrances to the Sound to stop the anti-logging activists from setting up their own illegal blockade. By August 3, 160 people had been arrested at the blockade. A week later, on August 9, three hundred of seven hundred protesters were arrested at the Kennedy River Bridge in the largest blockade of the summer and the largest mass arrest at a political demonstration in BC history. Virtually all those arrested were lying in front of logging trucks and had to be carried away. The sheer numbers strained police to the limit. In addition to a special eight-member Clayoquot arrest squad, RCMP had to call on eight other people from the provincial sheriff's office and corrections department. The Ucluelet detachment's single holding cell was too small, so police took over the local athletic centre to hold all those arrested.

Two hundred and eight were charged with criminal contempt, bringing the total charges for the summer to more than four hundred. BC Environment Minister John Cashore said the government was not going to change its mind on Clayoquot, no matter how many people got hauled away.

In the meantime, the three Native bands in the area asked the BC Supreme Court for injunctions to halt logging in key parts of the Sound until their land claims were settled, a process that could take years.

The Rendezvous '93 event held in Ucluelet on August 14 drew about five thousand people from communities throughout BC. It was an impressive display of support for the Clayoquot compromise. But the two-day event, which was the largest gathering to date by either logging or anti-logging supporters, received little media coverage from Vancouver or Victoria. In an apparent effort to discredit Rendezvous '93, FOCS accused MB of paying employees to attend the rally. The company conducted a survey and discovered there was no foundation to the accusation.

On August 30, 1993, the Crown opened its case in BC Supreme Court before Mr. Justice John Bouck against the first of more than four hundred blockaders who had been charged with criminal contempt for disobeying a court injunction. The protest group became known as the Clayoquot 44. Forty-three received jail sentences of forty-five days and fines ranging from $1,000 to $2,500. Tofino doctor Ron Aspinall was given sixty days and fined $3,000. The judge singled out Aspinall for condemnation, accusing him of being narrow-minded, intolerant, and obsessed with saving the forests. "Like so many of the defendants, he is preoccupied with his real or imagined charter rights and indifferent to his responsibilities as a Canadian citizen."[4] He also reprimanded NDP MP Svend Robinson for sitting at counsel tables during the Clayoquot trial and falsely claiming to be a member of the Law Society of B.C.

Jack Munro, at this time the head of the Forest Alliance of British Columbia and former president of the IWA, said he took no pleasure in the conviction of the protesters. MB spokesman Dennis Fitzgerald said the convictions were well deserved because the accused had consciously and openly defied the injunction.

As the court handed out sentences, the Nuu-chah-nulth Tribal Council signed an interim agreement with the Harcourt government. Alberni MLA Gerard Janssen, who had succeeded Bob Skelly, was happy and surprised with this outcome. He said it was the first time in Canada a government had entered into an interim agreement before treaty negotiations. The Nuu-chah-nulth had won the right to be consulted in a meaningful way on all approvals for harvesting in Clayoquot Sound. This had been a sore point, with them claiming they had been shut out of the decision making when the cabinet decided on the Clayoquot Sound compromise.[5]

For about half an hour on September 1, about two hundred forest workers—frustrated at having been prevented from working for almost two months—stopped two busloads of Victoria business and professional people who were on their way to join the blockade on the west coast.

The tide seemed to be turning in favour of a more reasoned approach to land-use decisions. FOCS organizers who hoped a cross-country Clayoquot Caravan would recruit 250 new supporters to the blockade were disappointed when only forty arrived. About the same time, MB loggers stayed home in a successful attempt to thwart FOCS plans for publicity in a day of mass arrests. The "peace camp" was finally dismantled by FOCS, so ending the summer-long blockade. However, the group vowed the fight was far from over.

In an extraordinary courtroom statement, Chief Justice William Esson of the BC Supreme Court denounced government leaders, defence lawyers, and others for their "ignorant" claims that the courts had initiated the Clayoquot Sound criminal contempt trials.[6] Esson said the trials were in fact launched and conducted by the Attorney General's ministry according to a precedent dating back to 1992. As a result of the judge's comments, Premier Harcourt ordered his ministers and MLAs to make no further comments on the trial proceedings.

New Angus Reid polls showed that a solid majority (59 percent) of British Columbians supported the decision to allow logging in Clayoquot Sound. The polls also suggested that the environmental movement might be discrediting itself in the public eye because of its protest tactics. Environmentalists attributed the results to public ignorance of the issues.

On October 22, Premier Mike Harcourt announced the creation of a scientific advisory panel to improve and monitor forest practices in Clayoquot Sound.[7] He said the creation of this independent panel was another step toward providing a sustainable future for Clayoquot, and ensuring that forestry activities in the Sound stand up to world scrutiny.

The nineteen-member panel would include scientists from BC and Washington State, internationally recognized leaders in their fields of expertise, and four members designated by the Nuu-chah-nulth Tribal Council. The panel's final recommendations on new forest practices for Clayoquot would be due on June 30, 1994.

On December 10, the BC government announced a two-year "government-to-government" agreement with the Nuu-chah-nulth Tribal Council to provide Native logging opportunities in Clayoquot Sound. The agreement let six bands co-operatively manage 60,000 cubic metres (2.1 million cubic feet) of annual timber harvest in the Clayoquot River Valley, and 10,000 cubic metres (353,150 cubic feet) on Flores Island. It also created a $1.25 million fund to provide technical training for band members and established a community resource board with NTC participation. The deal was seen as an interim step toward a permanent resolution to the tribal council's outstanding land claim on the west coast of Vancouver Island.

The interim agreement was good news for MB president Bob Finlay, who issued a press release congratulating the premier and the Nuu-chah-nulth chiefs. He said that Clayoquot had been a difficult issue for the company, but recognized the opportunity to demonstrate acceptance of change. He did not anticipate further reductions in employment in the Clayoquot area. To secure the compromise the company had already lost four hundred direct jobs and 300,000 cubic metres (10.6 million cubic feet) a year removed from the area.[8]

ANOTHER SHOCK AT MB

On June 21, 1999, MacMillan Bloedel Limited announced that it had agreed to merge with Weyerhaeuser. The combined company was expected to be the most powerful forest products company in the world. Shock and disbelief at the announcement resonated throughout MB divisions. Employees had felt loyalty toward the company with its great history and accomplishments over the years, but it was no longer the company of H.R. MacMillan. In 1981 Noranda had purchased 49 percent of MB shares, and within a few months Brascade Resources Inc. purchased 42 percent of Noranda. It was this complex ownership that Weyerhaeuser wanted to merge with. When it came forward with an attractive proposal the MB Board of Directors felt compelled to take it forward to its shareholders for a vote. The final agreement was reached only after several interim proposals had been rejected.

According to letters sent to employees, the "deal was a no-brainer. It's good for MB shareholders and good for Weyerhaeuser shareholders. The business of the two companies fit together hand in glove and the synergistic value is enormous."[9]

Weyerhaeuser, an US company, had been a big part of the BC Forest Products business for years, particularly in the province's Interior region. It would now have a huge presence across the country, employing about twelve thousand people, with its head office in Vancouver.

MB employees got a further shock when they heard that the name of MacMillan Bloedel would be dropped in favour of Weyerhaeuser. Public meetings were held to allow employees to express their feelings about the merger and the upcoming changes in the company. Weyerhaeuser did a good selling job and managed to convince many, though not everyone, of the positive outcome of the merger, which many saw as a takeover.

In August 1999 Weyerhaeuser issued a statement confirming it would continue the forest practices started by MB on the coast, including the phasing out of clearcutting. It also stated it would support the Clayoquot Memorandum of Understanding, and would honour MB's agreements with environmental groups and with Native and local communities.

However, the $3.6-billion bid by Weyerhaeuser to buy out MB depended on a number of approvals being granted. These included shareholder approval: they had to approve the deal by 66 and two-thirds percent of votes cast. It needed court approval: MB must apply to the BC Supreme Court asking for a court order to implement the merger. And under the Forest Act in BC, the consent of the minister of forests was required prior to any change in control of a company holding a forest tenure. Until these were all approved, MB worked to keep focused.

The public debate had just begun. Environmentalists, MB employees, retirees, even the Raging Grannies from Victoria had an opinion. These ranged from vehement opposition to enthusiastic support. Environmentalists were opposed to creating larger forest companies and worried that Weyerhaeuser would use provisions under the Free Trade Agreement to seek damages from Canadian governments for application of certain environmental laws and land-use policies. Bill Gaynor, Weyerhaeuser president, quickly disputed this. Taking such action would not be in the company's best interest, he said.

Stan Coleman, manager of Nanaimo Woodlands, favoured the merger. "When I first heard about the deal, I got a deep feeling of regret in my heart. Then I had a feeling of tremendous opportunity to create a much stronger company and to learn from each other to deal with complex issues."[10]

The break up of MB had already begun the year before, in 1998, with the sale of the Alberni Pulp & Paper Division to Pacifica Papers Inc. In 2001, the paper mill changed hands again to Norske Skog Canada Ltd. (Norske Canada), and in 2005 it became Catalyst Paper Corp.

Ultimately the merger went through. But Weyerhaeuser did not stay long in the region. In 2004, its private lands were removed from TFL 44 and sold to Brascan, which moved them to Island Timberlands. TFL 44 was the old TFL 20 and 21 and the primary source of timber for the Alberni mills; removing its private lands now allowed, under federal rules, the export of logs from those private lands. TFL 44 and the mills were sold to Cascadia Forest Products, which was then sold to Western Forest Products.

Port Alberni residents were angry when they saw logs being trucked to the east side of the island, or being barged out of the Alberni Inlet to the US, while local mills were curtailed due to log shortages.

One company that has managed to take advantage of the strong market for cedar lumber is Coulson Forest Products.

COULSON: A FORESTRY SUCCESS STORY

Once Port Alberni had the largest forest company in the British Commonwealth as its major employer, with mills stretching along the waterfront. Today it is fragmented with the mills under new ownership. However, one forest company not only survived the 1980s recession but is becoming known throughout North America. With fifty years under its belt, Coulson Forest Products Limited is now one of the last family-owned forest companies still operating in Port Alberni and on the west coast.

When the Port Alberni Airport opened in September 1993, Cliff and Mae Coulson were there to cut the large cake in celebration not only of the new airport but also for the Coulson Aircrane headquarters and maintenance shop located nearby. For the Coulsons this was a historic event in their family history.

Clifford Coulson, the patriarch of the family, was born in 1919 in Victoria to Anne and Scott Coulson, and spent his early years on the small family farm in Oak Bay with his siblings Margaret, Eleanor, Doris, and George. He began working in the forest industry in 1934. During the Second World War, he served with the Canadian Scottish Regiment. He married the love of his life, Mae, in 1947 and they had four children: Barry, Ron, Wayne, and Darlene.

In 1960 Cliff started a small logging company in partnership with John Prescott under the name Coulson Prescott Logging Limited. The company did contract logging for MacMillan Bloedel in the Sproat Lake Division. When Prescott retired in 1970, the company was renamed Coulson Forest Products Limited (CFP).

The company's first forest licence was obtained in 1972 in the Toquart River Valley, where it continues to operate and maintain this licence as the basis of its timberlands operation. Another forest licence was purchased in 1984 when Hecate Logging Ltd. was formed as a joint venture with the Ehattesaht First Nation people. This was the first successful joint venture of its kind in BC between Native and non-Native interests in the forest industry. Based on the success of this venture, the licence was returned to the Ehattesaht in 2006.

In 1997 CFP formed another joint partnership with Toquaht First Nation in Ucluelet. E-cha-peh Forest Resources Ltd. was awarded 50 percent of a community forest licence in 2000. The success of this company represented a breakthrough in structuring Native participation in the forest industry. CFP again extended its expertise in 2007 to another five Native bands in Clayoquot Sound, an unprecedented partnership where CFP was a 49 percent owner of TFL 54 along with the five bands.

Following the death of Mae Coulson in 2005, and of Cliff in 2006, the Coulson Group of Companies came under the leadership of son Wayne, who is now the president and CEO with headquarters in Port Alberni. Besides the logging enterprises, the company operates a sawmill plant at Polly Point, south of the city, and a new remanufacturing plant. It has reopened the old Somass mill once owned by Weyerhaeuser. All three facilities are now incorporated into Coulson Manufacturing.

Coulson was one of the first logging companies on the coast to get into helicopter logging, and in 1985 established Coulson Aircrane Ltd with a fleet of five Sikorsky S61 helicopters and two Bell Jet Rangers. It is now North America's biggest commercial operator of the S61.

In 2007 a new division was formed when the company purchased the world-renowned Martin Mars flying tankers, the largest flying boats in the world. Each can carry an enormous 7,200 US gallons per load. The purchase ensured the venerated flying tankers would continue to fight forest fires. The company also supplies helicopter services in isolated locations across BC and in other provinces, and within the US, Australia, and Azerbaijan. The purchase of a Hercules C130J aircraft by Coulson Aviation (USA) Inc. is targeted to fight wildfires in the US beginning in 2013.

The forest industry has changed dramatically in Port Alberni over the past decades. With Coulson and other forestry companies continuing to find new and innovative ways to benefit from the surrounding forests, and with Natives increasing their involvement in the industry, the town will be well served for years to come.

EPILOGUE

Port Alberni is an incredible community. Located in a stunning landscape, it has seen good times and bad, depending on market conditions in the forest industry. It may never again have the highest wage earners in Canada, and residents may never again experience the prosperity they once enjoyed through the forest industry, but they are proud of their town and its place in British Columbia history.

During one of its telethons, the BC Variety Club named the city the "Community with a Heart"—the town had raised $45,000 at a time when there was high unemployment and the soup kitchen had become a way of life for some. A large number of volunteer organizations continue to work in the community to make life better for everyone.

Forest workers have memories of MacMillan Bloedel, some good, some bad, but they recognize the long history the company had in Port Alberni and the good living they once enjoyed. The company tried to be a good business partner, donating the former Alberni Plywood Division site to the city, a move it hoped would be a major step in a drive to expand and diversify the town's economic base. The old IWA Local 1-85 is gone, merged into the United Steelworkers Union in September 2004. Alberni Pacific Division, Somass, and the paper plant still operate but with different owners. There are no more MB logos on lumber.

The west coast is quiet now, the anti-logging demonstration of Clayoquot Sound relegated to the history books. On May 5, 2000, municipal, provincial, and federal government officials, including Prime Minister Jean Chretien, and Native representatives joined residents and guests from around the world to officially commemorate the designation of Clayoquot Sound as a UNESCO Biosphere Reserve.

Whatever else, MB left a legacy of giving that would be hard to equal. Nearby, MacMillan Park's Cathedral Grove, generously donated by H.R., draws thousands of visitors every year to see the giant trees. The company encouraged volunteering; employees supported local agencies, and thousands of hours were contributed that could never be put into dollars and cents. Countless community venues and projects owe their success to Port Alberni MB employees who donated their time and energy quietly, without remuneration and often without recognition. Elsewhere in the province, the MacMillan name is attached to sixteen scholarships and bursaries at UBC, as well as UBC's MacMillan Library and MacMillan Bloedel Atrium. Over the years the MacMillan family and MB gave over $9.6 million to the university, plus millions more to support other educational institutes and programs.

The physical city of Port Alberni has also changed considerably. There is now a new fifty-two-bed West Coast General Hospital and a separate thirty-two-bed multi-level care facility, "Westhaven," located on the Port Alberni Highway at the entrance to the city. The site of the old hospital on Eighth Avenue became home to a new RCMP detachment building; the former extended care wing is now an Abbeyfield house.

The ice arena at Recreation Park closed when the Alberni Valley Multiplex, named the Weyerhaeuser Arena, was constructed on Roger Street. Nearby is a new Alberni Athletic Hall replacing the one that burned down on Beaver Creek Road. And a new Alberni District Secondary School, which includes a five hundred-seat theatre, opened in December 2012, also on Roger Street. The old school is being demolished and the land sold.

Perhaps the biggest change in town for residents is the shopping experience with the building of Walmart and other retail outlets on Johnston Road, across from the old Alberni Mall in North Port. On Third Avenue in South Port, once the major shopping area in town, the Woodward's/Zellers building is now owned by Coulson Group of Companies and is being renovated by the company.

The town's heritage groups, working with the Alberni Valley Museum, have proved that history can boost tourism. The McLean Mill National Historic Site, in tandem with the Alberni Pacific Railway steam train, created a destination attraction known throughout BC. The Alberni Harbour Quay and the Maritime Discovery Centre are located on the waterfront of Stamp Harbour, combining venues for history and tourism. The venerated *Lady Rose* ship has retired, but the *Frances Barkley* still sails the Alberni Inlet carrying freight and passengers to the coast. Cruise ships have now found their way up the inlet bringing thousands of visitors to experience homegrown hospitality.

At Victoria Quay, where the old Alberni City Hall was located, two carved Nuu-chah-nulth "Welcoming Figures" and a carved canoe are strategically placed at the foot of Johnston Road, the gateway to the west coast—perhaps a reminder that the Nuu-chah-nulth community has taken a seat at the table of future economic prosperity in the region.

The biggest stumbling block for future development remains the need for another transportation link with the east coast, something the early settlers already debated with government for decades. With only one road in and out, the town will always be hog-tied.

There are other challenges ahead as well. Today the forest industry is weakened by the worldwide recession—particularly in Europe, the United States, and Japan, the province's biggest markets for forest products—and faces some difficult choices. But Port Alberni is still a good place to live, work, and raise children. It has cast the image of "just a mill town" aside. In fact, the town's biggest resource is—perhaps always has been—its people. The spirit of the valley remains strong and optimistic.

The future of Port Alberni is waiting to be written . . .

ACKNOWLEDGEMENTS

Writing this book has been a personal journey. Having published four history books on Port Alberni, I felt I had more to tell about the city than its historic background. After living and raising three children there, I wanted to give a personal perspective on some of the events and situations that overshadowed three decades in the city. The town's main employer, MacMillan Bloedel Ltd., was a large part of our lives and the town. I set out to explore what happened to the company and how it changed life in Port Alberni. Working as a reporter for the *Alberni Valley Times* gave me privileged access to people and events that has enabled me to present a different viewpoint.

Throughout this journey there were many people who helped me either with photographs or recollections of events. I thank the *Alberni Valley Times* for giving permission to use my interviews and articles that were used as a resource. Also my sincere thanks to the Alberni District Historical Society Archives volunteers for their ongoing support and for previewing some of the material in the book. Thanks also to Dave Lowe for his help in documenting the establishment of the McLean Mill. I also appreciated the help I received from Trevor Jones in recalling the sequence of events that eventually solved the floodplain dilemma. The Coulson Group was helpful in my efforts to tell the family story.

To all my friends and acquaintances who contributed photographs for the book, I thank you. Sorry we couldn't use them all! The Alberni Valley Museum deserves special recognition, particularly Shelley Harding who was most helpful in searching for photos! Finally, thanks to my editor, Renate Preuss, for her expertise and for providing an excellent working relationship. And to Rodger Touchie and the staff at Heritage House, my thanks for continuing to support writers in British Columbia.

ENDNOTES

two—A MacMillan Bloedel Town
1. K. Drushka, *HR: A Biography of H.R. MacMillan*, 270.
2. I. Mahood and K. Drushka, *Three Men and a Forester*, 153–54.
3. L. Geigle, ed., *Be My Guest. The Memoirs of Marie Jacobson, Alberni Hotelier*, 125.
4. Alberni District Historical Society, *Place Names of the Alberni Valley*, 18.

three—Getting to Know the City
1. *Alberni Advocate*, March 22, 1912.
2. D.E. Harker, *The Woodwards: A Family Story of Ventures and Traditions*, 173.
3. *West Coast Advocate*, October 10, 1946.
4. Harker, *The Woodwards*, 172–79.
5. "Bill Patenaude Retiring, Not Leaving," *Alberni Valley Times*, November 4, 1983.
6. J. Peterson, *Twin Cities: Alberni-Port Alberni*, 213.
7. *Alberni Valley Times*, May 29, 1979.
8. Gillian Trumper interview with author, *Alberni Valley Times*, Oct. 15, 1981.
9. Gord Crann, *Toronto Star*, Apr. 12, 1987, p. B3.
10. Stu Keate interview with author, *Alberni Valley Times*, June 29, 1981.
11. Peterson, *Twin Cities*, 302.
12. *MB Journal*, October 1990.
13. Sandra McCulloch, *Times Colonist*, September 14, 2013.
14. Ibid., August 23, 2012.

four—Unions and First Nations
1. George McKnight speaking to the Select Standing Committee of Aboriginal Affairs in Port Alberni, October 17, 1996.
2. J. Peterson, "Walter Behn Relives 20 Years of Labour History."
3. J.E. McIntosh, "Mark Mosher's Reconstruction of the Development of the Woodworkers Union in the Alberni Valley 1935–1950: A Participant's History."
4. J. Munro and J. O'Hara, *Union Jack*, 133.
5. Paul George interview with author, "No Doubt We Are Running Out of Timber."
6. J. Peterson, "Air Pollution Questions Include Workers' Contract."
7. J. Peterson, *Harbour City: Nanaimo in Transition: 1920–1967*, 47–48.
8. Les Leyne, *Times Colonist*, December 9, 2006.
9. "NTC won't log Meares," *Alberni Valley Times*, February 6, 1985.
10. "Like David Beating Goliath. MB Denied Meares Island Timber," Canadian Press, Vancouver, March 27, 1985.
11. D. Francis, ed., *Encyclopedia of British Columbia*, 758.
12. J. Peterson, *Journeys Down the Alberni Canal to Barkley Sound*, 259.
13. Adam Shewish interview with author, September 22, 1989.
14. R. Fred, "Remembering George Clutesi."
15. J. Lavoie, "Elder Revives Vanishing Language."

five—Community Recreation and Preserving Heritage
1. Stella Teindle interview with author, February 23, 1982.
2. Peterson, *Twin Cities*, 327.

3. Ibid., 58.
4. Personal communication with Dave Lowe, October 30, 2012.

six—The Arts Community
1. Pat Miller interview with author, *Alberni Valley Times*, May 15, 1981.
2. *Alberni Valley Times*, September 21, 1982.

seven—Sugar in the Fridge; Mice on the Table
1. "Conrad Black" and "David Radler," *Wikipedia*.
2. R. Wade, "Once Upon a Time . . ." column.
3. Bill Young interview with author, August 20, 1982.

eight—The Recession Hits
1. Drushka, *HR*, 385.
2. D. MacKay, *Empire of Wood. The MacMillan Bloedel Story*, 318.
3. Ibid., 329.
4. Ibid., 324–25.
5. *Vancouver Sun*, June 5, 1982.
6. A. Zimmerman, *Who's in Charge Here, Anyway?*
7. MacKay, *Empire of Wood*, 341.
8. Drushka, 388.
9. Douglas Belshaw and David J. Mitchell, "Chapter 10: The Economy since the Great War" in H.J.M. Johnston, ed., *The Pacific Province: A History of British Columbia*, 334.
10. *Alberni Valley Times*, September 10, 1981.
11. "Labor militant: Behn," *Alberni Valley Times*, [n.d.].
12. *Alberni Valley Times*, October 1, 1982.
13. "The Organization of Unemployed Workers," *Alberni Valley Times*, May 4, 1984.
14. "OUW Packs Council Meeting, Slams Mayor," *Alberni Valley Times*, January 11, 1983.
15. "Mayor Denies Avoiding the OUW," *Alberni Valley Times*, January 13, 1983.
16. G. Wilson, "Jobless chant . . ."
17. *Alberni Valley Times* unemployment series (May 3–14), May 3, 1984.
18. G. Wilson, "Looking for Wage Controls."
19. Statistics Canada 1986.

nine—Fighting Back
1. J. Peterson, "We're Fighting Back."
2. J. Peterson, "Fed Up with Gloom: Barrett."
3. Paper: "The Day of Discovery," January 1982.
4. J. Peterson, "Faber Parents Lash Out at SD 70 Closures."
5. J. Peterson, "Is Education Revamping a Threat to Democracy?"
6. J. Peterson, "Count 'Em—Five Schools Will Close."
7. J. Peterson, "No Reprieve."
8. Gary Swann, *Alberni Valley Times*, March 23, 1982.
9. Bob Moss, *Alberni Valley Times*, April 30, 1982.
10. Advertisement in *Alberni Valley Times*, July 26, 1983.

ten—Foresty in the Hot Seat
1. "Report argues for Meares preservation," *Alberni Valley Times*, May 10, 1983.
2. H.J.M. Johnston, *The Pacific Province*, 334.
3. Ibid., 335.

4. "Meares Island to be Logged," *Alberni Valley Times*, November 10, 1983.
5. "Meares Fight Broadens Threat," Canadian Press, Vancouver, January 8, 1984.
6. "Meares Island Fight Far from Over for Residents," *Alberni Valley Times*, March 20, 1984.
7. "Loggers Back MB Island Cut, but Won't Fight," *Times Colonist*, October 16, 1984.
8. "NTC Won't Log Meares," *Alberni Valley Times*, February 6, 1985.
9. "Alberni's Findlay Takes Meares Pitch onto TV," *Alberni Valley Times*, February 19, 1985.
10. "Munro Blames 'Kooky Environmentalists.' Meares: Bloody Disaster," *Alberni Valley Times*, March 28, 1985.
11. G. Mason, "Battle for Meares Island Is Key to Settlement of Claims."
12. Wolfgang Zimmerman and Sven Frederickson interview in "Layoff Seeks Precedent for Disabled Workers," *Alberni Valley Times*, December 1, 1982.
13. *MB Journal*, September 1987.
14. Zimmerman and Frederickson interview, December 1, 1982.

eleven—The Floodplain Dilemma
1. J. Peterson, *Alberni Valley Times*, March 21, 1983.
2. Trevor Jones interview with author, April 8, 1983.
3. Author's "City Notebook" column, *Alberni Valley Times*, November 18, 1983.
4. Ibid., January 13, 1984.

twelve—A Year of Celebration
1. Port Alberni 1986 Forestry Capital of Canada Souvenir Edition, 3.
2. Ibid., 6.
3. Ibid., 8.
4. D. Murray, *The Expo Celebration*, 5.
5. B. Miller, "2-Spot Steam Ride: A Journey to Yesterday."

thirteen—Interviews of Note
1. Stu Keate interview with author, *Alberni Valley Times*, June 29, 1981.
2. Jack Webster interview with author, *Alberni Valley Times*, July 25, 1985.
3. "Happy Birthday . . . " (Cougar Annie), *Alberni Valley Times*, June 20, 1984.

fourteen—People of the Alberni Valley
1. Helen Patenaude interview with author, *Alberni Valley Times*, November 30, 1982.
2. G. Wilson, "Hope Porter Given Award."
3. Doris Gray interview with author, *Alberni Valley Times*, December 6, 1982.
4. G. Wilson, "Helen, Armour Ford Work Quietly."
5. "Peter Szachiv—A True Artist," *Alberni Valley Times*, July 8, 1983.
6. *Alberni Valley Times*, July 15, 1983.
7. "Devereux Reminisces on Early Arts," *Alberni Valley Times*, May 13, 1981.
8. "Opening Night Highs for Lady and Her Art," *Alberni Valley Times*, July 17, 1981.
9. "Reynolds Reaps Award," *Alberni Valley Times*, May 1981.
10. Dr. Dick Garner interview with author, *Alberni Valley Times*, 1984. Reprinted in *British Columbia Medical Association News*, August 1984.
11. "Dean O'Banion," *Wikipedia*.
12. Alberni Valley Times, January 18, 1984.
13. Ibid., January 19, 1983.

fifteen—A Changing Forest Industry

1. MB & Clayoquot Sound Briefing notes. Vancouver Island Regional Reference Library: R.333 7509711 MAC.
2. D. Suzuki, "Those Anti-Logging 'Thugs' Are Our Kids."
3. Premier Make Harcourt news release, dated April 13, 1993.
4. Steve Weatherbe, "Court Convicts 44 Clayoquot Sound Protesters," *Alberni Valley Times*, October 7, 1993.
5. R. Diotte, "Janssen Calls Agreement Historic."
6. Statement on the Clayoquot trials by Chief Justice William Esson, Supreme Court of British Columbia, October 22, 1993.
7. Premier Mike Harcourt news release dated October 22, 1993.
8. MacMillan Bloedel Limited press release December 10, 1993.
9. MacMillan Bloedel Limited letter to MB retirees June 22, 1999.
10. *MB Journal* 19 (October 19), no. 10, 1.

BIBLIOGRAPHY

Books, Articles, and Pamphlets

Alberni District Historical Society. *Place Names of the Alberni Valley.* Port Alberni, BC, 1988.
Crann, Gord. "Skelly New NDP leader." *Toronto Star,* April 12, 1987.
Diotte, Rob. "Janssen Calls Agreement Historic." *Alberni Valley Times,* October 7, 1993.
Drushka, Ken. *HR: A Biography of H.R. MacMillan.* Madeira Park, BC: Harbour Publishing, 1995.
Francis, Daniel, ed. *Encyclopedia of British Columbia.* Madeira Park, BC: Harbour Publishing, 2000.
Fred, Randy. "Remembering George Clutesi." *ABC Bookworld,* 2007.
Geigle, Lillian. *Be My Guest. The Memoirs of Marie Jacobson, Alberni Hotelier.* Qualicum Beach, BC: SP, 2010.
Harker, Douglas E. *The Woodwards: A Family Story of Ventures and Traditions.* Vancouver: Mitchell Press, 1976.
Johnston, Hugh J.M., ed. *The Pacific Province: A History of British Columbia.* Vancouver: Douglas & McIntyre, 1996.
Lavoie, Judith. "Elder Revives Vanishing Language." *Times Colonist,* October 18, 2006.
Leyne, Les. "George Watts Led the Way in Long Land-Claim Journey." *Times Colonist,* December 9, 2006.
MacKay, Donald. *Empire of Wood. The MacMillan Bloedel Story.* Vancouver: Douglas & McIntyre, 1982.
Mahood, Ian and Ken Drushka. *Three Men and a Forester.* Madeira Park, BC: Harbour Publishing, 1990.
Mason, Gary. "Battle for Meares Island Is Key to Settlement of Claims." *Times Colonist,* June 16, 1985.
McIntosh, Jean E. "Mark Mosher's Reconstruction of the Development of the Woodworkers Union in the Alberni Valley 1935–1950: A Participant's History." Vancouver: UBC thesis, 1987.
Miller, Barry. *2-Spot Steam Ride: A Journey to Yesterday.* SP Booklet.
Munro, Jack and Jane O'Hara. *Union Jack.* Vancouver: Douglas & McIntyre, 1988.
Murray, Derik. *The Expo Celebration: The Official Retrospective Book.* Vancouver: Whitecap Books, 1986.
Peterson, Jan. *Harbour City: Nanaimo in Transition: 1920–1967.* Surrey: Heritage House, 2006.
———. *Journeys Down the Alberni Canal to Barkley Sound.* Lantzville: Oolichan Books, 1999.
———. *Twin Cities: Alberni-Port Alberni.* Lantzville: Oolichan Books, 1994.
———. "Walter Behn Relives 20 Years of Labour History." *Alberni Valley Times,* December 21, 1982.
———. "Fed Up with Gloom: Barrett." *Alberni Valley Times,* October 28, 1982.
———. "No Doubt We Are Running Out of Timber." *Alberni Valley Times,* August 4, 1982.

———."We're Fighting Back." *Alberni Valley Times*, June 28, 1982.
———. "No Reprieve." *Alberni Valley Times*, April 28, 1982.
———. "Is Education Revamping a Threat to Democracy?" *Alberni Valley Times*, April 27, 1982.
———. "Faber Parents Lash Out at SD 70 Closures." *Alberni Valley Times*, March 23, 1982.
———. "Count 'Em—Five Schools Will Close." *Alberni Valley Times*, March 18, 1982.
———. "Air Pollution Questions Include Workers' Contract." *Alberni Valley Times*, July 24, 1981.
Suzuki, David. "Those Anti-Logging 'Thugs' Are Our Kids." *Toronto Star*, April 10, 1993.
Wade, Rodney. "Once Upon a Time . . . " *Alberni Valley Times*, October 29, 1982.
Weatherbe, Steve. "Court Convicts 44 Clayoquot Sound Protesters." *Alberni Valley Times*, October 7, 1993.
Wilson, Gavin. "Helen, Armour Ford Work Quietly." *Alberni Valley Times*, December 8, 1983.
———. "Jobless Chant . . ." *Alberni Valley Times*, April 11, 1983.
———. "Looking for Wage Controls." *Alberni Valley Times*, April 15, 1982.
———. "Hope Porter Given Award." *Alberni Valley Times*, December 7, 1981.
Zimmerman, Adam. *Who's in Charge Here, Anyway?* Toronto: Stoddart, 1997.

Author Interviews

Walter Behn, *Alberni Valley Times*, December 21, 1982.
Cougar Brown, *Alberni Valley Times*, May 1984.
Archie Clouston, *Alberni Valley Times*, January 18, 1984.
Pat Cummings, *Alberni Valley Times*, January 19, 1983.
Aileen Devereux, *Alberni Valley Times*, May 13, 1981.
Angie Dick, *Alberni Valley Times*, July 1981.
Dr. Dick Garner, *Alberni Valley Times*, 1984.
Doris Gray, *Alberni Valley Times*, December 6, 1982.
Trevor Jones, *Alberni Valley Times*, April 8, 1983.
Stu Keate, *Alberni Valley Times*, June 29, 1981.
Margaret Kelly, *Alberni Valley Times*, September 21, 1982.
Ada Annie Lawson (Cougar Annie), *Alberni Valley Times*, June 20, 1982.
Marianne McClain, *Alberni Valley Times*, July 17, 1981.
Pat Miller, *Alberni Valley Times*, May 15, 1981.
Bill Patenaude, *Alberni Valley Times*, November 4, 1983.
Helen Patenaude, *Alberni Valley Times*, November 30, 1982.
Dr. Garnet Reynolds, *Alberni Valley Times*, May 1981.
Chief Adam Shewish, September 22, 1989 (unpublished).
Peter Szachiv, *Alberni Valley Times*, July 8, 1983.
Gillian Trumper, *Alberni Valley Times*, October 15, 1981.
Jack Webster, *Alberni Valley Times*, July 25, 1985.
Wolfgang Zimmerman and Sven Fredrickson, *Alberni Valley Times*, December 1, 1982.

Newspapers, Periodicals, and Magazines
Alberni Advocate, Alberni
Alberni Valley Times, Port Alberni
British Columbia Medical Association News, Vancouver
Canadian Press, Vancouver
MB Journal, Vancouver
Times Colonist, Victoria
Toronto Star, Toronto
Vancouver Sun, Vancouver
West Coast Advocate, Port Alberni

Papers, Speech, News Releases
"Day of Discovery" paper, January 1982.
George McKnight's speech to the Select Standing Committee of Aboriginal Affairs, Port Alberni, October 17, 1996.
MacMillan Bloedel Limited letter to MB retirees, June 22, 1999.
MacMillan Bloedel Limited news release, December 10, 1993
Premier Mike Harcourt news release, October 22, 1993